BIBLE STORIES

Author
Martin Manser

Storytellers
Andrew Bianchi and Emma Peterson

Designer
Sarah Crouch

Project Management
Raje Airey

Editorial Team
Penny Clark; Jenny Hyatt and Derek Williams (ADPS)

Artwork Commissioning
Raje Airey; Susanne Grant

Picture Research
Janice Bracken; Liz Dalby; Kate Miles

Editorial Assistant
Liz Dalby

Additional editorial help from
Lesley Cartlidge; Rosalind Desmond; Lynda Drury;
Lynn Elias; Libbe Mella

Image Coordination
Ian Paulyn

Production Assistant
Jenni Cozens

Editorial Director
Paula Borton

Design Director
Clare Sleven

Director
Jim Miles

This is a Parragon Book
This edition published in 2000

Parragon
Queen Street House
4 Queen Street
Bath
BA1 1HE, UK

24681097531

Copyright © Parragon 1999

Produced by Miles Kelly Publishing Ltd
Bardfield Centre, Great Bardfield, Essex CM7 4SL

British Library Cataloguing-in-Publication Data
A catalogue record for this book is available from the British Library

ISBN 0-75254-207-9 (hardback)
ISBN 0-75254-488-8 (paperback)

Printed in ITALY

CONTENTS

Introduction to the Bible 8-9

THE OLD TESTAMENT

THE NEW TESTAMENT

BIBLE REFERENCE

Introduction to the Bible

The Bible: a library of books

The word *Bible* comes from the Greek word *biblia*, meaning "books". The Bible is not one book but a collection of many books of different kinds of writing. It is divided into the Old Testament and the New Testament (*testament* is a word that means "agreement"). The Old Testament contains books about God's law, books of history, books of poetry and wisdom and books of the prophets.

The New Testament contains books of the life of Jesus Christ, the history of the first Christians, letters and a book of prophetic visions.

The Bible's writers

The Bible has a dual authorship. The immediate authors were writers coming from different countries, walks of life and social positions: kings like David and Solomon; prophets, like Isaiah and Ezekiel; Matthew, a tax-

The caves at Qumran
Many of the Dead Sea Scrolls were found in 1947 in caves in the Qumran area. It is thought these ancient manuscripts were the remains of the library of a Jewish community called the Essenes.

collector; Luke, a doctor; and apostles like Paul. But the ultimate author of the Bible is God: it is his message which he wrote through many different people at different times.

The Bible's original languages

The two main original languages of the Bible were Hebrew and Greek. The Old Testament was mostly written in Hebrew but some was also written in Aramaic. The entire New Testament was written in Greek, the language commonly spoken and written throughout the Roman empire in the 1st and 2nd centuries AD.

The Bible's message

The Bible has one central message: God's salvation of his people. The Old Testament tells of God's chosen people (the people of Israel) and their relationship with God. It describes the problem of human disobedience and God's preparation of a solution to this problem through the promise of his Messiah. The New Testament describes the fulfilling of God's plan of salvation in the coming of his Son, Jesus, who Christians believe to be the Messiah: his life, death, resurrection and ascension, and the growth of the church, God's redeemed people.

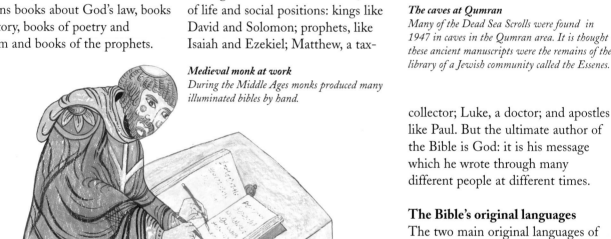

Medieval monk at work
During the Middle Ages monks produced many illuminated bibles by hand.

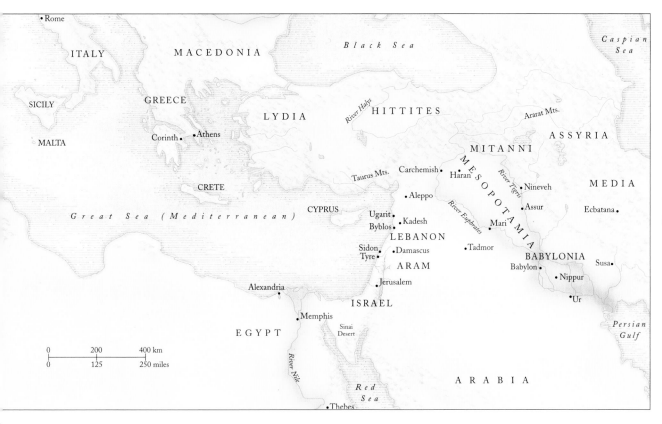

The Bible and archaeology

Archaeology is the scientific study of ancient people and cultures by discovering, studying and interpreting remains from the past. Archaeologists work by locating and dating these remains, like pottery, inscriptions, tools, weapons and coins for example.

Many remains from Palestine and its neighbouring countries have been discovered. Important buildings

The lands of the Bible
All the events of the Bible take place in the Near East. The Old Testament is focused on Israel and countries to the north and east. The New Testament is focused on Israel and countries in Europe to the northwest.

that have been preserved include the theatre at Ephesus where the apostle Paul was judged, whilst texts like the 14th century BC Amarna letters or the manuscripts from the Dead Sea Scrolls, all tell us a great deal about the people, the places and the

common ideas of Bible times. Through all these discoveries, we can form a picture of what life was like.

A library of books
The Bible is a collection of 66 separate books inside the cover. These are in two main sections, the Old Testament and the New Testament.

THE LAW	HISTORY	POETRY	ISAIAH — PROPHECY	HISTORY	ROMANS — LETTERS
GENESIS	JOSHUA	JOB	JEREMIAH	MATTHEW	1 CORINTHIANS
EXODUS	JUDGES	PSALMS	LAMENTATIONS	MARK	2 CORINTHIANS
LEVITICUS	RUTH	PROVERBS	EZEKIEL	LUKE	GALATIANS
NUMBERS	1 SAMUEL	ECCLESIASTES	DANIEL	JOHN	EPHESIANS
DEUTERONOMY	2 SAMUEL	SONG OF SONGS	HOSEA	ACTS	PHILIPPIANS
	1 KINGS		JOEL		COLOSSIANS
	2 KINGS		AMOS		1 THESSALONIANS
	1 CHRONICLES		OBADIAH		2 THESSALONIANS
	2 CHRONICLES		JONAH		1 TIMOTHY
	EZRA		MICAH		2 TIMOTHY
	NEHEMIAH		NAHUM		TITUS
	ESTHER		HABAKKUK		PHILEMON
			ZEPHANIAH		HEBREWS
			HAGGAI		JAMES
			ZECHARIAH		1 PETER
			MALACHI		2 PETER
					1 JOHN
					2 JOHN
					3 JOHN
					JUDE
					REVELATION — PROPHECY

OLD TESTAMENT   **NEW TESTAMENT**

THE BIBLE

THE OLD TESTAMENT

Here we read about God's
creation, about the call of Abraham
and God's promise to make Abraham's
descendants into a great nation, Israel.
The Old Testament tells the story of these
people, of how God worked through
them, revealing more and more of
his character and purpose.

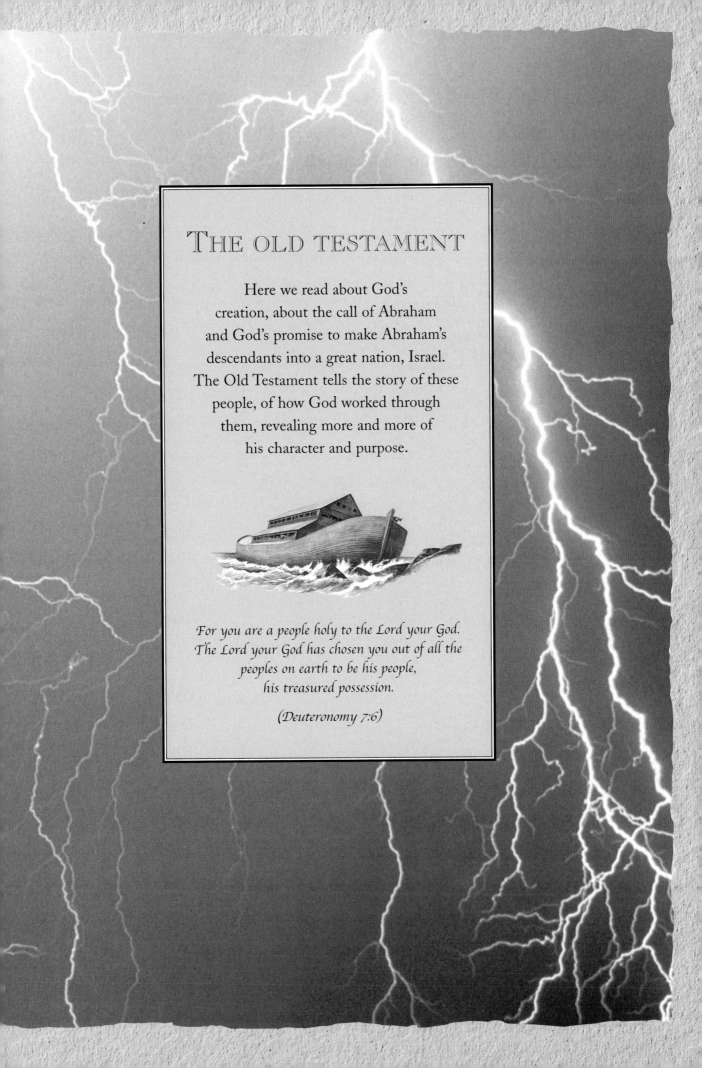

For you are a people holy to the Lord your God.
The Lord your God has chosen you out of all the
peoples on earth to be his people,
his treasured possession.

(Deuteronomy 7:6)

THE OLD TESTAMENT

The *Old Testament* contains 39 books: books of the law, history, poetry, wisdom and prophecy. The books were written by different authors over a long period of time. The *Old Testament* is full of lively stories, of love, hope, family life, jealousy, anger and disobedience. It is made up as follows:

The Books of the Law
The first five books of the Bible are known as the "pentateuch" and describe the origin of the Jewish people and culture. *Genesis*, the book of beginnings, goes back to the creation and describes the first disobedience towards God and God's choosing of Abraham and his descendants. *Exodus* shows God's rescue of his people from slavery in Egypt under Moses' leadership. *Leviticus* contains laws for the Israelites' worship, especially about the sacrifices to be made to God. *Numbers* describes the Israelites' wanderings in the wilderness for forty years. *Deuteronomy* records Moses' speeches to the Israelites when they were about to enter the Promised Land.

The Books of History
This section covers twelve books concerned with the history of the Israelites from about 1200–400BC. *Joshua* shows how the Israelites took possession of the Promised Land after Moses' death. *Judges* relates how the new nation was disobedient to God and how he chose leaders or "judges". *Ruth*, a story of love and loyalty, is followed by *1 and 2 Samuel*, a history of Israel from the last of the judges, through the leader Samuel and to Israel's first king, Saul, followed by King David, "a man after God's own heart". The two books of *Kings* describe the reign of Solomon, and the later division into the northern kingdom (Israel) and the southern kingdom (Judah). Later Israel fell to the Assyrians and Judah (Jerusalem) to the Babylonians. The two books of *Chronicles* parallel the events of *2 Samuel* and the books of *Kings*. *Ezra* tells of the rebuilding of the temple in Jerusalem. *Nehemiah* describes his leadership in rebuilding the walls of Jerusalem. *Esther* was a Jew who became queen of Persia and managed to save her people from a plot.

The Books of Poetry and Wisdom
These books deal with important

OLD TESTAMENT TIMELINE

BC ... **AD**

2000	
	c. 1950 Abraham's son Isaac born
1900	
1800	*c.* 1820 Jacob and Esau fall out
	c. 1750 Joseph sold into slavery
1700	*c.* 1720 Entry into Egypt
1600	
1500	
1400	*c.* 1350 Birth of Moses
1300	*c.* 1280 Exodus
	c. 1240 Crossing of Jordan
1200	*c.* 1160 Gideon defeats Midianites
1100	*c.* 1120 Samson dies
1000	
900	*c.* 930 Division of kingdom
	c. 860 Elijah's contest on Mt Carmel
800	*c.* 750 Amos prophesies Israel's fall
700	*c.* 722 Fall of Samaria (end of Israel)
	c. 620 King Josiah reforms Judah's worship
600	*c.* 587 Judah into exile in Babylon
	c. 538 Return to Jerusalem
500	*c.* 470 Esther foils Haman's plot
	c. 450 Ezra returns to Jerusalem
400	
300	*c.* 323 Alexander the Great dies
	c. 250 Old Testament translated into Greek
200	*c.* 167 Maccabean revolt in Judea
100	*c.* 63 Pompey captures Jerusalem
	c. 4 Jesus is born
0	*c.* 30 Jesus is crucified
100	*c.* 70 Destruction of Jerusalem

Eras: PATRIARCHS · GROWTH OF NATION IN EGYPT · WILDERNESS · JUDGES PERIOD · UNITED MONARCHY · JUDAH ISRAEL · EXILE · RESTORATION UNDER PERSIAN EMPIRE · MACEDONIAN RULE · EGYPTIAN RULE · SYRIAN RULE · ROMAN RULE questions of life. *Job*, a good man, grappled with the difficult question, "Why do the innocent suffer?" The *Psalms* are prayers, hymns, and poems that cover the full range of human emotions. *Proverbs* is a collection of wise sayings by different authors on a variety of everyday themes. *Ecclesiastes*, considers the age-old question, "What is life all about?" The *Song of Songs* is a poem that celebrates the physical love that a couple find in each other.

King Solomon was famous for his wisdom.

The Books of the Prophets

The prophets predicted future events, especially about the coming Messiah, but their main task was to call God's people back to him. *Isaiah* describes the threat of the Assyrian conquest, God's promises to exiles in Babylon, and a message of hope to the Jews after they had returned from the exile. The warning messages of *Jeremiah* came in the closing years of Judah. The book of *Lamentations* is a song of sorrow about the destruction of Jerusalem by the Babylonians. *Ezekiel* records the visions and prophecies of the prophet in exile in Babylon. *Daniel*, captive in Babylon, lived a life of integrity and faithfulness to God.

Hosea records prophecies to the northern kingdom of Israel: even though the people were faithless, God was still faithful. *Joel* describes a devastating plague of locusts, seen as a

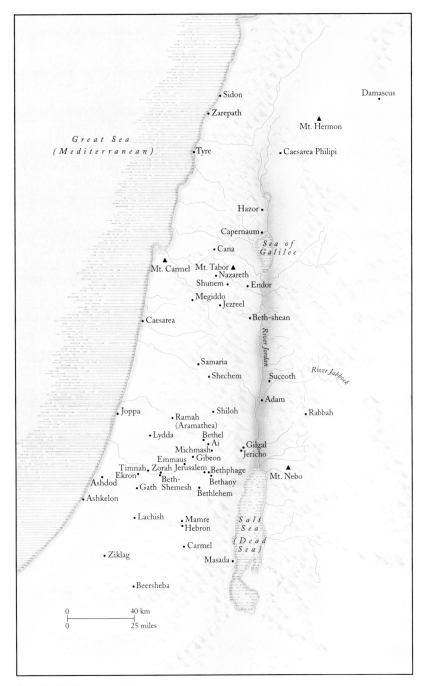

Israel in Old Testament times
The Israelites moved into Canaan in about 1240BC. After Solomon's death in 930BC, the country split into two. The northern part (based on Samaria) was then called Israel, and the southern part (based on Jerusalem) was called Judah. The Bible deals with both countries.

sign of the coming final "day of the Lord". *Amos* preached a message of social justice to the affluent society of Israel. *Obadiah* is a prophecy against Edom, a country bordering Judah. *Jonah* describes his reluctance to go and preach in Nineveh, the capital of Assyria, Israel's enemy. *Micah* records prophecies against injustices in society yet also contains a message of forgiveness and restoration. *Nahum*

foretells the destruction of Nineveh. The prophet *Habakkuk* questions God about how he could use the wicked Babylon to punish people who were better than them. *Zephaniah* prophesied against Judah; *Haggai* and *Zechariah* urged the people on to rebuild the temple; and *Malachi* questioned the people's religious apathy and challenged them to wholehearted obedience to God.

Creation stories

Since time began many cultures have invented stories that explain the origin and order of the universe. One of the most famous is the Babylonian epic of creation, "Enuma Elish". The Babylonian version features the god Marduk. A later Assyrian version substitutes the national god Asshur for Babylon's Marduk. The story opens in the time before the earth and order have been brought into being.

Fruit

The law of Moses declared that for the first three years after a tree was planted, its fruit was forbidden. In the fourth year, the fruit belonged to God, and it was only after five years that people could eat the tree's fruit. Fruit trees were so valuable that even during war, special efforts were made to protect them. Figs, grapes, dates and olives are all important crops, but citrus fruits did not come in until New Testament times.

Leopard

The Bible tells us that every living creature was created by God, although it does not tell us how different species of animal changed over time. The expression that "leopards don't change their spots" has its origins in the Bible.

GOD MAKES THE WORLD

✦ Genesis 1-2 ✦

At the beginning of time, God created heaven and earth. The earth was completely dark, without any shape, and empty. Complete darkness hung over the ocean waters.

God then made everything simply by the power of speaking out his commands.

"Let the light shine!" God said on the first day, and light came. He saw that the light was good. He separated the light and the darkness. He called the light "day", and the darkness "night". Then came evening and morning.

On the second day, he said, "Let the oceans divide," and a great space appeared between the waters. God called this space "sky".

On the third day, God said, "Let there be dry ground," and he called the dry ground "land". Then the land produced many different kinds of trees and flowers. Fruit and crops started to grow.

On the fourth day, God commanded, "Let the sky be filled with lights," and he made the sun, and the moon, and set brilliant stars and galaxies around them.

On the fifth day, God filled the oceans with fish and the sky with birds. He blessed them all and told them to roam free and to increase in number and to fill the earth and skies and oceans.

Finally, on the sixth day, God made animals of all shapes and sizes, both tame and wild, to live on the land. And he made men and women, and told them, "Go and have many children so you can take care of the earth and all the fish, birds and animals and all living creatures."

At the end of the sixth day, the heavens and the earth were completed in all their glory. God looked back at everything he had made and was extremely pleased with what he saw.

By the seventh day, God had finished making the universe. So he rested from all his work and made this day a special day. It was a holy day, a day for rest and for stopping to give thanks for all the wonders of his magnificent creation.

The fifth day of creation
*The opening words of the Bible
declare that God made heaven
and earth. Everything around
us did not come about by mere
chance but is the result of God's
purpose and design.*

ADAM AND EVE SPOIL CREATION

✤ Genesis 2-3 ✤

The tree of knowledge
According to tradition, the fruit that Adam and Eve ate from the tree of knowledge was an apple. But the Bible does not tell us what kind of tree or fruit it was. Some experts now think the fruit may even have been a pomegranate.

God made a beautiful garden called Eden, a paradise full of animals and fruit trees. At the centre of the garden stood a tree with the special power to give the knowledge of good and evil to anyone who ate its fruit. God told Adam, the first man, to look after the plants, but warned him, "You may eat fruit from any tree you like, but not from the tree of knowledge. If you do, you will die."

When God realized that Adam was lonely by himself, he made him fall into a deep sleep. He took out one of Adam's ribs and from it he made a woman called Eve, to be Adam's wife. Although they were both naked, they were not in the least embarrassed, and they were very happy living in the garden.

Now in the garden was a snake, who was the most cunning of all the animals. He used his powers of persuasion to get Eve into trouble. "You won't really die if you eat fruit from the tree of knowledge," he said. "Instead you will be just like God, knowing what is good and what is evil."

Eve was so tempted by the tasty fruit that would make her clever that she picked some and ate it. She offered some to Adam, who ate it too. Immediately, they realized that they were naked and were ashamed. They sewed fig leaves together as clothes to cover themselves.

When God came walking in the garden that evening, Adam and Eve hid themselves behind the trees in fear. "Adam, where are you?" God called. "Have you eaten the fruit I told you not to eat?"

Reluctantly, Adam had to admit that he had. "The snake tricked me into giving it to him," Eve explained, sadly.

God was angry that Adam and Eve had disobeyed him, and told Adam, "I will curse the ground with weeds, so that you will have to work hard to grow your food." Then God told Adam and Eve to leave the Garden of Eden for ever.

CAIN MURDERS ABEL

✤ Genesis 4 ✤

Adam and Eve started a new life outside the Garden of Eden. They had two sons: Abel, who grew up to be a shepherd, and Cain, who worked in the fields as a farmer.

When the time came to make an offering to God, Cain brought a few of his harvest crops, but he did so with a careless attitude. Abel, on the other hand, brought only the very best pieces of meat from his sheep, showing his deep, heartfelt trust in God. So God was pleased with Abel's offering but not with Cain's. This filled Cain with anger.

"Why are you so angry?" God asked Cain. "If you make the right offering I will accept it, but be careful, because if you do not, sin is waiting to pounce on you and rule you."

But Cain would not listen. Burning with rage and jealousy, he lured his brother Abel into a field and killed him.

"Where is your brother?" God asked him, but Cain pretended not to know.

"Don't ask me," he replied. "Am I supposed to look after him?"

"Look what you've done!" said God, angrily. "I can plainly see Abel's blood on the ground, so now I must punish you. From now on your crops will no longer grow and you will have to wander through the world without a home."

Cain trembled with fear. "My punishment is too much for me to bear," he pleaded with God. "Because you are no longer my friend, whoever finds me will kill me."

"Don't worry," God replied, showing mercy by putting a special mark on Cain to protect him. "If anyone kills you, he will suffer seven times more than you." So, with tremendous sadness, Cain left and went to live in the land of Nod.

Cain kills Abel
After Adam and Eve were expelled from the Garden of Eden, sin entered the world for the first time. This is shown when Cain became jealous of Abel and committed the first murder. Cain's punishment for killing his brother was to become a wanderer with no home. He was forced to lead a nomadic existence in the land of Nod.

The Garden of Eden
We do not know the precise location of the Garden of Eden. A popular theory is that it lay in the lush and fertile area of land between the rivers Tigris and Euphrates in Mesopotamia.

NOAH BUILDS THE GREAT ARK

✤ Genesis 6-8 ✤

Carpenters' tools
More than three thousand years ago, the Egyptians used tools like this adze and chisel. Noah would have used an adze to hack and plane the wood, and a chisel to carve and shape it.

Boat building
In many parts of the world, boats are still built by hand using methods and tools that have hardly changed over thousands of years. The ark that Noah built was enormous. It is estimated that it was about as long as two jumbo jets and higher than a five-storey building. The framework was sealed with tar to make it watertight.

God saw that people were becoming more and more wicked and he began to regret making them.

But there was one good man, called Noah, who loved and obeyed God. "I have decided to destroy the men and women that I have created," God told him. "Every living animal will die too. I want you to make a wooden boat, because I am going to send a flood to cover the whole world. Only you and your family, and the animals that are inside the boat, will be kept safe."

With the help of his three sons, Noah obeyed God and began to build an enormous boat, called an ark. He followed the plans that God had given him for its construction precisely. When the ark was finished, God sent two of every kind of animal and bird – one male and one female – and they all went into the ark. As soon as the last animals were on board, God told Noah and his family to

get in, too. God himself closed the door behind them.

Then it began to rain. Water poured down from the sky and burst up from springs deep under the earth's surface. Soon the ark was floating free on the swirling waves that crashed against it. The water kept rising until even the tallest mountains were covered and the last remaining animals and people had drowned.

After several months, the rain stopped and the water began to go down. The ark drifted silently over the calm waters until finally it came to rest on the mountains of Ararat. Noah sent out birds to see how much of the earth was free of flooding. When a dove returned with a fresh olive leaf in its beak, Noah knew that the trees were growing again. Their voyage was over. Soon they could all leave the ark and explore the earth.

A RAINBOW OF PROMISES
✤ Genesis 8-9 ✤

"You must leave the ark now," God said to Noah and his family. "Bring the animals, too, as they must find new homes and raise their young." So Noah climbed down the gangway and stepped onto the earth. He was so glad that God had saved him from the flood that he built an altar and made an offering to God.

"Even though people will never change, and will continue to behave wickedly, I will not destroy the world in this way again," God said. "From now until the end of time I promise that the rhythm of nature will continue. There will be a time for sowing seeds and for reaping the harvest, and the hot summer will follow the cold winter as surely as the day follows the night."

Then God told Noah and his family, "Make a fresh start. The whole world belongs to you and your children. Use it wisely and enjoy its resources."

Then God made a covenant with Noah, his children, and all the animals. "I will never again send a flood to destroy the world. If ever it rains for a long time and you begin to worry that I have forgotten this promise, all you need to do is look upwards. I will put a sign in the sky to remind you of what I have said. Whenever you see the colourful rainbow shining out in the middle of dark rain clouds, remember my promise."

The rainbow
There are lots of covenants in the Bible, but God's covenant with Noah is the first one. A covenant is an agreement in which people promise to do certain things. The rainbow was the sign of God's covenant promise never again to destroy the earth with a flood. The word that the Bible uses for rainbow also means a "war-bow". This symbolizes God lowering his bow to declare peace.

BABBLING TONGUES

✦ Genesis 11 ✦

Mud bricks
Today in the Middle East people still make bricks in the same way as they would have done to build the tower of Babel. The wet mud or clay is shaped in a wooden mould and then pressed out to dry in the sun or baked in kilns for greater durability.

The tower of Babel
The tower of Babel may have been a type of Babylonian temple, called a ziggurat. Ziggurats were pyramid-shaped and some may have been over 100 metres high. They had steps on the outside and a temple at the top. Sometimes each level was painted a different colour so the building would have looked like a large rainbow.

Sites of ziggurat towers
From earliest times, people have known they should worship God, so they built temples. Ruins of these temples have been found all over ancient Mesopotamia, which lies in modern-day Iraq. The traditional site of the tower of Babel was Babylon, one of the chief cities founded by Nimrod.

At first, Noah's descendants roamed from place to place in the east. But many years later, one group reached a fertile plain in Babylonia and decided to settle down there.

The people held a meeting and decided to build themselves a large city to live in. They would use bricks made of mud and straw baked hard in the fiercely hot sun, and they would stick them together with tar. The grandest building was to be a spectacular tower, so tall that its top would reach to the clouds.

So the people eagerly set to work building their new city.

"Now we will have a proper home and will no longer have to keep on wandering through the world. And when people realize how clever we've been to build such a grand city, then we'll be famous," they told each other, proudly.

But their pride was to be their downfall. When God looked carefully at their growing city with its elaborate tower, he was not pleased.

"These people are vain. They have forgotten me and only think of how important they are," said God. "If I let them continue, soon they will want to control everything in the world. But I will stop them by mixing up their words so that they cannot understand each other. Then they will not be able to carry out their plans."

Soon all that could be heard across the city was a confused babble of voices. Building work had to come to a halt, because no one could understand what his neighbour was trying to say. The people all spoke different languages, and could not communicate with each other, so they went to live in different parts of the world.

GOD CALLS ABRAHAM

♣ Genesis 12-13 ♣

One of Noah's descendants was a man called Abraham, who grew up in the city of Ur in Mesopotamia. His father decided to move the family to Canaan, but on the way they settled in the city of Haran. There, Abraham and his wife Sarah enjoyed a life of wealth. They had many servants, and owned large flocks of cattle, sheep and donkeys.

One day, when Abraham was seventy-five years old, God told him something that would change his life for ever. "You and your family must leave your country and travel to the land of Canaan. There I will bless you and make you the father of a great nation."

Abraham had a deep faith that what God said would come true. So he loaded all his possessions onto his camels and set out on the long journey with Sarah, his nephew, Lot, and all their servants.

When they reached Canaan, God appeared to Abraham and made him the wonderful promise that one day Abraham's children would live there. Sarah had not been able to have any children, but being a man of faith, Abraham believed that in the future God's promise would come true.

But it was proving difficult to find enough grazing pasture for all the animals. Abraham's shepherds started to fight Lot's shepherds for each piece of grass.

Abraham settled the argument wisely. "We should split up and go our separate ways," he told Lot, and he gave Lot first choice as to where he could go.

So Lot set off with his flocks for the fertile Jordan Valley, while Abraham stayed in Canaan.

Golden bull's head
Archaeologists have found the site of Ur, the city that Abraham came from. There they have discovered royal graves containing many exquisite gold objects, such as this golden head of a bull, set with precious stones. It once formed part of a lyre – a musical instrument similar to a harp. These finds show that Ur was a powerful, wealthy and sophisticated city.

GOD'S CHOSEN PEOPLE

Mosaic from the royal tombs at Ur

The book of Genesis narrates the lives of the "patriarchs", or fathers. The origins of the people of Israel are traced back to Abraham and his descendants, Isaac, Jacob and Joseph.

God promised Abraham that he would make him the father of a great nation, that he would bless him and his descendants and that through them, all people would be blessed. In return, God called on Abraham to obey God and to be faithful to him.

Abraham

Abraham came from Ur, a city in southern Mesopotamia. God called him to leave his home so he moved first to Haran and later to Canaan, the land promised by God. For many years, Abraham and his wife Sarah had no children. But Abraham's faith never wavered and eventually Isaac was born. God then tested Abraham's faith by telling him to sacrifice Isaac. Abraham was prepared to obey God.

Abraham prepares to kill his son

Isaac

God confirmed the promises that he had given to Abraham to his son, Isaac. When Isaac was forty years old, Abraham, in accordance with the customs of the time, arranged his marriage to Rebekah, a girl from his family in Haran. She was childless for a long time, but eventually gave birth to twin boys, Esau and Jacob. When he was old and almost blind, Isaac was tricked into giving the blessing of the firstborn to his younger son, Jacob, instead of to his elder son, Esau.

Isaac gives his blessing to Jacob

Jacob

After tricking Esau out of his inheritance and getting his father's blessing, Jacob fled north. While he slept he had a vision of his descendants standing on a ladder between heaven and earth. God's promise to Abraham was confirmed. Jacob was given the new name of Israel after he had spent the night wrestling with God by the river Jabbok. Jacob was tricked on his wedding night into marrying Leah, instead of Rachel, whom he loved. The twelve tribes of Israel were descended from his twelve sons born to Leah and Rachel and to their two slave girls.

Joseph interprets dreams

Joseph

Joseph was the son borne by Rachel and was Jacob's favourite son. Jacob's preference for Joseph provoked the jealous hatred of his eleven brothers, who sold him into slavery in Egypt, where he worked for Potiphar. Later he used his God-given abilities to interpret dreams and he became a wise ruler in Egypt, second only to the king or Pharaoh. Eventually he was reconciled to his brothers and saved his family in a time of severe famine.

A typical bedouin tent dwelling

Tent dwellers

Tents are among the earliest dwelling places made by people. When God called him, Abraham exchanged his settled life in the city of Ur for a nomadic tent-dwelling existence. Tents were a practical solution for a people constantly on the move. They were made out of goats' hair, stretched over wooden poles and pegged down at the edges with guy ropes.

Places

Excavations reveal that several of the towns mentioned in the Bible in connection with the patriarchs were already established centres of population. What life was like in these places can be learnt from the pottery, ruined houses, tools, weapons and occasional written records that have been unearthed. Clay tablets which have been found refer to a number of settlements in Canaan with which trade existed, like Megiddo, Hazor, Lachish, Gezer, Jericho and Shechem.

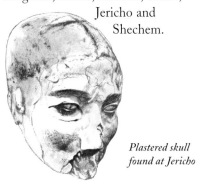

Plastered skull found at Jericho

Camel trains crossing the desert

Travel, trade and commerce

Commercial trade was well developed all over the Near East at this time and travel was fairly extensive. It is known, for example, that trade in wool and copper between Asia Minor and Assyria existed as early as 2000BC. Major routes, like the King's Highway, which ran from Syria to the Gulf of Aqaba, crossed the region and were used by armies as well as traders and travellers. Travellers would either walk, or travel by ass, ox wagon or camel. Road conditions were poor and to travel alone was dangerous.

The lands of the patriarchs
To travel from Ur to Beersheba, Abraham walked over 1,500 kilometres up the Euphrates valley to Haran before turning south. This route was known as the Fertile Crescent where there was water, food and towns. The direct route from east to west was across hostile desert.

Customs

Information about the customs of the time has emerged with the discovery of the Nuzi tablets. These are tens of thousands of clay tablets which document all aspects of everyday life – commercial, legal, religious and private. In particular, they tell us a great deal about the customs concerning adoption, marriage and inheritance. For instance, a childless man could adopt his slave as his heir, or the son of his wife's slave-girl, but it was more usual to marry a second wife or to take a concubine.

The servant Hagar, mother of Ishmael

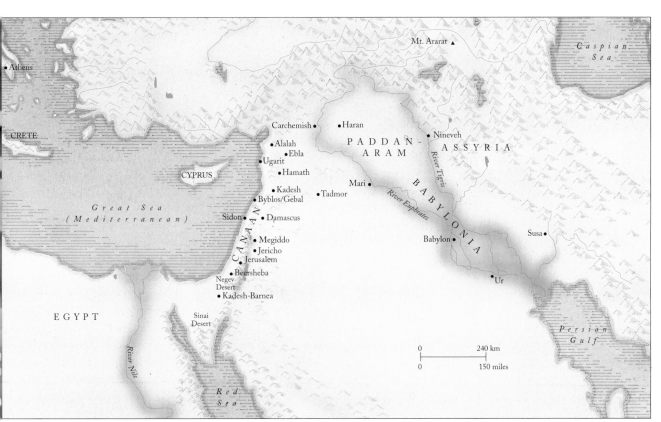

LONGING FOR A SON

✦ Genesis 15 ✦

The sphinx
The sphinx, built in about 2550BC, is a massive stone statue with the body of a lion and the head of a man. It stands by the pyramids at Giza in Egypt and represents the Egyptian god Horus guarding the city of the dead. Abraham and Sarah went to live in Egypt when there was a famine in the land of Canaan, and they may have seen it there.

Many years went by, and still Abraham and Sarah had no children. Abraham began to wonder who would take over from him, if he had no son and heir. God's promise of building a great nation through him and his descendants seemed impossible to fulfill.

But God appeared to Abraham in a vision and reassured him, saying, "Do not be afraid. You will have a son of your own. Look up at the night sky and count the millions of stars, if that is possible. That's how many descendants you will have. And look out at the land as far as you can see to the north, south, east and west. It will all belong to your family."

Because Abraham was a man who trusted God, he believed what God had told him with all his heart, but he still wanted more reassurance. "How will I know that the land will be mine?" he asked God.

ABRAHAM'S TRUST IN GOD
Abraham is known for his faithfulness and obedience to God. Although Abraham and his wife, Sarah, were old and had not been able to have any children, God promised that Abraham would have many descendants and that they would become a great nation. Abraham couldn't see any human way of making this happen, but he knew that somehow God would do what he had promised. He firmly trusted in God's promise and so was considered right with God.
God kept his promise to bless Abraham's descendants, as Abraham became the father of the nation of Israel.

To show Abraham that his promise would come true, God told him to sacrifice some animals. Abraham killed a cow, a goat and a ram, and cut them in half, and also brought a dove and a pigeon.

That evening, Abraham fell into a deep sleep, but instead of relaxing, he was gripped with fear. While he slept, God spoke comfortingly to Abraham about the future.

At first, God said, Abraham's descendants would live a hard life as slaves in a strange land. But God would eventually punish the nation that had enslaved them. "And then I will bless them and they will come back to Canaan with enormous wealth. And you, Abraham, will live to a ripe old age and die in peace."

Then God sent a cooking pot billowing with smoke and a torch ablaze with fire through the animal pieces to seal his promise with a visible sign.

ISHMAEL IS BORN TO A SERVANT

✤ **Genesis 16** ✤

Women in captivity
This frieze shows mothers and their children being led away into captivity. Women sold into slavery had no rights. Like Hagar, they could be given to the head of the household to secure the birth of a male heir. This child would then belong, not to its mother, but to her owner.

problem by letting Hagar start a family for us with you as the father?" Abraham agreed and treated Hagar as his wife.

When Hagar realized that she was having Abraham's baby, she began to think of herself as very important. "She is so rude to me," Sarah complained to Abraham. "This is your fault! Now she is having your baby, she thinks she is better than me!"

"She is your slave," Abraham answered. "You can treat her how you like."

So Sarah began to treat Hagar unkindly, until Hagar could stand it no longer and ran away in despair. When Hagar stopped to rest at a spring in the desert, God's angel appeared and asked, "Where are you going, Hagar?"

"I am escaping from my owner, Sarah," she replied.

Arab man
According to tradition, modern-day Arab people are the descendants of Ishmael, Abraham's son by Hagar. Ishmael later had twelve sons of his own. They became the rulers of the nomadic Ishmaelite people.

After so many long years of waiting to have a child, Abraham's wife, Sarah, began to feel disappointed and impatient. Would she really be the mother of Abraham's son, she wondered. Perhaps the great nation that God had promised would come through her Egyptian slave, Hagar, instead.

"God has not given me any children and now I am too old," Sarah told Abraham, "so why don't we solve the

"God has heard your unhappiness," the angel said. "Go back to Sarah and obey her. You will bear a son, called Ishmael, and you will have many descendants."

Hagar was delighted that God had noticed her troubles, so she willingly went back to Sarah. Shortly afterwards, she gave birth to a son and called him Ishmael, just as the angel had said.

CIRCUMCISION
Circumcision means "cutting around" and refers to cutting away the foreskin of a male child. In the Old Testament, circumcision is seen as a sign of belonging to God's people. Israelite boys were to be circumcised eight days after their birth. Abraham and Ishmael would both have been circumcised.

Later in the Old Testament, the prophets emphasized that circumcision alone was not enough. People must also show commitment to God through humility, trust and obedience to him.

THE CITY OF SODOM

❖ Genesis 18-19 ❖

One day, God spoke to Abraham and told him that he was concerned about the people who lived in the cities of Sodom and Gomorrah. "These people don't respect me at all," he said. "Instead they do as much evil as they like. I will destroy them and their cities."

Abraham knew that his nephew, Lot, and his family lived in Sodom and was horrified at the thought of them dying. He asked, "Lord, are you really going to destroy the good people along with the guilty? I know you are a fair and just judge. What if there are fifty good people living there? Would you punish them, too?"

God replied, "No, if I find fifty good people living in Sodom I will allow the city to remain standing."

Abraham trembled before God, wanting to ask him to be even more merciful. "Forgive my boldness, and do not be angry with me, but what if there are only twenty good people, or even only ten?"

God replied, "If there are just ten good people, I will not destroy the city."

That evening, two angels, who looked like ordinary men, went to Sodom and met Abraham's nephew, Lot, at the city gate.

Lot bowed before them, and said, "Gentlemen, I am here to serve you. Please come to my house and stay the night." So they went, and Lot prepared a meal for them.

Later, a large crowd of rowdy men from the city gathered outside the house and demanded that Lot hand over the two strangers so that they could ill-treat them.

Lot pleaded desperately with them not to do such a terrible thing, saying, "I must protect my guests, at all costs. You can even take my daughters instead!"

But the crowd only grew wilder and prepared to force their way into Lot's house. Then the two angels came to Lot's rescue. They pulled him back into the house and blinded the men outside, so that they could not find the door and break in.

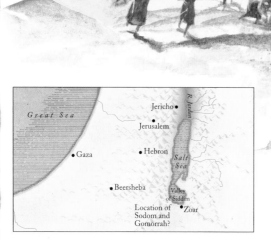

The cities of Sodom and Gomorrah
Sodom and Gomorrah were probably once located at the south-east end of the Dead Sea. The remains of the two cities may now lie under its waters. Archaeological evidence shows that this was once a fertile, well-watered area with a large population.

LOT AND HIS WIFE

✤ Genesis 19 ✤

The two angels now gave Lot a serious warning. "If you have any family living in Sodom, you must hurry and get them out of here," the angels urged him. "God has sent us to destroy this city and every wicked person who lives in it!"

As dawn broke the next morning, the angels again urged Lot to leave. But he still was not sure what to do. It was hard to believe that God was about to destroy his home. Seeing his hesitation, the angels grabbed Lot, his wife and his two daughters by the hands and led them out of the city.

"Quickly!" the angels shouted. "Time is running out. Run into the hills and save your lives! And there is one thing you must remember – do not look back!"

Lot and his family hurried away, and as the sun rose high in the sky, God sent a devastating storm of burning sulphur raining down on the cities of Sodom and Gomorrah. Nothing survived the inferno. Everyone died and all the buildings and land lay in ruins.

Sensing the destruction behind her, Lot's wife could not resist turning round and looking back at the city, disobeying the angels' warning. Immediately, she was transformed into a solid pillar of salt.

Early the next morning, Abraham looked down at Sodom and Gomorrah. All he could see were puffs of smoke rising up from where the cities had once stood. At least his nephew Lot had escaped to safety, he thought with relief.

Salty Dead Sea
At 392 metres below sea-level, the Dead Sea is the lowest point on earth. It has no outlet, so it loses water only through evaporation. This leaves such a high concentration of minerals and salts in the water that nothing can live there. The pillars of salt in the water are reminders of the fate of Lot's wife.

ISAAC'S BIRTH BRINGS GREAT JOY

✤ Genesis 18-21 ✤

Home in a tent
Nomadic people like Abraham and his family lived in tents made of cloth or animal skins. The tents were held up on poles and were kept secure by cords stretched from the poles to pegs or stakes embedded in the ground.

BIBLE NAMES
The name Isaac means "he laughs" or "laughter". Here are the meanings of some other names in the Old Testament.

Abel	breath *or* son
Abraham	father of a multitude
Adam	man *or* of the ground *or* taken out of red earth
Daniel	God is my judge
Elijah	the Lord is God
Elisha	God is salvation
Esau	hairy
Eve	life *or* living
Ezekiel	God strengthens
Isaiah	the Lord is salvation
Ishmael	God hears
Israel	he struggles with God
Jacob	supplanter
Jeremiah	may the Lord exalt
Jonah	dove
Jonathan	the Lord has given
Joseph	may the Lord add
Joshua	the Lord is salvation
Judah	*possibly* praised
Laban	white
Leah	wild cow
Levi	joined
Moses	son *or* drawn out
Rachel	ewe
Rebecca	knotted cord
Ruth	*possibly* companion
Samson	sun child
Samuel	name of God *or* heard by God
Sarah	princess
Saul	asked for
Solomon	peaceful

Butter churn
Sarah would probably have used a churn similar to this one to make butter from sheep or goats' milk. Butter was made by adding a small amount of sour milk to heated milk and stirring it in the churn until the butter separated from the liquid.

As Abraham sat at the entrance of his tent one hot, sunny day, he looked up and saw three men close by.

He hurried out to meet them and bowed, saying, "Gentlemen, I am here to serve you. You have honoured me by coming to my home. Let me bring you water to wash your feet, and food to give you strength for your journey."

The men agreed, so Abraham told Sarah to bake some bread, while he spread out a feast of his tenderest meat and milk for them to eat, under the welcome shade of a tree.

"Where is your wife, Sarah?" the men suddenly asked Abraham.

"She is in the tent," he replied, wondering why they wanted to know.

Now one of the men was really God. He gave Abraham the news that he had been longing to hear for many years. "When I come back here in nine months, Sarah will have a son," he declared.

Sarah had been listening to their conversation, and chuckled to herself. "That is impossible!" she said. "I am much too old to have children."

"Why did Sarah laugh?" God asked Abraham. "Nothing is too difficult for God. I promise that in nine months from now Sarah will have a son."

"I did not laugh," Sarah lied, embarrassed that God had heard her doubting laughter.

"Yes, you did. I heard you," God replied, firmly.

But nine months later, God's promise came true and Sarah gave birth to a little baby boy. "God has brought me joy and laughter," Sarah cried in delight.

Abraham was overjoyed to have a child, especially as he was now an old man of one hundred years.

He named his son Isaac, which means "he laughs", because Sarah had laughed.

SACRIFICE YOUR SON

✤ Genesis 22 ✤

At last God had given Abraham and Sarah a precious son, and they watched with great delight as Isaac grew up into a happy young boy. But then one day God decided to test Abraham's faith.

"Take Isaac to a mountain in the land of Moriah, and offer him to me as a sacrifice," God commanded him.

Who can imagine how Abraham must have felt as he considered killing his only precious son? But Abraham trusted God, so the next morning he obediently loaded his donkey with wood for the sacrifice and set out with Isaac and two servants on the journey to Moriah.

On the third day, Abraham saw the mountain God had told him about in the distance, so he left the donkey and the servants behind. Isaac carried the wood, while Abraham carried a knife and hot coals for lighting the fire.

As they walked on together, Isaac asked Abraham, "Father, where is the lamb for the sacrifice?"

Abraham thought carefully, and answered, "I am trusting that God will provide that."

When they arrived, Abraham built an altar of stones and wood. Then he tenderly took Isaac, tied his arms together and laid him on the altar. He took his knife and summoned up his courage to kill Isaac.

Suddenly, an angel called out from heaven, "Abraham, Abraham!"

"Here I am," he replied.

"Do not hurt Isaac," the angel said. "You have passed the test. Now I know that you truly love God, because you were willing to give up your son. I will bless you with as many descendants as there are stars in the sky or grains of sand on the beach."

Abraham breathed an enormous sigh of relief. He looked round and saw a ram caught by its horns in a bush. Gratefully, he offered the ram as a sacrifice instead of his dear son.

So with great rejoicing Abraham named the place "the Lord provides". Then he and Isaac came down from the mountain and returned home.

SACRIFICES
Sacrifices were an important religious ritual in Old Testament times. The life of an animal was offered to God to give thanks for God's goodness or to bring forgiveness for sin.

Abraham found a ram, or male sheep, caught by its horns in a thicket as it was feeding. He sacrificed this animal as a burnt offering to God, in place of his son, Isaac.

Keeping sheep
Sheep are mentioned more than 400 times in the Bible. Their wool was very valuable, as it was the most useful and easily available fibre for making clothes. Their tanned skins were also used to make tents, shoes and clothing. Sheep's milk was a basic part of the diet. It was more important than their meat, which was only eaten on special occasions.

A BEAUTIFUL BRIDE FOR ISAAC

✤ Genesis 24 ✤

When Abraham was nearing the end of his life, he began to think about finding a wife for his son, Isaac. He did not want Isaac to marry a woman from Canaan, where they were living.

So Abraham sent for one of his servants. He told the servant that God would help him to find a bride for Isaac among the family's relatives in their homeland of Mesopotamia.

The servant set off, and when he arrived outside the city where Abraham's brother Nahor lived, he let his tired camels rest near a well.

He prayed, "Lord God, please may one of the young women coming to the well be the bride you have chosen for Isaac. When I ask her for water, let her offer to water my camels, too, so that I may know she is the right woman."

Even before he had finished praying, a beautiful young woman called Rebecca who was Nahor's granddaughter, arrived to fill the water jar on her shoulder.

"Please give me a drink of water from your jar," the servant said.

"Gladly, sir," Rebecca replied, "and I will also bring water for your camels."

The servant was delighted that his prayer had been answered. Rebecca was the right one! He praised God, and gave her gifts of jewellery. "Is there room for me to stay at your father's house?" he asked.

"You are very welcome," she replied. Rebecca's father and brother welcomed the servant, who gave them gifts from Abraham. They listened carefully to his story about how God had chosen Rebecca to be Isaac's wife, and they happily agreed to the marriage. The next morning, Rebecca said goodbye to her family and travelled back to Canaan with the servant.

When they drew near, they saw Isaac walking in the fields. Rebecca got down from the camel to meet her new husband, shyly covering her face with her scarf.

When he heard the servant's story, Isaac was delighted to meet his beautiful bride, and took Rebecca into his tent and married her. And Isaac loved Rebecca very much.

Water jars
Pottery water jars like these have been used for centuries to fetch water from wells. Their size and shape has changed little over the years. In many dry parts of the world today, wells are still the main source of water for people and their animals.

JACOB TAKES ESAU'S BLESSING

✤ Genesis 25-27 ✤

For many years, Isaac's wife Rebecca was unable to have children. Then at last she gave birth to twin sons, Esau and Jacob. Before they were born, God told Rebecca that he planned to make Jacob the head of the family, even though he was younger than his brother Esau.

One day, Esau came home from hunting feeling very hungry, so he asked Jacob to give him a portion of the lentil stew he was cooking.

"Only if you give me your rights as the first-born son," Jacob replied.

"All right," agreed Esau, greedily taking the food without caring too much about losing his inheritance. "I am about to die of hunger anyway. What good would my rights be to me then?"

Years later, when Isaac knew he was coming to the end of his life, he wanted to put his affairs in order. "Go and kill an animal for me, Esau, and cook me a tasty meal. Then I will give you my final blessing before I die."

Rebecca was listening, and decided to make God's plan for Jacob come true. "I will cook your father a meal," she told Jacob, "then you can pretend to be Esau and receive your father's blessing instead."

Jacob protested, "Father is almost blind, but I am not hairy like Esau, so he will know that it is me."

Rebecca answered by dressing Jacob in Esau's best clothes, and putting goat-skins on his arms and neck to make him feel hairy.

"Are you really Esau?" Isaac asked, when Jacob took him the meal.

"I am," Jacob lied, hoping to trick his father.

Isaac recognized the smell of Esau's clothes and felt his hairy arms. Believing it was Esau, he gave Jacob his blessing to be in charge of the family when he died.

So when Esau arrived home shortly afterwards and brought his father his meal, Isaac was shocked to discover he'd been tricked. "Your cunning brother deceived me and stole your blessing," Isaac told him, in great distress.

Esau exploded with anger and begged his father, "You must bless me, too!" but there was nothing Isaac could do.

CHEATING

Cheating is dishonest. It's not fair if someone at school gets a better mark than us because they have cheated. We may feel angry with them and that we can't trust them any more. People who cheat never get away with it; in the end they usually get found out and punished.

Lentils and beans
Lentils and beans are a favourite food throughout the Near East. They can be boiled to make stew, like the one that Jacob gave to Esau, or they can be mixed with other ingredients to make bread.

Lentil plant
The lentil is a member of the pea family. It is a small plant, with five or six pairs of tendril-bearing leaves on each stem. It has white-and-violet striped flowers with flat pods which encase the lentils.

JACOB WORKS LONG AND HARD

❖ Genesis 28-29 ❖

Angels
In the Bible, angels sometimes appear to people in dreams or visions, like the one that Jacob had at Bethel. Angels are spiritual beings with superhuman powers. They often act as God's messengers. Although they are often pictured by artists as men with wings growing out of their shoulders, the Bible gives little detail about what angels look like. However, their appearance must have been unusual enough to distinguish them from ordinary people.

Esau was so angry that Jacob had stolen his blessing, that he threatened to kill his brother. But Rebecca overheard his plans and warned Jacob. She told Jacob to leave at once and go to stay with his uncle, Laban, in Haran.

On the journey, Jacob lay down to sleep with his head on a stone and had a vivid dream. He saw a vision of a gigantic stairway, with its bottom on the earth, and its top reaching all the way up to heaven. Angels were climbing up and down it.

At the top was God. He spoke to Jacob and promised, "I will give this land to you and your many descendants."

When Jacob woke up, he felt amazed that God had spoken to him, and worshipped God by making the stone he had used as a pillow into an altar. He called the place Bethel, which means "the house of God".

Then Jacob continued on his journey until he reached a well where shepherds were waiting to water their sheep. "Do you know my uncle, Laban?" he asked them.

"Yes, we do," they replied, "and here comes his beautiful daughter, Rachel."

Jacob lifted the heavy stone from the well to help Rachel give her sheep some water, then introduced himself as her cousin. Rachel ran to fetch her father, Laban, who invited Jacob to stay in Haran and work for him.

Jacob soon fell in love with Rachel. When Laban offered him payment for his hard work, all Jacob asked for was to marry her. He even offered to work for nothing for seven years. Laban agreed, and because Jacob loved Rachel so much, the seven years seemed like only a few days.

But when the wedding took place, Laban tricked Jacob into marrying his eldest daughter, Leah, who was not beautiful.

"Why have you broken our agreement?" Jacob asked, angrily.

"The elder daughter must marry first," Laban explained. "But do not worry. You can marry Rachel at the end of this week if you work for me for another seven years."

Jacob was disappointed, but he loved Rachel so much that he agreed to work the extra years.

Now Jacob had two wives, Rachel and Leah, but he loved Rachel more.

WELCOME HOME, BROTHER

✤ Genesis 32-33 ✤

Despite Jacob's hard work as a shepherd, Laban continued to cheat him, so after Rachel gave birth to their son Joseph, Jacob decided to return home to Canaan.

Jacob set off with Rachel and Leah and their children, his servants, and his large flocks of animals, but worry filled his mind. Did his brother, Esau, still want to kill him for stealing his inheritance? He sent Esau a message that he hoped they would now be friends.

But his messengers returned with a warning that Esau was coming to meet him with four hundred men. Jacob was frightened at the thought of an army attacking his family, and prayed earnestly, "Lord God, I do not deserve your help, but please save me and my loved ones!"

Wisely, Jacob divided his people into two groups so that if one group was attacked, at least the other could escape. Then he told his servants to present some of his animals to Esau, hoping that this generosity would soften his brother's anger.

In the middle of the night, Jacob sent his family and everything he owned across the river Jabbok to safety, but he stayed alone on the other side.

Suddenly a man appeared, and began wrestling with Jacob. They fought all night, and when the man realized he could not beat Jacob, he struck Jacob's hip, which was thrown out of joint. The man cried out for Jacob to let him go, but Jacob insisted, "Not until you bless me."

Then the man said, "Now that you have wrestled with God and won, you will be called Israel instead of Jacob."

Jacob asked who he was, but the man simply blessed him and would not answer. "I have seen God face to face and am still alive!" Jacob said, filled with awe and wonder, as he limped away on his injured hip.

Later that day, Jacob bravely went ahead of his family to meet Esau, bowing humbly and hoping that his brother had forgiven him.

But Esau was no enemy. Instead he threw his arms around Jacob in a friendly hug and welcomed his family, and soon they were both crying with happiness.

Rachel
Jacob was tricked into marrying Leah, but later married Rachel too. This placed a terrible strain on their home life. Leah was desperate for a son to win her husband's love. She eventually had four sons, but Rachel was childless for many years. Jacob was caught between the two of them.

KEEPING SHEEP
The first shepherd mentioned in the Bible is Abel. Being a shepherd was hard work. In such a dry and stony land, it was always difficult for him to find enough grass and water to feed his flocks.

JOSEPH'S DREAMS

♣ Genesis 37 ♣

Jacob had twelve sons, but it was Joseph who had a special place in his heart, because he was Rachel's son. To show everyone that Joseph was his favourite, Jacob gave him a fabulous coat to wear. It had long sleeves and was made of fine material woven in all the colours of the rainbow.

All Joseph's brothers were jealous of him, and it didn't help that Joseph told Jacob every time his brothers did something wrong. In fact, his brothers hated Joseph so much that they were hardly pleasant to him at all.

One night, Joseph had an unusual dream. "In my dream," Joseph told his brothers, "we were all working in the fields, tying up bundles of wheat, when suddenly my bundle stood up straight and your bundles bowed down to it."

His brothers were not impressed. "Do you really think you are going to rule over us?" they asked, and hated him all the more.

Later, Joseph boasted to his eleven brothers about another dream, which made them even more angry. "Listen to this!" he said. "In my dream I saw the sun, the moon, and eleven stars bowing down to me!"

He told his father about the dream, but even Jacob was annoyed with him and told Joseph off. "Do you really think that your mother and I and all your brothers are going to bow down to you? Don't be so ridiculous!"

But once Jacob had calmed down, he wondered about the dream. Perhaps Joseph had been specially chosen by God to be a leader and the dream would come true, after all.

JOSEPH SOLD AS A SLAVE

✤ Genesis 37 ✤

One day, Jacob sent Joseph to check on his brothers. They were in the fields, looking after their flocks of sheep. By now, Joseph's brothers were so full of hatred and jealousy that they wanted to kill him. They were just waiting for a good opportunity to put their plan into action.

"Look, here comes the dreamer," they sneered, spotting Joseph in the distance wearing his fancy coat of many colours. "Let's kill him and throw his body into a dry well, then all his dreams will come to nothing! We can pretend that a wild animal killed him, so that we do not get into trouble."

But the eldest brother, Reuben, protested, saying, "Don't kill him. Let's just throw him into one of these wells." He secretly hoped to come back later and help Joseph to escape.

Dyes
Bright and colourful dyes like these can be found on sale in many Middle Eastern markets today. But the Bible only mentions four colours of dye – purple, blue, crimson and scarlet. These dyes would have been made from natural products such as shellfish, insects and plant roots.

Coat tassels
The Greek translation of the Bible describes Joseph's coat as a "coat of many colours", but it would be more accurately translated as a richly decorated, long-sleeved robe. It was probably made from cloth woven with coloured thread and fringed with tassels around the hem.

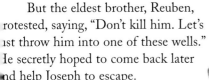

So when Joseph arrived, the brothers pulled off his fine coat and threw him into a dry well. Then they sat down to eat, ignoring Joseph's cries for help.

A little later, one of the brothers, Judah, noticed a group of Ishmaelite traders passing by on their camels, on their way to Egypt. He said to the others, "I have an idea. Why don't we sell Joseph as a slave, instead of murdering him, then we won't feel so guilty. After all, he is our brother."

His brothers agreed, so when the next group of Ishmaelite traders came past, they pulled Joseph out of the well and sold him to them for twenty pieces of silver. The brothers did not care that Joseph would face a hard life as a slave.

To cover up what they had done, they killed a goat and dipped Joseph's coat into its blood, then took it to show their father.

Jacob was horrified when he saw it. "It is Joseph's coat!" he wailed. "He has been torn to pieces by a wild animal!"

Jacob was so upset that no one could comfort him, and he mourned his favourite son for a very long time.

Camel traders
Traders like this Bedouin with his camels would have been a familiar sight in Joseph's day. Camels allowed traders to carry heavy goods through desert areas. The Ishmaelite traders in this story would probably have been carrying spices and incense to sell in Egypt.

THROWN INTO PRISON

✦ Genesis 39 ✦

Egyptian queen
Wall paintings discovered from ancient Egyptian tombs tell us a lot about how these people lived. Fine linen clothes and elaborate jewellery were typical dress for noblewomen like Potiphar's wife. This queen holds the ankh symbol, which represents eternal life. Only gods, kings and queens could carry this symbol as only they had the power to give or take away life.

Eye make-up
Egyptian women wore a lot of make-up. Different minerals, like galena or lead ore – which makes kohl, for example – were ground down and then mixed with water to make a paste. The paint was kept in a tube and applied with a little stick of wood or bronze. Archaeological discoveries from Egypt have unearthed many examples of tubes and pots like this one made from painted pottery.

Once they reached Egypt, the Ishmaelite traders sold Joseph as a slave. He was bought by a man called Potiphar, who had an important job as captain of the guards at the Egyptian king's palace. Potiphar soon realized that Joseph was a hard-working man, and that God was making him successful in everything he did. So he put Joseph in charge of his house and trusted him with everything he owned.

But trouble lay ahead. Because Joseph was a strong, attractive man, Potiphar's wife began to desire him and tried to persuade him to make love to her.

Joseph was horrified and told her firmly, "Your husband has trusted me with everything in this house, but he certainly has not given you to me. I will not sin against God by doing such a terrible thing!"

But Potiphar's wife would not give up. Every day, she kept trying to persuade him. But still Joseph would not give in to temptation, and he did his best to avoid being near her.

Then one day, when none of the other servants were around, Potiphar's wife grabbed Joseph by his coat and insisted that he go to bed with her. Luckily, Joseph managed to escape from her, but as he ran off he left his coat behind in her hands.

"Look what Joseph has done!" Potiphar's wife cried out to her servants,

pretending to be very upset. "He tried to force me into bed, but I screamed and he ran off!"

When her husband, Potiphar, came home, she showed him Joseph's coat and told him the same terrible lies, and he believed her. Angrily, he ordered Joseph's arrest and had him thrown into prison.

Calamity had struck Joseph, but God was with him, even in prison. The prison guard soon realized that Joseph could be trusted, and helped him by putting him in charge of all the other prisoners. Everything in the prison ran smoothly, because God helped Joseph succeed in everything that he did.

TELL ME WHAT MY DREAMS MEAN

✤ **Genesis 40-41** ✤

While he was in prison, Joseph became servant to the Egyptian king's wine steward and to his chief baker. They had both angered the king and were in prison waiting to hear their fate. One night, both men had strange dreams which they could not understand, so Joseph offered to explain their meaning.

The wine steward said, "In my dream, I squeezed the juice from the grapes on three branches into the king's wine cup."

Joseph was delighted to tell him, "God is saying that in three days, the king will give you your job back."

Then the chief baker said, "In my dream, I was carrying three baskets of pastries for the king, but the birds were eating them up."

Joseph told him, sadly, "God is saying that in three days, the king will cut off your head."

And three days later, the king did exactly what Joseph had told them.

Joseph was still in prison two years later when, one night, the king had a puzzling dream which none of his wise men could interpret. When the wine steward told him that Joseph could explain dreams, the king summoned Joseph from prison. "I have been told that you can explain the meaning of dreams," he said.

Joseph carefully replied, "I cannot, but if you give me the details, God will tell me the meaning."

So the king began to relate his dreams. "I dreamt that I was standing by the river Nile, when seven fat cows came out of the river to eat grass. Then seven thin cows appeared and ate the fat cows. I also dreamt that I saw seven ripe ears of corn, which were swallowed

by seven thin, scorched ears of corn. Tell me, what does it all mean, Joseph?"

"God is telling you to prepare yourself for seven years of plentiful harvests, followed by seven years of terrible famine," Joseph explained. "You must put a clever man in charge of the country at once. Only if you save food wisely while it is plentiful will your people be saved from starvation during the famine."

Bread stamp
This is the kind of bread stamp that the chief baker would have used. His job was to grind and sieve flour, then knead it with water and yeast to make a dough. He shaped the dough into loaves, then stamped them and baked them in an oven.

JOSEPH PUT IN CHARGE

✤ **Genesis 41-42** ✤

Signet ring
A signet ring was a symbol of office. Joseph was given the king's ring as a sign that the king had transferred his royal authority to him. The ring was used to stamp the king's personal seal on official documents. Joseph would have worn it on his finger, or on a cord around his neck.

Crops
Along the banks of the Nile, conditions were ideal for growing crops. The climate was sunny, and there were lots of workers. Every year, the Nile flooded and water spread on to the land around it. This made the soil rich and fertile. Farmers cut special canals and channels to spread the flood waters on to the fields.

Egyptian cat goddess
The Egyptians worshipped many gods. Some of them represented particular powers of nature, such as the sun, or the Nile floods. The cat goddess, Bastet, was the daughter of the sun god, Re. Bastet was believed to have the power of the sun to ripen crops.

Now Joseph could put God's plan into action. He opened up the storehouses and sold the corn that he had carefully kept from the plentiful harvests. In fact, there was so much corn that many people from other countries came to Egypt to buy some for themselves because they were suffering from famine, too.

Joseph's family in Canaan also had no food, so Jacob told his sons, "Go to Egypt and buy some corn, so that we will not starve to death."

So Joseph's brothers travelled to Egypt. But remembering the tragic loss of his favourite son, Joseph, Jacob kept his youngest son, Benjamin, safely at home.

O nce Joseph had explained his dreams to him, the king realized what a wise man Joseph was. Clearly, he could hear God and was the right person to make sure that Egypt did not fall into ruin because of the coming famine.

"I now make you chief minister over all of Egypt!" the king declared, giving Joseph some smart clothes, a gold chain, and even putting one of his own royal signet rings on Joseph's finger to show his new authority. What a change – from prisoner to minister!

Now Joseph had to set about making sure there was enough food to feed the people. For the next seven years, there were plentiful harvests, just as God had said there would be. Joseph travelled around the country, collecting food from the fields and taking it to the cities to be stored. Corn was piled so high that it looked like millions of grains of sand on a beach, and Joseph gave up trying to measure how much there was.

Then, just as God had said, there were seven years of dreadful famine, when the crops in the fields did not grow. The Egyptian people were in danger of starving and they cried out to their king for food. The king told them to go to Joseph.

JOSEPH FEEDS HIS FAMILY

✤ Genesis 42-45 ✤

Joseph's brothers did not recognize him as they bowed before the mighty Egyptian minister. Joseph pretended not to know them either. "You are spies," he accused them, harshly.

"No!" they protested. "We are an honest family. We have just come to buy food. There were twelve of us, but one of our brothers is dead, and our youngest brother is at home."

But Joseph had his brothers thrown into prison. After three days, he said to them, "If you want to save yourselves from death, bring your youngest brother to me. I will keep Simeon here as a hostage until you return to prove your honesty."

"Now we are paying the price for what we did to Joseph," Reuben sadly told his brothers. Joseph overheard this, and wept. He felt sorry for his family, so he let his brothers take home some corn.

Once they were back in Canaan, the family soon ate all the corn and Jacob reluctantly had to agree to let the brothers take Benjamin back to Egypt.

When Joseph saw Benjamin again, he was so pleased that he went outside and wept tears of joy. Then he treated his brothers to a magnificent feast.

Later, Joseph had their sacks filled with food. He also hid his special silver cup in Benjamin's sack, to test whether his brothers had become better people. When the missing cup was found in Benjamin's sack, the brothers were all arrested.

"You are guilty, so now you must become my slave," Joseph told the frightened Benjamin.

Judah was worried. "Our father has already lost Joseph. If he loses Benjamin too, he will die of grief. I will become your slave instead." All those years ago, Judah had been the one who suggested selling Joseph into slavery, yet now he wanted to sacrifice himself to free Benjamin.

Joseph cried with relief. "Don't you see? It is me, Joseph! God sent me to rule Egypt so I could save you from starving." He hugged his excited brothers. "Tell my father that you must all come and live here in Egypt, where there is plenty of food."

Egyptian silver cup
At the time of Joseph, silver was a precious metal that had to be imported into Egypt from Syria, so it was very valuable. Only noble men and women would have drunk from silver cups; ordinary people had cups made of pottery. The theft of Joseph's cup was a serious matter, not only because it was very valuable, but also because of Joseph's important position as chief minister.

POWER TO HELP OTHERS
In this story, Joseph is able to use his powerful position to help his brothers. You may sometimes be in a powerful position, too. For example, if a new boy or girl joins your class at school, they may feel lonely, or even a bit scared. If you have a big group of friends and know your way around the school, you are in a much more powerful position. It is good to use this power properly, by being kind to the new person and helping them to settle in.

A BABY IN THE REEDS

✦ Exodus 1-2 ✦

The king of Egypt was frightened by the many Israelites living in his country. He treated them very cruelly, making them slaves. Then the king told the midwives who helped the Hebrew women give birth to kill the babies if they were boys. But the midwives respected God so did not obey the king.

Finally, the king ordered, "Drown their baby boys in the river Nile!"

One Hebrew woman had a lovely son and didn't want him to be killed. She kept him at home until he was three months old and she could hide him no longer. She made a floating papyrus basket, placed him in it and gently pushed it off into the Nile.

"Watch what happens," the mother said to her daughter Miriam. As the boat bobbed in the reeds near the bank, the king's daughter and her servants came to swim. She noticed the basket, and as she peered inside the baby began to cry.

"It's a poor Hebrew baby," the princess exclaimed in amazement.

Seeing that she felt sorry for the baby, his sister bravely approached the princess and asked, "Shall I fetch a Hebrew lady to nurse the child?"

"Yes, go," she replied and so Miriam raced off to fetch her mother.

"Look after this child for me and I will pay you," the king's daughter told her. So the child's natural mother cared for him until he was older. The king's daughter adopted him and named him Moses.

Nile crocodile
Crocodiles are no longer found in the waters of the Nile below the Aswan Dam, but in the time of Moses they were numerous. Regarded as sacred by the Egyptians, crocodiles are the largest of all existing reptiles and can grow to well over 6 metres. Leaving a baby in a basket in the reeds of the Nile was very risky.

The finding of Moses
Moses was found in the papyrus reeds of the Nile by the king's daughter. She adopted him as her son, and gave him the name Moses, which sounds like the Hebrew for "drawn out of the water".

MOSES STANDS ON HOLY GROUND

✤ **Exodus** 3-4 ✤

When Moses grew up, he left Egypt and became a shepherd. One day he saw a bush on fire, but despite the flames the bush wasn't burning up at all.

He went over to get a closer look and the voice of God from inside the strange bush called to him, "Don't come any nearer! Take your sandals off because you are standing on holy ground. I am the God of Abraham, Isaac, and Jacob." Moses trembled with fear.

"I have seen the sorrow of my people in Egypt. I have heard their cries of suffering at the hands of their cruel masters and have decided to rescue them from Egypt and take them to a wonderful land full of everything that they will need. I have chosen you to go to the king and demand that he allows them to leave."

Moses thought up one excuse after another. Every time he thought of a reason for not going, God overruled it.

When Moses asked him how to reply if he was asked who had sent him, God told him to say, "Tell them 'I AM WHO I AM' has sent you." God also assured him that he would prove his power by performing great miracles.

Moses was still unsure. "I really don't want to do it. Please send somebody else!"

This time God became angry and thundered, "Very well then. I will send your brother Aaron to do the talking." So the two of them set out nervously for Egypt.

Shepherd and flock
Sheep were important animals because they provided people with milk, meat and wool for clothes. They were not kept in fields but roamed over the land, which was also home to wild animals. Shepherds protected their flocks and found them fresh water and grass.

Sandals
These sandals from the time of Moses are made from woven papyrus, palm leaves and grass. From their open design it is easy to understand how dusty the feet would get on a journey and to appreciate the need for the ritual foot washing. Removing one's sandals was a sign of respect in the presence of God, a custom still observed in Muslim, Hindu and Buddhist temples today.

יהוה

Yahweh
These letters are Hebrew for "Yahweh" which translates as "I am who I am". There are several names for God in the Bible, but Yahweh is considered to be his most sacred name by the Jewish people and they do not pronounce it. In English bibles it is usually written as "The Lord".

41 ✤

PLAGUES STRIKE AT EGYPT

✤ Exodus 5-10 ✤

Ramses II

Ramses II was also known as Ramses the Great because of the enormous temples and statues he built during his 67-year reign. Records show that much of this building work was done using slave labour. He was also a great military leader. The date of the Exodus is uncertain, so while some scholars believe that it happened during the reign of Ramses II, we cannot be certain.

Cobra

A cobra was one of the symbols of the Egyptian king's power and a representation of it was worn on the front of his royal head-dress, supposedly to spit fire at his enemies. The venom of the cobra works by paralyzing the nervous system. When Aaron turned his staff into a snake it was probably a cobra.

Aaron and Moses presented themselves to the king of Egypt. "The Lord God of Israel says you are to let his people go so that they may hold a festival in the desert to honour him."

But the king replied, "Who is this God? I certainly will not let the Israelites go."

So incensed was he by the request that he made the life of the slaves even more difficult. From now on they even had to make the bricks for the great temples they were being forced to build.

When Moses realized how distressed they were, he prayed again to God.

"Go back to the king. Even though he will do everything he can to resist me, he will eventually see my power and let you go," came the reply from God.

Once more Moses and Aaron appeared before the king of the Egyptians. While they were there, Aaron threw down his staff and it became a snake, but when the king saw his own magicians do the same thing he was unimpressed and stubbornly refused to listen to Moses.

God then told Moses to announce to the king that the river Nile would turn into blood. When it happened the king was still unmoved and so God brought a succession of dreadful plagues upon Egypt: he sent frogs that found their way into the people's houses; then irritating gnats appeared from

nowhere; after they had gone flies swarmed throughout the land covering all the people and animals; then the animals of Egypt were struck down with a mysterious disease; next horrible boils broke out on all the Egyptians; hail destroyed crops and killed the livestock in the fields; then a dark cloud of locusts came down and stripped the countryside of vegetation; finally the whole land was shrouded in darkness for three days.

During each plague the king said that the people could leave, but when Moses stopped it, he changed his mind.

When Moses went to see the king after this final plague, the king said the people could go.

Moses told him, "We must also take our animals with us so that we can make sacrifices to God."

DEATH PASSES OVER GOD'S PEOPLE

✤ Exodus 11-12 ✤

Before his last meeting with the king, God had told Moses, "I will send one last plague upon Egypt, after which the king will expel you from his country."

At the end of his interview with the king, Moses told him what the final plague would be: "At midnight God will pass throughout your country and every first-born male from the highest to the lowest will be killed. The whole of Egypt will resound to the anguished tears of mourning parents. Only my people will be spared this tragedy. Then you will send your officials to me begging us to leave."

Moses then stormed out of the king's presence for the last time and went to his people to prepare them for the dramatic events of the night.

"Listen carefully to everything I have to say," he told the Israelites. "Each family is to choose a lamb and kill it this evening. Then they are to coat some blood on the doorposts. Then you must go inside and close the door tightly; no one is to venture out because God will pass through the land. Wherever he sees blood on the doorpost he will pass over that house. Every year you must do the same thing to remind you and your children of the way in which God killed the Egyptians, yet spared his own people the Israelites."

The people did as Moses told them and that night God kept his promise. Every Egyptian household lost a son, struck dead by God.

Early next morning the king sent messengers to Moses, pleading with him to leave. As the sun rose, the Israelites set off, driving their flocks past anguished groups of Egyptians who watched them walk off to freedom in the desert.

Hyssop

Although hyssop is mentioned many times in the Bible we are not certain of the plant's identity. Hyssop was used in the passover rites, for the purification of lepers, as a cure for plague, and in sacrifices. The herb we know as hyssop today grows throughout southern Europe.

PASSOVER FESTIVAL

The deliverance of the Israelites (the Jewish nation) from slavery in Egypt is commemorated by the Passover Festival. The word "passover" recalls how God allowed the plague to pass over the homes of the Israelites. Each year the festival is celebrated in Jewish households with a special meal of roasted lamb, unleavened bread and bitter herbs.

43 ✤

THE JOURNEY TO THE PROMISED LAND

The descendants of Jacob – the twelve tribes of Israel – increased in number when they settled in Egypt. But in due course the Egyptians felt threatened by the increasing numbers of the Israelites, so they put slave drivers over them hoping to wear them out under the heavy burdens. It was the exodus from Egypt, under the leadership of Moses, that marked the birth of Israel as a nation.

Moses

Born of Israelite parents in Egypt, Moses was placed in the Nile in a basket and found and brought up by Pharaoh's daughter. Trying to bring peace between two fellow Israelites, Moses killed an Egyptian and fled to Midian, where he spent forty years in isolation. God called him at the burning bush and he returned to Egypt to confront Pharaoh and to lead the Israelites out of slavery in Egypt through the Red Sea. He received the law, including the Ten Commandments, from God on Mount Sinai, and supervised the building of the Tabernacle. He was not allowed to go into the Promised Land because of his disobedience in carrying out God's instructions.

God calls Moses

Egyptian religion

The Egyptians had many gods and were very superstitious, wearing charms for good luck. They held a materialistic view of the afterlife. At death, a body's vital organs like the heart and liver were taken out and put in canopic jars. The rest of the body was then mummified and buried in coffins along with all the belongings a person might need in the afterlife.

Canopic jars

Culture

From the well-preserved pictorial records of Egyptian everyday life and religious practices, we know a great deal about their culture and beliefs. Archaeological excavations have uncovered quantities of beautiful articles, revealing their high level of skill in metal-working, carpentry, weaving, pottery, and building. Literature and the arts flourished, and they had knowledge of many other subjects such as medicine and mathematics.

Egyptian painting

Pharaoh

Pharaoh was the name given to the king of Egypt. He was seen as an intermediary between the gods and ordinary people. His position as civil and religious ruler gave him absolute power and authority. We can't be sure which Pharaoh oppressed the Israelites, but it may have been Ramses II.

Slaves

Women in captivity

The nation of Israel prospered and increased during their 400 years in Egypt, to the extent that the Egyptians began to see them as a threat. They were forced into slavery, making bricks for the king's building projects. A law was made to drown their newborn babies in the Nile to try and reduce their numbers.

Plagues

God sent a series of natural disasters, or plagues, upon the Egyptians to persuade Pharaoh to let the Israelites leave. After the tenth plague, the Egyptians heaped clothing and precious jewellery upon the Israelites, only too glad to see them go. Through the plagues, God showed his supremacy over the gods of Egypt.

Quails and manna

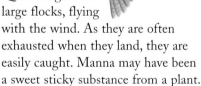

Quail

In the wilderness, God fed his people with manna and quails. Quails migrate in large flocks, flying with the wind. As they are often exhausted when they land, they are easily caught. Manna may have been a sweet sticky substance from a plant.

Climate

For forty years in the desert, the Israelites endured extreme climatic conditions. Hot days and cold nights for most of the year gave way during the rainy season to mists, fog and dews. The mountains of granite rock and the barrenness of the surroundings were relieved by occasional oases and wadis where vegetation flourished around a water source.

The spies return

Joshua

Moses' assistant and military commander Joshua, was one of the spies sent to explore the land of Canaan. He encouraged the people to go in, and as successor to Moses, was chosen to lead the people of Israel into the land. He is known especially for the miraculous victory at Jericho and for his obedience in leading Israel.

Caleb

Caleb was also one of the twelve spies Moses sent to explore Canaan. Although all the spies brought back a good report of the land, only Joshua and Caleb had the faith to believe that God would enable them to conquer it, and only these two were eventually allowed to settle there – all the other Israelites born in Egypt died in the wilderness.

The land of Canaan

Canaan was a land of hills and valleys rising from the coastal plains and then falling sharply away again to the rift valley of the river Jordan. The temperate to tropical climate and the seasonal contrast between hot dry summers and wet winters meant that snow could lie on the mountain tops while tropical fruits could ripen in the valleys. A great variety of crops could be grown, including cereals, fruit trees, vines and vegetables. The land seemed like a garden paradise after the desert.

Tabernacle

In the desert, Israel constructed the Tabernacle, or tent of meeting, for the worship of God. It was based on the design that God gave to Moses on Mount Sinai. It consisted of a tent made of linen and goats' hair curtains, overlaid with two waterproof coverings of animal skins, draped over a supporting frame of acacia wood. The tent was divided into the Holy Place and the Most Holy Place, where the Ark of the Covenant was kept. Everything had to be portable so that it could be easily transported.

Canaanites

Various peoples, like the Hittites, Amorites, Girgashites, Perizzites, Hivites and Jebusites for example, were known collectively as Canaanites. They were originally the descendants of Noah's grandson Canaan. Because of his disrespect, he and his descendants were cursed.

Canaanite religion

Baal

Canaanite religion involved the worship of many gods and goddesses. Chief among these was Baal, the god of the weather, who was thought to hold the key to a successful harvest – essential for survival. Canaanite fertility rites were also widespread.

The journey to the Promised Land
After forty years in the Sinai desert the Israelites probably went south, but we do not know their exact route. They avoided the coastal region because of fear of attack from the Philistines.

Great Sea (Mediterranean)

Jericho
Ashdod
Salt Sea
CANAAN
Gaza   Hebron
Arad?
MOAB
The way to the Land of the Philistines
Bene-jaakan/ Beeroth
Ra'amses
Qantir
Baal-zephon
the way to Shur
Kadesh-barnea ('Ain Qudeirat)
EDOM
GOSHEN
Pithom
Succoth
Great Bitter Lake
Mt. Sinai?/ (Jebel Helal)
The King's Highway
Wilderness of Paran
EGYPT
SINAI
MIDIAN
(Gulf of Suez)
Mt. Sinai?/ Mt. Horeb
(Gulf of Aqabah)

—— Exodus route
—— Alternative exodus route

0   50   100 km
0   30   60 miles

River Nile

Red Sea

CROSSING THE RED SEA

✤ Exodus 13-15 ✤

Chariot horse
Egyptian chariot horses drew two-wheeled vehicles which were used not only in warfare, but also for hunting, or as a means of transport for wealthy or noble people. The battle chariots of the Egyptian army which pursued the Israelites were designed to be stable, fast and easy to manoeuvre. They were fitted out to hold bows, arrows and spears and were used as firing platforms.

When he led the Israelites out of Egypt, God directed them towards the Red Sea along the desert route. During the day he gave them a bright pillar of cloud to follow and at night they were to follow a glowing pillar of fire.

When the king of Egypt was informed of the departure of the people, he regretted his decision to let them go.

"What have I done? We need those Israelites to work for us. Let's go and bring them back." So he assembled his army and, leading the way in his chariot, set off after the Israelites.

When the people saw dust in the distance they knew that the king had changed his mind. With the Egyptians behind them and the Red Sea in front of them they realized that they were trapped. Terrified, they shouted at Moses, "Why have you brought us all this way to die in the desert? It would have been better to be slaves of the Egyptians rather than be slaughtered here in this dreadful place."

Moses replied, "Don't be afraid. God will rescue us today and kill every one of those Egyptians galloping towards us."

God then said to Moses, "Point your staff over the sea and I will push back the water so that my people can pass safely over on dry land." When Moses did as God commanded, the water divided in the middle leaving a dry path. Nervously at first, and then with increasing confidence, the Israelites scurried across to the other side between the two walls of water.

When the Egyptians attempted to cross too, God told Moses to raise his staff towards the sea again. As he did so the water crashed over the Egyptians, sweeping them away to their deaths.

The Israelites were so thankful for their remarkable deliverance that they joyfully celebrated their victory over the Egyptians with singing and dancing before continuing on their journey.

GOD FEEDS HIS PEOPLE

✤ Exodus 16-17 ✤

After a few weeks in the desert the Israelites began to grumble to Moses. "In Egypt we were never hungry, but since we have been following you we haven't had enough to eat. It would have been better to have died in Egypt!"

Moses replied, "This evening you will see how God looks after you even though you are complaining about him. When you eat meat tonight and fresh bread tomorrow morning, then you will realize that God cares for you."

Later that evening birds called quails appeared and the next morning the Israelites found food called manna lying on the ground.

"This is the special food that God is sending you," Moses told the people. "You are to collect as much as you need each day and once a week you must gather double so that you don't have to work on the Sabbath, which is to be a day free from work." For all the time that the Israelites were in the desert God provided manna and quails for them, and they were never hungry again.

The desert was hot and sticky and the Israelites needed water as well as food, but it was difficult to find. One day they camped where there was no water anywhere. Again they began to complain, "We're dying of thirst. We have come all this way only to die."

Moses asked God what he should do, for the people were ready to kill him. "Go to Horeb and strike the large rock there. When you do, enough water will come out for everyone to drink."

Moses followed God's command and enough water gushed from the rock for everyone to quench their thirst. So despite their moaning, God ensured that the Israelites had plenty to eat and drink during their travels.

THE TEN COMMANDMENTS

✤ Exodus 19-20 ✤

God said to Moses, "Lead the people to Mount Sinai. They are to wait at its foot while you and Aaron climb to the summit." When they had reached the bottom God descended upon the mountain, covering it in a thick cloud of smoke. There was a crashing of thunder and the ground shook violently. Then God called Moses up to speak with him. This is what God said:

I am the Lord who rescued you from Egypt. You are to have no other gods before me.

Do not try and represent God by making an idol or any other image of him.

Do not misuse the name of the Lord your God.

Remember the Sabbath day by keeping it holy.

Respect your father and your mother.

Do not murder.
Do not commit adultery.
Do not steal.
Do not tell lies.
Do not long to have anything that belongs to another person.

Moses
Moses was the first and greatest leader of Israel. Not only did he lead them out of slavery in Egypt, but he kept them together in the desert when they tried to rebel. Through Moses God gave the people of Israel his religious and social laws so that they could become God's special people.

Moses' burial place
This church is built on the site where Moses is thought to have died. The Bible says that he died on Mount Nebo, but that no one knew exactly where. Moses had hoped to take the Israelites into Canaan, but God would not allow him to because he once disobeyed God.

THE TEN COMMANDMENTS
The Ten Commandments are a summary of how God expects people to live in every age and every culture. They are not just rules for the ancient Israelites. People can fulfill the potential God has given them only when they honour God, keep to the rhythms of life he created, protect other people's lives and respect their rights and property. Respecting parents is another way of saying that family life is something to protect and cherish.

GOD'S HOLY LAWS

❖ **Leviticus 1-27** ❖

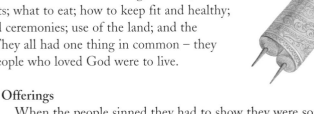

The Ten Commandments were the most important rules that God gave to the Israelites. There were many others which gave practical details of how these rules were to be obeyed. The rules covered every aspect of life: how to make appropriate sacrifices and offerings to God; the ordination and conduct of priests; what to eat; how to keep fit and healthy; religious practice and ceremonies; use of the land; and the importance of rest. They all had one thing in common – they were to show how people who loved God were to live.

Talmud
The Talmud is the code of Jewish civil and religious law and is kept strictly by orthodox Jews. It is composed of the oral law, the "Mishnah", and the rabbis' comments on this, the "Gemara".

Offerings

When the people sinned they had to show they were sorry by sacrificing an animal or some grain to God. They took their gift to the priest who would burn it. By doing something that cost them money and time they showed him that they realized how serious sin was, and it served as a reminder to them not to make the same mistake twice.

Priests

Aaron, Moses' brother, was the first priest. All the priests came from his family. Before beginning work they attended a special ceremony. Their tasks were to make sure the people obeyed God, to teach them the difference between right and wrong, and to accept offerings on God's behalf. By doing this they would keep the Israelites holy.

Carrying the Torah scrolls
The Torah (Jewish law) is read publicly every Saturday at a synagogue. Before the reading, the scrolls are carried in a procession around the building. It is divided into fifty-four portions and is read through once a year.

Food

God did not allow his people to eat everything. Some animals and birds were considered unsuitable for eating. This may have been because they often had diseases in them which could have been passed on to human beings. By following God's rules the Israelites would have shown that they were holy and obeyed him.

Staying healthy

In a hot country disease can spread very quickly. It was vital to control illness as soon as possible. One of the best ways to stop others from becoming ill was to isolate the sick person from them until they were feeling better. The Israelites had to wash things thoroughly, especially if they had been somewhere dirty or were about to eat.

Holidays

God knew that everyone needs holidays. He told the people to have holidays throughout the year when they could forget about their work and think particularly about him. Once every fifty years there was to be a holiday that lasted for a whole year. No one was to work for all that time. This gave the earth a rest, too. God promised to provide enough food during these long breaks.

The feast of Tabernacles
This is also called the feast of Booths. It takes its name from the shelters made of branches, like makeshift tents, which the Jews had to live in for a week as a reminder of the nation's forty years living rough in the desert.

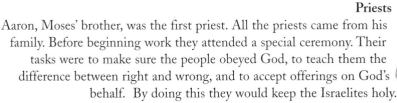

49 ❖

THE GOLDEN CALF ANGERS GOD

✦ Exodus 32 ✦

Metalworkers
Our knowledge of how the Israelites worked metals comes from Egyptian wall paintings like this one. Gold is soft and easy to shape into intricate designs. It was some of this gold which Aaron melted down to make the golden calf, probably by hammering flat sheets of gold over a wooden model of a calf.

Almond tree
The Hebrew name for the almond tree can be translated as "waker". This is because it is the first fruit tree to flower after winter is over. The almond tree is associated with Aaron in the Bible, because his almond rod came into flower overnight.

Bronze mirror
The Israelites left Egypt with huge quantities of gold and jewellery, much of which was melted down to make the golden calf. This fine mirror survived. The reflective surface is highly polished bronze and the handle is a servant girl holding a bird.

The people became restless when they realized how long Moses had been up on the mountain. They decided to approach Aaron, saying, "For all we know we may never see Moses again. Make us some gods that will be able to lead us on from here."

"Bring me your jewellery," Aaron replied, and the people did as he told them. He collected all that they took him and created a beautiful golden calf. He then built an altar and declared, "Tomorrow we will hold a festival to the Lord our God."

The next day the Israelites began to celebrate with offerings and sacrifices, after which they sat down to eat.

But God saw all that was going on and alerted Moses, "You must go back down the mountain, because the Israelites have made themselves an idol and begun sacrificing to it as though it had been responsible for bringing them out of Egypt. They are proud and wicked. Leave me, for I have decided to destroy them and make a nation out of your children alone."

But Moses pleaded with God, "If you do this, then the Egyptians will believe that you rescued us only to destroy us in the desert. Please don't do such a thing to your people. Remember the promises you made to Abraham, Isaac and Israel, when you said that you would create a great nation

from their offspring."

God listened to Moses' words and did not carry out his threat. Moses then hurried down the mountain carrying the two pieces of stone on which the Ten Commandments had been written. When he saw the golden calf and the wild dancing he threw the tablets to the ground shattering them into hundreds of tiny fragments. He then proceeded to destroy the calf by melting it in a fire.

Moses then turned angrily on Aaron, "What on earth have you done?"

"Don't get cross," Aaron replied, trying to make excuses. "The people were wondering where you were and told me to make some gods for them. They brought me their gold jewellery which I threw in the fire. Then out came this calf!"

Moses announced to the people, "You have been exceedingly wicked. I will go to God and plead on your behalf."

So he went up onto the mountain again and asked God to forgive the people's sin. When he had finished, God gave him this answer: "Whoever has sinned against me will be punished."

Later God kept his word by bringing a plague down upon the Israelites.

Manna
A jar of manna was kept in the Ark of the Covenant to remind the Israelites of God's provision for them during their wanderings in the wilderness. Manna was white, like coriander seed, and tasted like wafers made with honey. Some people think it may have come from the hammada shrub. This bush grows in the Sinai peninsula and produces a white substance which the Bedouins still use as a sweetener.

PLAGUES AND PUNISHMENT
We do not know what illness the Israelites suffered, but they saw it as God's punishment for their sin. Sometimes today illness can be triggered by the way we live. However the Bible never says that all illness is a punishment from God. There are bad things in the world which can affect anyone. God promises that in heaven there will be no more illness or death.

Mount Sinai
It was on Mount Sinai, or Mount Horeb as it is sometimes known in the Bible, that God gave Moses the Law and the Ten Commandments. This photograph shows the traditional location of the mountain in the southern Sinai peninsula, but we cannot be certain that this is the exact site.

WE WILL NOT ENTER CANAAN!

✤ Numbers 13-14 ✤

"Choose one man from each tribe to go and explore the land of Canaan," God commanded Moses.

So Moses selected twelve leaders from the tribes and sent them off on their mission. "Investigate the land thoroughly," he told them. "Discover as much as you can about its inhabitants, and whether their towns are well protected. Find out if the land is fertile, and bring back some of the fruit, so that we can taste it for ourselves."

Forty days later, they returned with their reports for Moses and all the people. "The country is all that we could have hoped for. It is covered in all kinds of wonderful fruit and crops. Here is some of the fruit. But the people who live there are extremely powerful, and their towns and cities are formidable fortresses. They are too strong for us."

Then two of the spies, Caleb and Joshua, interrupted the others. "We should go ahead and capture the land. God will give it to us as he has promised," they said.

But the people were afraid. "Let's choose a new leader and go back to Egypt," they cried.

Then God became angry with the Israelites because of their lack of faith. He threatened to kill them all. Moses pleaded with him, "Do not destroy us. If you do, the other nations will say that the only reason you rescued us from Egypt was to murder us in the desert. Even though they do not deserve it, pardon your people, just as you have done ever since we left Egypt."

"Very well," God replied, "but not a single one of them will set foot in the Promised Land. Only Caleb and Joshua will be able to enter it, because they trust me unquestioningly."

Moses and Aaron reported to the people what God had told them. "God has decreed that none of you will ever live in the Promised Land. Instead you are destined to roam aimlessly in the desert for forty years, until the last one of you is dead and buried. Then your children will take possession of the land."

The people were overcome with sorrow. "We have sinned against God; let's make amends by entering the Promised Land now." Moses pleaded with them not to go, but they refused to listen to him.

When the Israelites set out to conquer the land, the inhabitants fought them and defeated them easily.

GOD MAKES IT POSSIBLE
In this story, the Israelites are not able to capture the Promised Land because they lack faith in God. We all face challenges in life, such as taking an exam. But sometimes we lack the confidence to succeed. We think about all the difficulties, instead of praying to God and trusting him to help us to do our best.

The spies and the fruit
Fruit grew abundantly in the warm climate of Canaan. The spies that Moses sent out brought back a vine branch, bearing a single cluster of grapes. It was so large that two men had to carry it on a pole between them! They also brought pomegranates and figs. These and a variety of other crops, such as apples, olives, nuts and vegetables, were part of people's everyday diet in the Promised Land.

Pomegranate
A pomegranate is an orange-coloured fruit, which contains lots of seeds in a red pulp. Pomegranates are grown throughout the Middle East for their juice.

Sand viper
The sand viper is one of about twenty types of poisonous snake found in Israel. If someone is bitten by a sand viper, its poison attacks their lungs. Moses put the bronze serpent on a pole so that people who had been bitten by real snakes could look at it and be healed.

THE BRONZE SNAKE

✤ Numbers 21 ✤

The Israelites spent many long years travelling in the unwelcoming desert, and they were often discouraged and unhappy. Once, when they were retracing their steps to the Red Sea, they grew particularly impatient and started complaining about God and Moses.

"Why did you make us leave the safety of Egypt in order to die in this awful desert? We never have any bread, and there is hardly ever any water. We are sick and tired of this disgusting food."

When God saw how ungrateful they were, he sent poisonous snakes to bite them. A good many of the Israelites died after they had been bitten. They realized how foolish they had been to speak out against God, and went to Moses to admit their mistake.

"We realize now that we made a mistake when we became angry with you and God. Please ask him to take these dangerous snakes away from us."

So Moses prayed on behalf of the people. When he heard Moses' prayer, God answered, "I will not take away the snakes; if I do, the people will just start to misbehave again. But I want you to make a bronze snake and place it on the top of a pole. If anyone is bitten by a snake, all they have to do is to look at this snake and they will not die."

Moses did as God commanded him and erected the snake where people could easily see it. And whenever anyone who had been bitten by a snake looked at the statue perched on top of the pole, they were healed.

THE DONKEY THAT SPOKE

✤ Numbers 22-24 ✤

During their wanderings the Israelites camped near the lands of Balak, king of Moab. He was terrified they would invade his territory, so he sent a message to Balaam the prophet, saying, "I fear we will be overpowered. Come and curse them so I can drive them away."

Balaam asked God what to do. "The people he wants you to curse are blessed; you must not do as he says," God replied.

Dismayed, Balak sent a second message, but again Balaam was unmoved.

However, that night God said to him, "You may go with the messengers, but you must only say what I tell you to say."

The next day Balaam set off, but an angel stood in the road. When the donkey Balaam was riding saw the angel, it shied off the road, but Balaam forced it back. Again, the donkey shied away and Balaam forced it back. Finally the donkey lay down.

As Balaam was beating it, God made it say, "Why are you beating me?"

Furious, Balaam said, "Because you are making a fool of me."

"Do I usually behave like this?"

"No," Balaam admitted.

Then God let Balaam see the angel. Balaam fell to his knees as the angel asked, "Why were you beating your donkey? If it had not seen me and tried to avoid me, I would have killed you and spared the donkey."

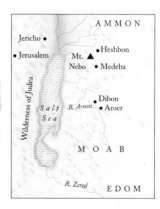

Donkey
The donkey that was a beast of burden in biblical times was quite different from the European ass with which we are familiar. It was a beautiful, graceful and friendly animal, with a reddish-brown coat. Capable of carrying heavy loads, it was also used for ploughing and threshing grain. Donkeys were held in high regard and were a measure of a person's wealth.

The lands of the Moabites
The Moabites were descendants of Moab, Lot's son. Their territory was quite a small area east of the Dead Sea, stretching about 100 kilometres from north to south and 30 kilometres from east to west. The Israelites were camped on the plains of Moab. They had no intention of attacking the Moabites, but it is easy to understand the Moabites' fear, particularly as they had just lost control of the land north of the Arnon to the Amorites.

"Forgive me. If you want me to return home then I will."

"No, but only say what I tell you," came the response.

When Balaam met the king, Balak told him to curse the Israelites. Balaam refused, blessing them as God ordered. Balak repeated the order. Again it was refused. And again, and again. Balak was furious. "Go. You have done the opposite to what I ordered!"

Balaam left and returned home.

A NEW LEADER IS CHOSEN

✤ Deuteronomy 31-34 ✤

"I am a hundred and twenty years old and can no longer lead you," Moses said to the people. "God has told me that I cannot enter the Promised Land. He has chosen Joshua to lead you there. You must obey him totally. Be brave and resolute, for the Lord God will never leave you."

Then God said privately to Moses, "Take Joshua to the Tabernacle ready for me to commission him."

When they got there, God appeared and said, "Moses, you will soon die and the people will wander away from me. When they do so, I will bring many difficulties upon them. Write down this song and teach it to them as a reminder of the wrong they have done."

God then encouraged Joshua, "Be brave and resolute. I will always be there to help you."

After their meeting with God, Moses assembled the leaders of the people. "Throughout my life you have rebelled against God and you will do so even more when I am gone. Take this book in which I have written all that has happened to us since we left Egypt,

and put it in the Ark to remind you how you should live."

Moses then blessed each of the twelve tribes of Israel before leaving his people for the last time. Slowly he climbed Mount Nebo from where God showed him the Promised Land.

When Moses died, the Israelites mourned for a month, for they knew there would never be another prophet like him.

The Promised Land
Canaan, the Promised Land, was a rich, fertile country with many olive groves. Olive trees grew profusely and were one of the ancient Hebrews' most valuable trees. They were regarded as a symbol of strength, beauty, divine blessing and prosperity.

SEND IN THE SPIES

✤ Joshua 1-2 ✤

Flax plant
Flax is the oldest known textile fibre. It was used for making linen and rope. The plants were pulled up by the roots, soaked in water, and beaten to separate the fibres from the stalk. Women usually did this work. Then they would spread the fibres on the flat roofs of their homes to dry before spinning.

FLAT-ROOFED HOUSES
The traditional flat roof was constructed by laying branches or reeds across wooden rafters. This formed a secure base which would then be covered with a thick layer of mud plaster. The roof had to be replastered every year. In the summer, the family would often sleep on the roof, as it was the coolest place in the house. The roof was also used to dry flax or foods, such as figs and raisins, in the hot sun.

After Moses had died, God told Joshua that he would lead him and the people to victory. Knowing that Joshua faced many difficult situations, God spoke to him many times about the need to be brave and full of courage.

Before the Israelites entered the Promised Land, Joshua secretly called two men and told them to go and spy out the land, especially the city of Jericho.

The two spies did as they had been commanded. In Jericho, they stayed at the house of a woman called Rahab. But the king of Jericho heard that there were spies in the city. He sent his messengers to tell Rahab to hand over the men.

Rahab replied, "Two men did come to me, but they left late this afternoon and I do not know where they went." In fact she had hidden the spies under some bundles of flax on her roof.

When the messengers had gone, Rahab climbed up onto her roof to talk to the men. "The whole country is terrified of the Israelites," she said. "No one thinks that we can resist you, for your God is the only God in the whole world. Promise me that you will repay the kindness I have shown you – do not kill my family."

The men replied, "You have saved our lives, and we will save you. We will make sure that you and your family are not harmed when God gives us your land."

Rahab's house was built into the city wall and so she was able to let them down on a rope from her window. As they left, the men said, "You must gather all your relatives in your house. Then place a scarlet cord in the window, so that we know not to attack your house. Above all, do not tell anyone what we are about to do."

Rahab agreed, and the men went back to Joshua. He was delighted when he heard their news. "If the people are all afraid of us, then God will certainly give us the land," he exclaimed.

THE RIVER STOPS FLOWING

♣ Joshua 3-4 ♣

Joshua moved the people to the banks of the river Jordan. Before long the order rang out throughout the camp: "When you see the priests carrying the Ark of the Lord your God, everyone is to pack up and follow it. Prepare yourselves, because tomorrow God will perform a great miracle."

Then God said to Joshua, "Tell the priests to take the Ark to the edge of the water."

Joshua called out to the Israelites, "Listen to what God says. The Ark is going ahead of you into the river. As soon as the priests set foot in the water, the river will stop flowing."

Even though the river was in full flood, as soon as the soles of the priests' feet touched the water, it stopped flowing. The priests continued walking until they were in the middle of the river. Then they stopped, and all the people crossed over.

When the last of the people had reached the other bank, God spoke to Joshua again. "Pick a man from each tribe and tell them to find twelve stones from the middle of the river. They are to carry them to the other side and set them up as a memorial where you camp tonight."

When this had been carried out, Joshua ordered the priests to join the rest of the people. No sooner had their feet touched dry ground, than the river started to flow as it had done before.

Joshua then moved the whole Israelite camp to Gilgal. He ordered that the stones from the Jordan be placed there, and then he addressed the people. "When your children ask you the significance of these stones, you are to tell them that the Israelites crossed the river Jordan on dry ground. God did this, just as he dried up the water of the Red Sea for Moses all those years ago. He did it to show his great power and to remind you to honour him."

From that day on, the Israelite people respected Joshua, just as they had respected Moses, because they saw that God was with him.

Frogs
There are several species of frog in Israel. They live near water and in rivers like the Jordan. Frogs are only mentioned once in the Bible, in the story of the ten plagues of Egypt.

The river Jordan
The Jordan is the biggest river in Israel, and it is mentioned many times in the Bible. The Israelites approached the Jordan Valley from the east, and the river formed a natural boundary to the Promised Land. It was not an easy river to cross, as it could be forded only in certain places. Even these fords were useless when the river flooded its banks at harvest time.

Priest's breastplate
An Israelite priest wore a breast-plate, studded with twelve gemstones, one for each of the twelve tribes of Israel. It contained pockets for the Urim and Thummim, special stones used by the priests to cast lots.

THE WALLS FALL DOWN

✣ Joshua 6 ✣

Death mask
Archaeological evidence shows that Jericho was occupied as early as 8000BC, making it one of the world's oldest cities. Skeletons without skulls have been discovered in burial sites there. The skulls seem to have been used as moulds for death masks of clay or plaster. Shells had been added to some to make eyes. These masks may have belonged to ancestors whom Jericho's inhabitants worshipped, or they could have been enemy trophies.

Joshua and his army had surrounded Jericho, preventing anyone from entering or leaving the city. God explained to Joshua how he was going to capture it.

"I am going to give you the city and all its inhabitants. March your army around its walls once a day for the next six days. Seven priests are to carry trumpets in front of the Ark. At the end of the week, you are to march around the city seven times with the priests blowing the trumpets. On the final blast tell the people to shout out loud. Then the walls will collapse and you can charge inside."

Joshua told the people to follow God's instructions, and so for the next six days they marched silently round the walls of the city.

On the seventh day the army circled the city seven times. On the final circuit Joshua addressed the army: "Shout with all your strength, for God has given us the city. Kill everyone except Rahab and her family; don't spare anyone. Don't loot anything for yourself but hand everything of value over to our treasury."

When the people shouted and the trumpets sounded, the walls collapsed and the soldiers scrambled over the debris into the city. When they had finished ransacking the city, they set fire to it until all that was left was a smouldering ruin.

The conquest of the Promised Land had begun.

DISASTER AT AI

♣ Joshua 7-8 ♣

After Joshua had captured Jericho, he sent some men to see how they should attack the next city, Ai. On their return they gave him their report: "Only a few thousand soldiers need go to take Ai, as there are not very many men there."

So Joshua sent three thousand soldiers to capture the city but they were easily defeated by the inhabitants.

Joshua was dismayed and distressed. He prayed to God, "Lord, why didn't you let us stay on the other side of the Jordan instead of bringing us across to be defeated by our enemies? Now our enemies will hear that we have lost a battle and will join together to drive us away."

God replied, "The reason you were defeated is that someone has sinned against me by stealing some of the goods that should have been destroyed. You can no longer rely upon me unless that person is punished. You must assemble the people tomorrow and I will show you who the thief is."

Joshua did as he was told and the next day a man called Achan was exposed as the thief and taken away to be stoned to death.

Now the Israelites were able to go and attack Ai. Joshua divided his army into two. Some of them went and showed themselves to the defenders of the city who, when they saw them, rushed out to fight them as they had done before. Joshua and his men pretended to flee and let the enemy pursue them. As they did so, the rest of Joshua's men entered the city unopposed and destroyed it.

When smoke began to rise from Ai, Joshua and his men stopped retreating and turned upon the men of Ai.

With some of his men in the city and others fighting outside, Joshua soon killed all the people of Ai, just as God had commanded him to do.

Palm tree
Date palms are tall, unbranched trees. At the top they have a huge 'crown' of feathery leaves, and clusters of fruit. The hot climatic conditions of the Jordan valley make ideal growing conditions for these trees. Although they flourish in groves, there are numerous references to them growing by themselves in biblical times. Jericho is also known as 'the city of palms' as many palm trees grew there.

MAKING A HOME

✤ Joshua 13-24 ✤

Division of the kingdom
The national unity and the strength of Israel lay in the nation's common worship of God and obedience to his laws. In later years it split into two nations, and both were destroyed because of Solomon's idolatry.

Lots
Lots were cast when important decisions had to be made. It was believed that God directed the lots. These pottery fragments, each inscribed with a single name, come from Masada, where 960 Jewish zealots died rather than be taken prisoner to Rome. They cast lots to determine who would kill the others.

THE TRIBES OF ISRAEL
The twelve tribes were named after ten of Jacob's sons: Asher, Benjamin, Dan, Gad, Issachar, Judah, Naphtali, Reuben, Simeon, and Zebulun. Joseph's two sons Ephraim and Manasseh also became heads of tribes. Jacob's son Levi became head of the priestly family which was not allotted land in Palestine. In 722BC all the tribes except Judah and Benjamin were scattered by the Assyrians and have never been re-formed.

When Joshua was much older, God said to him, "You are old now and there are still vast areas of land to be captured." Some of the country had already been allocated to the tribes in accordance with what Moses had decided, but most of the tribes were still without their own territory. So Joshua began to distribute land to the twelve tribes.

While Joshua was sharing out the country, his old friend Caleb came to him. "Do you remember what Moses told me? He promised that I would receive land because I trusted God when we came back

from spying out this land all those years ago. God has kept his promise to me through all those long years in the desert and here I am today as strong and fit as I was then. Now give me the hill country as my inheritance from God."

Joshua blessed Caleb and fulfilled his request gladly. By this time there were still seven tribes without their own land so Joshua commissioned three men from each tribe to survey the land. "Go into all the

land. Write down everything you see. Divide it into equal parts and when you return I will draw lots to determine which tribe can have the different tracts of land."

When he had divided up the land the Israelites gave Joshua a piece of land just as he had given land to Caleb.

Before Joshua died, he called the people together for the last time and urged them to be faithful to God. "Remember th Lord your God. Pay attention to everything written in the Book of the Law. If you do not, then just as you have received blessings from his hands, so you will receive judgement and God will drive you from the land that he has given you."

After Joshua's farewell speech, all the people were then able to go to their new homes and live in peace. At last they could begin to enjoy the Promised Land.

SAVED FROM OUR ENEMIES

♣ Judges 3-4 ♣

Once in the Promised Land, the people of Israel disobeyed God.

So God sent Eglon, the king of Moab, to rule over them. When the Israelites prayed to God, he sent Ehud, a left-handed man, to deliver them. Ehud strapped a sharp sword to his right thigh underneath his flowing robes.

He presented a gift to the king and whispered, "I have a private message for you, sir." The king, eager to discover the secret, ushered all his attendants out of the royal chambers.

Ehud then humbly approached the throne. "This is the message from God," he whispered and plunged the sword into the king's stomach.

The king was so fat that the sword was lost in the folds of his belly. Calmly Ehud left the room, locking the doors behind him.

The royal attendants found the door locked, but were reluctant to go in as they believed the king was in the bathroom. When they finally entered they discovered their king dead on the floor.

Meanwhile Ehud had escaped. He called the Israelites to arms and they killed a vast number of Moabites. After this the Israelites were no longer enslaved by the people of Moab.

After Ehud's death the people forgot God again. This time God sent another foreign king, Jabin, to rule over them cruelly. Once more they cried out to God. He instructed Deborah to tell the army leader Barak, "Rise up and attack Sisera, the commander of your enemy's army."

Together with the army they defeated Sisera who, seeing that he was beaten, fled on foot. Exhausted by his flight, he fell asleep in the tents of Jael. While he dozed, Jael drove a tent peg through his head, killing him instantly. When Barak arrived in pursuit of Sisera, Jael showed him his opponent pinned to the ground. With Jabin's army in ruins and his commander dead, the Israelites easily overcame the oppression of Jabin and his people.

Battle weapons
Because of the hilly terrain, the army was made up mostly of foot-soldiers, equipped as slingers or archers. Bows were made of wood and bone, and quivers held up to thirty arrows with triangular-shaped bronze tips. For hand-to-hand combat, axes, short swords and daggers were used.

GIDEON BECOMES A WARRIOR

✦ Judges 6-7 ✦

Pottery jar
The jars that Gideon and his men took with them when they went to attack the Midianites may have looked like this one. It was found at a site called Megiddo in Israel, and was made in about 1550–1480 BC. Gideon's men would have used the pottery jars to hide the light from their torches as they approached the enemy camp. Then they smashed the jars to panic the Midianites.

ASHERAH POLE
The Asherah pole in this story would have been a carved image of the Canaanite goddess Asherah. The Canaanites worshipped many different gods. Most of them were connected with either fertility or war. Asherah, or Astarte, was the goddess of war, motherhood and fertility. Idols of her usually show her naked. She was one of the most important goddesses of the ancient Middle East.

When the Israelites disobeyed God, he handed them over to the Midianites, who ruled them for seven years. In desperation, the Israelites finally cried out to God.

He sent an angel to a man named Gideon. "The Lord God is with you, mighty warrior," said the angel. "I have chosen you to save Israel."

Gideon was shocked and protested, "But Lord, I am an insignificant member of the smallest tribe of Israel. How can I save the Israelites?"

"With you I shall indeed strike down the Midianites," declared God.

Gideon went away to prepare an offering of meat and bread for the angel. He placed it on a rock. The angel touched the offering with his staff and immediately it burst into flames. Then Gideon cried, "I have seen the Lord's face!" and feared for his life.

God assured him that he was safe, and told him to pull down the town's altar to Baal and cut down the Asherah pole beside it. Gideon did this at night, because he did not want to anger the townspeople.

But when they discovered what had happened, they soon realized that Gideon was responsible. "Your son must die," they screamed to Joash, Gideon's father.

"If Baal really is a god, then he can take his own revenge," replied Joash, and so Gideon was left unharmed.

Later, when the Israelites' enemies had crossed the river Jordan and were preparing to attack, Gideon summoned all the people of the nearby tribes to his side.

Despite his outer confidence, Gideon was still unsure of the outcome of the battle, so he spoke to God. "Tonight I am going to place a woollen fleece on the floor. Tomorrow morning, if the fleece is wet but the ground is dry, then I will know that you are going to use me to save Israel." The next morning, he went to the fleece and discovered that it was dripping with water.

Still nervous, Gideon spoke to God again. "If you really are going to use me to

WINNING AGAINST THE ODDS
Sometimes we find ourselves facing difficult circumstances, and wonder how we can possibly succeed. The odds seem stacked against us. Then we should remember the story of Gideon and his small band of men, which shows that God can help the weak to win great victories.
God may even deliberately put us in a weak position, so that we can enjoy seeing his power working for us. When we learn to rely on God, and not on our own strength, our obedience to him can release more of his power.

Drinking from the spring
God selected only three hundred men to fight the Midianites. This was to show the Israelites that it was God, and not their own efforts, that gave them the victory. Gideon watched to see how his soldiers drank from the waters of the spring. He chose the men who cupped their hands to drink, rather than those who put their faces down into the water. Perhaps these men seemed the most alert and ready for battle.

feat your enemies, then when I place the
ece out tonight, make it dry and the
ound around it wet with dew."

Again, God did exactly as Gideon
d requested. Then he said to Gideon,
here are too many soldiers in your army.
you win, the men will boast that the
ctory was theirs. Tell your soldiers that
yone who is frightened may leave now."

When they heard what Gideon told
em, twenty-two thousand men left. Then
od spoke again. "There are still too many
you. Lead your men down to the water
d I will tell you who can remain."

At the waterside, God told Gideon,
Choose only the men who lap the water
e dogs." So Gideon selected three
ndred men in this way and sent all the
hers home.

During the night, God told Gideon,
o to the enemy camp. Listen to what
ey are saying and then you will know that
am going to win a great victory for you."

So silently, Gideon sneaked into the
enemy camp, just as a man was telling a
friend of a dream he had. "As I slept, I saw
a loaf of bread roll into the Midianite
camp and knock a tent over."

"This must be Gideon," came the
reply. "God has given us all into his hands."

As he overheard this, Gideon praised
God. He returned to his own camp, and
called his men. "Wake up! God has given
the Midianites into our hands."

Then Gideon split them into three
groups and gave them orders. "Take a
torch, a jar, and a trumpet. When we reach
the enemy camp, wait for my command.
When I call, you are to blow the trumpets,
smash the jars and wave the torches,
crying, 'For the Lord and Gideon!'"

When the Midianites heard the
uproar, they panicked, thinking that they
were surrounded. They began attacking
each other and fled in utter disarray, with
Gideon's tiny band pursuing them.

So, with only a handful of men,
Gideon defeated the Midianites.

Shophar
*Gideon's men would have used a
special trumpet, called a shophar.
It is a wind instrument made
from a ram's horn, and it produces
a loud, strident noise. The
shophar was used to summon men
to battle, and also to call the
people to worship on the
Sabbath. It is still
sounded in some
Jewish synagogue
services today.*

STRONG ENOUGH TO KILL A LION

✤ Judges 13-14 ✤

A fter many childless years, God told Manoah and his wife that they were to have a son. "He must never cut his hair, for he is going to be a Nazirite, a man dedicated to God, and he will begin to free the Israelites from their enemies the Philistines." In due course, the child was born, and they called him Samson.

When he was older, Samson fell in love with a Philistine woman. He asked his parents to arrange a marriage. They were horrified. "What is wrong with one of our Israelite women?" they asked. "Why do you want to marry a foreigner?"

But he insisted, and so Samson and his parents went to visit the woman. As they approached the town where she lived, a lion attacked them. With the power of the Spirit of God, Samson ripped the lion to pieces with his bare hands and left its body lying on the path.

Later, Samson returned that way for the marriage ceremony. He was

intrigued to discover that a swarm of bees had settled in the lion's dead body. They had made some honey, which he scooped out and ate.

At his wedding, Samson remembered this unusual incident. He set some of the guests this riddle: "Eats from the eater, from the strong something sweeter."

None of the guests could guess the answer, so they secretly went to Samson's wife and threatened her: "Find out the answer or we will kill you and your family."

She rushed to Samson, weeping sadly. "If you really love me, tell me the answer to your riddle."

Eventually he told her, and she immediately went to the guests with the answer. They, in turn, found Samson and told him, "It is honey from a lion."

Samson was furious that he had been caught out. In a wild fury, he stormed out of his own wedding celebrations. He left his wife and went back to live with his parents.

Lion
In Samson's time, lions were common in Canaan. But their numbers declined and they eventually became extinct in the region in about AD1300. Lions normally lived in thickets along the river Jordan. But when the river flooded, they were forced out of their lairs and could be a real threat to people. Shepherds often had to kill lions to defend themselves and their flocks.

Honey bee
Honey bees were highly valued in Canaan. Honey was the main sweetener for food, and was considered one of life's necessities. A find of wild honey would have been a real treat. Wild bees often nested in clefts in rocks, but sometimes they would choose other odd places, like the carcass of the dead lion in this story.

SAMSON FALLS IN LOVE

✤ Judges 16 ✤

Once again Samson fell in love – this time with a woman called Delilah. The leaders of the Philistines came to her and offered to pay her to find the secret of Samson's strength.

So Delilah asked Samson, "Explain to me how you are so strong, and what someone must do to overpower you."

He replied, "If someone were to tie me up with fresh bow-strings then I would be as weak as the next man."

So Delilah tied him up with some fresh bow-strings and then cried out, "Samson, the Philistines are here!" Immediately, he sprang up and snapped the strings as if they were cotton.

"You have lied to me. Tell me the truth," complained Delilah.

She kept on asking him until, worn down by her nagging, Samson finally revealed the real secret. "If my hair is cut off then I will lose all my strength."

This time, Delilah realized that he had told her the truth and so she sent a message to the Philistines, "Come back tonight because he has told me everything."

That night, while Samson was asleep, the Philistines crept in and one of them cut off his hair. When Delilah woke him, he discovered that he was unable to resist the Philistines. They captured him, blinded him and threw him in prison. But slowly Samson's hair began to grow back.

Much later, the Philistine rulers were having a feast in their temple when they remembered him. "Let's bring Samson out to entertain us," they said. So Samson was led in, and stood between the pillars of the doorway.

He prayed to God, "Make me strong just one more time so that I can pay back the Philistines for having blinded me." Then he pushed against the pillars with all his might. They crashed down, bringing the roof down and killing everyone inside the temple, including Samson.

With this last dramatic act, Samson killed more of his enemies than he had done in all the rest of his life.

Nazirite
A Nazirite was someone who was dedicated to God for a special purpose. Sometimes this was for a specific period of time, but in Samson's case, it was for life. The name Nazirite comes from the Hebrew word meaning "separated" or "consecrated". Nazirites were forbidden to cut their hair or to drink alcohol. They also had to avoid all contact with dead bodies, so that they remained pure.

A CARING DAUGHTER

♣ Ruth 1-4 ♣

Ruth
The law in Israel stopped landowners harvesting to the very edges of their fields, so that foreigners, orphans, widows and poor people could gather, or glean, any leftover grain. In Israel, in the times of the Judges, there were many unscrupulous men who harvested everything in the fields, but there were still a few good men, like Boaz who offered Ruth work and protection.

Bethlehem
Bethlehem is built on one of the highest hills of the Judean plateau, about eight kilometres south-west of Jerusalem and eighty kilometres from Moab, where Ruth and Naomi lived. Little more than a village at this time, it was surrounded by fields of barley (a more drought-resistant crop than wheat), which gave way to the dry pasture of the Judean wilderness where nomad shepherds grazed their flocks.

Bronze sickle
Men cut the crops with sickles, while the women bound it into bundles. These were threshed – beaten with sticks and trampled by oxen to separate the grain from the straw. After threshing, the grain was winnowed by tossing it into the air so the chaff blew away. Then it was sieved to remove weed seeds.

Naomi, an Israelite, lived in Moab with her husband Elimelech and their two sons. After Elimelech's death, the sons both married Moabite women. Tragically Naomi's sons died and she decided to return to Israel.

When Naomi said goodbye to her daughters-in-law, one of them, Ruth, said she would go with Naomi, saying, "I have decided to go with you. Your people and your God will be mine too and when I die I wish to be buried alongside you."

So together the two women went to Bethlehem and settled there.

At harvest time, Ruth went gleaning in the fields. One day Boaz, the landowner, asked his servants, "Who is that woman?"

"Ruth, who lives with Naomi."

Boaz approached her and said, "Ruth! Stay by my servants and glean all the grain you like."

"Why are you being so kind to me?" she asked.

"I've heard how good you are to my relative Naomi."

Ruth blushed and went on gleaning That evening Naomi was delighted when Ruth told her about Boaz. She knew he would make Ruth a good husband. She told Ruth to put on her best clothes and go to see him one night after he had finished his meal.

As he was asleep, Ruth lay at his fee When he awoke, he was amazed to see he

"I would like you to marry me," he said, "but that right belongs to a closer relative of Naomi's. I will see if I can arrange to take his place as your husband.

Next day Boaz spoke to the other man in front of the town's leaders. According to custom the man had to buy field that Elimelech had owned. When he did so, he would also have to marry Ruth. As the man did not want the field he let Boaz buy it – which also meant that Boaz could marry Ruth.

Naomi was thrilled. "Praise God," sl said through her tears, "for through his kindness he will yet give me a grandchild.

HANNAH GIVES HER BABY TO GOD

✤ 1 Samuel 1-2 ✤

At that time in the hill country of Ephraim lived a man named Elkanah. Elkanah had two wives. Peninnah had children, but Hannah had none. Peninnah taunted Hannah, causing her great distress. It upset Elkanah too, because he loved Hannah. Each year they went to the temple at Shiloh to worship and make sacrifices to God. Peninnah would take advantage of the occasion to tease her rival even more. Elkanah tried to comfort Hannah, but she could not be consoled.

One year Hannah was overcome with sorrow and she prayed to God, "Dear Lord, if you look upon me with kindness and give me a son, then I will dedicate him to you for all his life."

As she prayed, her lips moved, though her words were silent. Eli, the priest, saw this and thought she was drunk. He rebuked her, saying, "Stop your drunkenness and throw away your drink."

Taken aback, Hannah replied, "I haven't been drinking. I am just a broken woman full of grief."

Eli apologized, "Then may God grant you whatever you have asked of him. Go in peace." So Hannah left the temple with her spirits raised.

In due course Hannah gave birth to a boy and called him Samuel, which means "heard by God".

When Elkanah made his annual pilgrimage to the temple, she stayed at home with the child, saying, "When he is weaned, I will take him to the temple to consecrate him to God."

When Samuel was older, Hannah did as she had said. She presented him to Eli at the temple doors, saying, "A few years ago you saw me praying silently to God. He has answered my prayer and so I have come here to fulfill my vow to him. I am giving my boy back to God in order that he might serve him all his life."

Eli was deeply moved by Hannah's faithfulness and praised God.

The high priest's clothes
A high priest, like Eli, wore special clothing to underline the importance of his role. All the clothes had a symbolic meaning. The beautiful breastpiece was studded with twelve gemstones, representing the twelve tribes of Israel, and also contained pockets for the Urim and Thummim. This was tied to a linen apron, or ephod, and worn over a blue robe fringed with gold bells and representations of pomegranates.

The menorah
The seven-branched lampstand, or menorah in Hebrew, stood in the Tabernacle. The menorah and all its accessories were made of pure gold, the cups shaped like almond blossoms. The menorah symbolized the glory of the Lord reflected in his people. Today it is the symbol of the Jewish state of Israel.

GOD CALLS SAMUEL

✤ 1 Samuel 3 ✤

Ancient lamp
A lamp was made from a small clay saucer, with part of its rim pinched together to form a spout. The lamp was filled with olive oil, which acted as a fuel, and a wick stuck out from the spout.

Inside a synagogue
The temple where Eli was priest was an early form of Jewish synagogue. The word "synagogue" means "a gathering together" in Greek. Today, Jews still gather together in the synagogue on the Sabbath to hear the rabbi (teacher) read from the scriptures and explain the law. Only men take an active part in the service. Women and children sit in a separate area of the synagogue.

Rabbi and pupil
This modern-day rabbi is teaching a young boy, just as Eli taught Samuel. When a Jewish boy reaches the age of 13 he is known as a Bar Mitzvah, which means "son of the commandment". To mark this event, the boy is called to read from the scroll of the law during the Sabbath service at the synagogue. Afterwards, his family often hold a big party to celebrate the Bar Mitzvah.

Samuel served under Eli the priest at a time when there were few visions from God. One night, Eli had gone to bed, and Samuel was asleep in the temple where the Ark of the Covenant was kept. In the quiet and darkness, God called to Samuel.

Samuel answered, "Here I am," and raced off to Eli. "Here I am," he repeated, "What did you call me for?"

Sleepily, Eli replied, "I did not call you. Go back to your bed and lie down."

Samuel settled down to sleep again, but almost immediately God called his name again. Once more, Samuel got up and walked through to where Eli was. But Eli repeated what he had said earlier: "I did not call you; go back and get some sleep."

Samuel trudged back, and a short while later the voice came yet again. He got up and went through to Eli. "Here I am. What is it that you want?"

Then Eli realized that it was God calling Samuel, so he said, "Go back, and if you hear the voice again, say, 'Speak, Lord. Your servant is listening.' " Samuel did as

he was told. When the Lord called out his name, he replied as Eli had told him to.

Then God told Samuel, "I have decided to judge the family of Eli because his sons are behaving in a wicked way and he has done nothing to stop them."

In the morning, Samuel was reluctant to talk to Eli, but the priest asked him, "What did God say to you last night? Do not try to hide anything from me."

So Samuel related exactly what the Lord had told him. When he had heard everything, Eli solemnly declared, "He is God. He must do what he thinks is right."

Samuel continued to serve at the temple and as he grew, God blessed everything that he did and said. And all the Israelites knew that the Lord had made a great prophet for them.

THE ARK IS SEIZED IN BATTLE

✣ 1 Samuel 4-6 ✣

The Israelites went to fight the Philistines. They took the Ark of the Covenant with them, believing that it would bring them victory.

When the Philistines heard about this they were afraid. "No one has ever brought their god into battle against us. We must all stand firm and not give in to fear if we want to win this battle."

So the Philistines fought fiercely. They slaughtered the Israelites and stole the Ark of the Covenant.

A survivor sped off to Eli with news of the defeat. "Our army has been massacred," the messenger reported. "Your sons have been killed and the Ark has been captured." When he heard this, Eli fell off his chair in shock. He fell awkwardly, broke his neck and died.

Meanwhile the Philistines took the Ark to the city of Ashdod, and put it inside the temple of their god, Dagon. During the night the statue of Dagon tumbled over. They placed the statue back in position, but the next night it fell over again, smashing into tiny pieces.

While the Philistines were in possession of the Ark, God made trouble for them. He afflicted the inhabitants of Ashdod with tumours, and when the Ark was moved to the city of Gath, he did the same there. Then the people of Gath tried to pass the Ark on to another city, but the citizens refused to let it inside the walls. "Return the Ark to its own people, otherwise we will all be killed!" they cried.

After seven desperate months, the Philistines came up with a plan. They loaded the Ark and some gold onto a cart pulled by two cows, and sent it back to the Israelites. The cows stopped near a field of wheat outside the town of Beth Shemesh.

Some Israelites collecting the harvest saw the Ark, and were overjoyed. "The Ark of the Lord has returned to its people!" they exclaimed. They sacrificed cattle and burnt them on an altar made from the cart and worshipped God.

Dagon
The chief god of the Philistines was Dagon, the god of grain and fertility. He was often shown as part fish, part man. The Philistines built many temples to him. The one at Ashdod, where the Ark was placed, may have been big enough to hold hundreds of people. But the statue of Dagon was unable to stand before the power of God. It fell over twice, and the second time it broke into pieces.

Oxen and cart
In many parts of the world owning an ox (a castrated bull) is still seen as essential for the most basic existence. Farmers use oxen to plough fields and to pull carts that have changed little since the time of this Bible story. For moving heavy objects, like the Ark of the Covenant, ancient peoples often preferred to use cows because they were more docile than oxen.

Clay coffin
Clay coffins like this one have been found at Bethshean and in the Trans-Jordan area. Dating from the 12th century BC, experts believe that they were made by the Philistines. The vertical strokes moulded into the clay above the face may represent the feathered head-dresses worn by the Philistine people.

KINGS OF ISRAEL

When Israel entered the Promised Land, authority was the responsibility of the judges. However, when Samuel was judge over Israel, the people asked for a king to rule over them, so that they could be like the other nations. Samuel would not give in to their demands at first but eventually after the people insisted, Samuel agreed.

David and Goliath

David
David was a shepherd boy when Samuel anointed him to be king in place of Saul. His victory over Goliath won him great popularity, and though Saul tried many times to kill him, he was eventually crowned king. David captured Jerusalem, and brought back the Ark of the Covenant to the city. He was not only a great king and military leader, but also a poet and musician who wrote many of the Psalms.

Anointing
Oil was used to anoint both people and objects to set them apart for sacred use. Prophets, priests and kings were consecrated for office by anointing. Objects that were used in the performance of religious ceremonies were also purified by being anointed with oil. Israel's king was often called "the Lord's anointed", his physical anointing being seen as a symbol of his divine anointing. Anointing was also done for medical and cosmetic reasons.

Rehoboam, king of Judah

Saul defeated

Saul
Saul was the first king of Israel. He was tall and handsome and a brave warrior. But as a king he grew proud and when he deliberately disobeyed God, Samuel the prophet was sent to tell him that God had chosen someone else to be king in his place. In his later years he suffered from fits of insanity, and he finally met his death alongside his son, Jonathan, in a battle against the Philistines.

Solomon
Solomon was the greatest and wisest of all of Israel's kings. Under his rule, the country enjoyed peace and unparalleled wealth and prosperity. He expanded trade, had a strong army and undertook many ambitious building projects, including the magnificent temple in Jerusalem. He sealed many political treaties by making marriage alliances with foreign princesses. They caused him to turn away from worshipping the God of Israel to worshipping their gods. When Solomon died the kingdom was split into two.

Solomon

Political situation
The reign of Solomon was Israel's golden age, but on his death the kingdom was divided. Ten tribes broke away to form the northern kingdom of Israel under Jeroboam, while the remaining two tribes formed the southern kingdom of Judah, under Solomon's son, Rehoboam. Various kings ruled over the following years. When they obeyed God things went well, but when they disobeyed him there was disaster. Their reigns were against the backdrop of the rise to power of Assyria and then Babylon. Samaria, the capital of Israel, fell in 722BC, and Jerusalem, Judah's capital, in 586BC.

*David brings back the
Ark of the Covenant*

transition in worship

hen the Israelites conquered Canaan and settled in one
ce, they no longer needed a portable temple they could
rry around and the Tabernacle remained at Shiloh for a
g time. The Ark of the Covenant was captured by the
ilistines, but they eventually returned it as it brought
em nothing but trouble. David later brought the Ark
Jerusalem and assembled the materials for constructing
magnificent temple in which to house it. However,
cause David was a warrior, God decreed that his son
lomon would be the one to build it. Its layout was
nilar to that of the Tabernacle, and the temple in
usalem now became the centre of worship for
e Israelites.

NGS AND QUEENS OF ISRAEL

ngs of United Israel

aul	1042-1000BC
avid	1000-961BC
olomon	961-922BC

ngs and Queens of southern kingdom (Judah)

ehoboam	922-915BC
bijah	915-913BC
sa	913-873BC
hoshaphat	873-849BC
horam	849-842BC
haziah	842BC
ueen Athaliah	842-837BC
ash	837-800BC
maziah	800-783BC
zziah/Azariah	783-742BC
tham	742-735BC
haz	735-715BC
ezekiah	715-687BC
anasseh	687-642BC
mon	642-640BC
siah	640-609BC
hoahaz	609BC
hoiakim	609-598BC
hoiachin	598-597BC
edekiah	597-587BC

ngs of northern kingdom (Israel)

roboam I	922-901BC
adab	901-900BC
aasha	900-877BC
ah	877-876BC
mri	876BC
mri	876-869BC
hab	869-850BC
haziah	850-849BC
ram	849-842BC
hu	842-815BC
hoahaz	815-801BC
hoash	801-786BC
roboam II	786-746BC
echariah	746-745BC
allum	745BC
enahem	745-738BC
ekahiah	738-737BC
ekah	737-732BC
oshea	732-722BC

The kingdoms of Judah and Israel
*Although Judah consisted of only two tribes, it
survived Israel partly because it was less
vulnerable to attack from the north.*

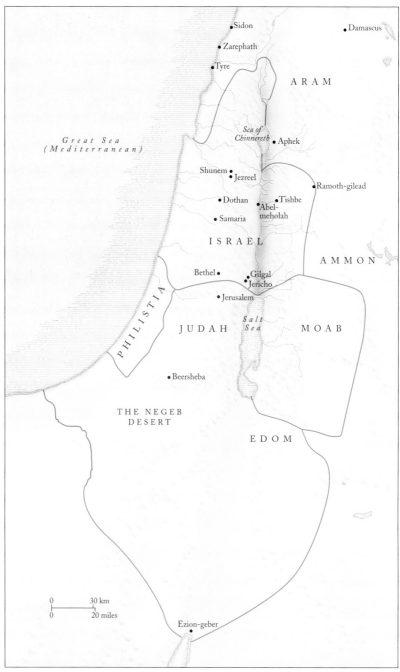

WE WANT A KING!

✤ 1 Samuel 8-10 ✤

Olive grove
An olive tree bears no fruit for the first fifteen years, but then it can produce fruit for hundreds of years. Olives were grown for their oil which was used in cooking and as a fuel for lamps, as a lotion for the skin and hair, and as a soothing ointment, as well as for anointing people to set them apart for God's service.

Cinnamon and Myrrh
The anointing oil was made from myrrh, cinnamon, cane and cassia. Myrrh yields a fragrant resin from its cut stems; cinnamon is obtained from the bark of the cinnamon tree; cane from the root of a reed plant; and cassia from the dried flowers of the cinnamon tree.

Anointing horn
Samuel anointed Saul to be the first king of Israel with sacred oil from an animal's horn like the one pictured here. As "the Lord's anointed", his leadership was to be spiritual as well as political. The horn of a ram, goat or wild ox could be used for religious or ceremonial purposes, but cows' horns were forbidden.

In his old age, Samuel appointed his sons to act as judges. But they were corrupt and used their position for their own purposes.

The leaders of the people met with Samuel and told him, "We don't want your sons, since they don't behave correctly as you do. We would prefer to have a king as the other nations do."

This request upset Samuel, but God said to him, "It is me that they have rejected, not you. Ever since they left Egypt they have been like this. You may choose a king for them, but warn them how he will mistreat them."

Samuel warned them of the consequences of having a king. "He will exploit you and order you to obey his every whim. He will take your land, your flocks, and your possessions. He will oppress you so that you will eventually call out to God for relief."

But the people could not be swayed.

"Very well," said Samuel. "Go to your homes and I will determine whom God has chosen to be your king."

Later, God told Samuel that he would soon meet the man who would become king. The next day Samuel met Saul, who was searching for some donkeys that his father had lost. Samuel invited him in for a meal.

Afterwards, as Saul was leaving, Samuel poured oil onto his head and said, "God has chosen you to be king. I have called all the people together and will reveal this choice to them. Make sure you are at the meeting."

When all the Israelites were ready, Samuel reminded them of what God had said earlier: "By choosing a king, you have rejected God's rule over you. But he has allowed you to go ahead with your plan. We will find the new king by drawing lots." They drew lots and Saul was chosen.

However, Saul was nowhere to be seen! He was so frightened that he had hidden himself among the tents and baggage that people had brought. So they brought him out in front of everyone.

"This is your king," Samuel proclaimed.

"Hurrah! Long live the king!" the people shouted at the top of their voices.

SAUL MAKES A MISTAKE

✤ 1 Samuel 13-14 ✤

Saul sent his son Jonathan to attack one of the Philistine outposts at Geba. He then sent messengers into all the land saying, "We have attacked the Philistines and now they are wanting to get revenge. All soldiers are to report to Gilgal at once."

Meanwhile, the Philistines prepared for battle. A vast army of them assembled, marched out and camped at Michmash. When the Israelite soldiers saw them they were terrified, and so they began to drift away back to their own homes. Those that stayed with Saul became increasingly scared. Samuel was due to come and offer a sacrifice to God before the battle. After a week he still had not arrived and so Saul decided to do it himself.

"What have you done?" Samuel asked Saul when he finally arrived.

"All my soldiers were leaving and you hadn't come. I thought I had better offer a sacrifice to God in order to seek his favour."

"You have done a foolish thing. You have disobeyed God. God will take the kingdom away from you and your children for ever. No one else in your family shall be king."

With that Samuel left Saul and his depleted army.

Meanwhile Jonathan went with his servant to ascertain the exact positions and strength of the enemy.

"With God on our side we can beat anyone, even though there are only two of us," Jonathan said to his servant. Stealthily they climbed up a hill and surprised a company of the enemy, killing about twenty of them. The Philistines panicked and ran for their lives. When Saul saw the confusion among them, he called all his men. They joined Jonathan and harassed the enemy all the way back to where they had come from.

Philistine head-dress
These Philistine warriors are shown wearing their characteristic battle head-dress of feathers rising vertically from a headband. The Philistines were warlike and a constant threat to the Israelites. Their military pressure was one of the reasons that Israel wanted a king. They had superior weapons made from iron.

Philistia
The Philistines lived in five cities to the southwest of the land of Israel and bordering the Mediterranean: Ashdod, Ashkelon, Ekron, Gath, and Gaza. They gave their name to the whole of the land, "Palestine". They probably migrated here from the Aegean Sea.

Goat
In the Old Testament, a sacrifice could be made for various purposes: as a gesture of thanksgiving, or to make up for past sins. Only certain animals were suitable for sacrifice, including goats, bullocks, sheep, doves or pigeons. Animals for sacrifice had to be physically perfect, and male animals were preferred over females.

A SHEPHERD BOY IS CHOSEN AS KING

✤ 1 Samuel 15-16 ✤

Saul disobeyed God, who then regretted that he had allowed him to become king. Samuel too was very upset, but God came to him and said, "I have rejected Saul as king. Wipe the tears from your eyes and go to Bethlehem where Jesse lives. I am going to make one of his sons the next king."

When Samuel arrived in Bethlehem, he met Jesse and asked him to bring his sons to him so that he could meet them. As soon as he set eyes upon the eldest boy, Eliab, Samuel thought to himself, "This must be the one that God has chosen to be the next king."

But God said to Samuel, "Don't be swayed by his appearance, he is not the one that I have chosen. I look at things from a different perspective. People look on a person's outward appearance, but I look at what a person is like on the inside."

Next Jesse called Abinadab, and then Shammah, but Samuel knew that neither of them had been selected by God. One by one seven of Jesse's sons were introduced to Samuel, but none of them was the special one chosen by God.

"Do you have any other sons?" he asked Jesse.

"Yes, there is one more. But he is out looking after the sheep at the moment."

Samuel asked Jesse to fetch him. When David arrived, God said to Samuel, "He is the one. Anoint him with oil for I have chosen him to be the new king of Israel."

So Samuel poured oil over David and God's Spirit came upon him.

DAVID AND GOLIATH

✤ 1 Samuel 17 ✤

The armies of the Philistines and the Israelites faced each other across the valley of Elah. Goliath, the Philistines' champion soldier, challenged Saul's army. "Pick one man to come and fight a duel with me. If he should beat me, then we will become your slaves, but if I beat him then you will become ours."

His words struck fear into the whole Israelite camp – no one was brave enough to go out to fight him. Every morning and evening for forty days Goliath kept up his taunts.

One day, as Goliath was yelling out his threats, David arrived at the Israelite camp with some food for his brothers who were serving in the army. He was amazed that no one would fight Goliath. "What right has that Philistine to pour scorn upon the army of the living God?"

When Saul heard that David was in the camp he sent for him. "I will go and fight that Philistine, sir," he said.

Saul said he was too young, but David persuaded him with stories of his bravery when protecting his father's sheep from wild animals.

"Very well then, may God bless you," said Saul. "But use my armour." David tried it on, but it was too big. Instead, with just a staff, a sling and five stones from a nearby stream, he advanced towards Goliath.

When Goliath saw David, he let out a volley of curses. "Who do they think I am? Why have they sent me out a mere boy that I should slaughter him and feed him to the birds?"

David replied, "You can rely on your weapons, but I will kill you today in the name of the Lord God of Israel. It will be you who is eaten by wild animals, not me. Then everyone will know that this battle is under the control of God and that he is going to give us complete victory."

He then ran towards Goliath, put a stone in his sling, and threw it with all his might. It flew through the air, hitting Goliath in the middle of his forehead. Instantly the Philistine fell to the ground. David raced up to him, drew out Goliath's sword and cut his head off. When the Israelites saw what had happened, they rushed down the valley and pursued the disheartened Philistines and plundered their camp.

Goliath
The Philistines' champion was almost three metres tall and well armed, but David's victory over him proves that it is more important to have faith in God than to rely on size or strength.

Chain mail
The Bible tells us that Goliath's armour weighed about 56 kg and was made of small bronze plates punctured with tiny holes and laced together onto a cloth or leather tunic. The armour was completed with bronze greaves to cover the shins and a bronze helmet to protect the head.

Sling
First used by shepherds to scare wild animals away from their flocks, slings soon became popular in wars because they were simple to make and use. David's sling was probably made of plaited wool, with a wider, reinforced middle piece for the stone. A skilled slinger could hurl a stone a distance of 182 metres.

SAUL BECOMES JEALOUS

✦ 1 Samuel 18-24 ✦

Water flask
David and his followers wandered through the hot desert countryside of Judea. A water flask, like this one dating from the 11th-12th centuries BC, would have been a vital piece of their equipment. A cord threaded through two small handles meant that it could be carried around the neck or across the body, leaving the hands free.

David's spear
A spear or javelin was the usual weapon of the hunter or warrior. The leaf-shaped metal tip, usually of bronze, was fixed to a long wooden shaft with a spiral of metal. Many spears of this period had a metal tip at the end of the shaft, so the spear could be stuck in the ground when not in use. In some circumstances, the spear was a symbol of royal authority.

After his incredible defeat of Goliath, David became a national hero. The people thought more highly of him than they did of Saul. This made Saul extremely jealous and he decided to kill David. He urged his son Jonathan to help him, but Jonathan and David were best friends.

Jonathan begged his father, "Don't kill David. Since he entered your service he has done nothing but good for you."

Saul relented and vowed, "I promise before Almighty God that I will not kill him."

So for a short time Saul and David were at peace. But the truce did not last long. Saul soon broke his promise and tried to murder him by throwing a spear at him.

David fled and this time it was Michal, David's wife, who came to his rescue. Saul had sent soldiers to watch his house but Michal warned him about them. "Run away. My father has sent his men to kill you," she said.

So David went to Jonathan. "Your father is trying to kill me again," David said.

"Are you absolutely sure?" Jonathan asked. "He promised me that he would not attempt such a thing again," said his friend "I'll go and find out what he is up to and come and tell you."

When Jonathan next saw his father he discovered that it was true – Saul was desperate to kill David.

"I'm so sorry," Jonathan cried when he met David again. "Even if my father hates you, I will be your friend for ever."

Saul kept chasing after David as if nothing else mattered but killing him. David had to be continually on the move, but wherever he went, Saul followed him up and down the country.

Once David had the chance to kill Saul when he found him in a cave. Instead he left him alone. This touched Saul so much that he asked David to forgive him and they became friends again. But after all that he had been through, David couldn't help wondering how long this change of heart would last.

Caves
The difficult, inaccessible terrain in the area around Ein Gedi gave David plenty of places to hide from Saul. In many places, natural openings in the rock form caves in which to shelter.

JEALOUSY – SOMETHING TO AVOID
David was so successful that Saul became jealous of him. First Saul tried to kill David, then sent him away to fight his battles, hoping the Philistines would kill him. Eventually Saul spent most of his time scheming to kill him. What began as simple jealousy became hatred and the wish to see David dead. The saddest thing of all was that David was very loyal and loved Saul. Becoming jealous is easy, but controlling it is difficult. If a brother, sister, or friend at school does well we should be glad for them, not jealous.

A WIFE FOR DAVID

❖ 1 Samuel 25 ❖

David lived near a very wealthy man named Nabal who had been away on business. On his return, David told some of his servants to visit Nabal and say, "Greetings to you and all your household from our master David. When your men were tending their flocks near our master he ensured that neither they nor the animals suffered in any way. Therefore he humbly asks that you give us some provisions from your stores."

But Nabal became angry: "Who is this David? Who does he think I am that I should hand out the food I have prepared for my own workers to a stranger?"

When David's servants told him what Nabal had said, he was furious. "Arm yourselves, men," David ordered, and about four hundred of his men prepared to go to help him teach Nabal a lesson.

One of Nabal's servants heard about this and told Nabal's wife, Abigail, "David sent some of his men to our master, asking for food. But he insulted them. While we were near David's camp he was kind to us. Now he is going to punish us all for Nabal's arrogance."

Immediately, Abigail prepared some food for David and went out hoping to see him before he attacked her husband. She met him by a mountain ravine.

"Kind sir," she said, falling on her knees, "please don't listen to what Nabal said. Had I met your men, I would have treated them as well as you treated our men. Give these things to your men and forgive Nabal's stupidity," she pleaded.

David replied, "Thank the Lord God that you have prevented me from killing your husband. And thank you for this food you have brought for me and my men. Go in peace." And he returned to his camp.

When Abigail told Nabal about her meeting with David, he fell into a deep state of shock and died soon afterwards. Hearing of this, David sent messengers to Abigail asking her to marry him. She agreed and left her old home to become the wife of David.

Fig tree
The fig is one of the most important trees mentioned in the Bible. It grew to a height of 6-9 metres and produced two or three crops of fruit each year. The first figs of the year were a great delicacy. They were usually eaten fresh, but were sometimes pressed into cakes to take on a journey. Abigail took pressed figs when she went to see David.

Wadi
Deep ravines or valleys cutting through the rocky landscape are typical of the region. In winter rain makes streams along the bottom of the valleys, but they dry up in the hot season. This dried-up river bed is known as a 'wadi'. Abigail went along a wadi or ravine on her donkeys when she took food to David.

Food strainer
This pomegranate-shaped food strainer dates from the time of Saul and David. Strainers were used in food preparation to strain out stalks, seeds and skins. Perhaps the design of this is a clue that it was used to strain seeds from the juice of red pomegranates which were commonly pressed to make a refreshing drink.

SAUL ASKS A WITCH TO TELL THE FUTURE

✤ 1 Samuel 28-31 ✤

Inscribed bowl
Magic spells and incantations were sometimes written on bowls and other household utensils to ward off evil spirits. This Aramaic inscription calls on Gabriel, Michael and other good spirits to protect the house and bring healing.

Battle axe
The most common way of fighting a battle in Old Testament times was by hand-to-hand combat. Soldiers were armed with weapons like hammers, sticks, swords and axes. Although the sword is the most frequently mentioned weapon in the Bible, bronze axe heads of various shapes and sizes have also been found.

Isis
The goddess Isis was the patron of Egyptian magic. Using magic or sorcery to attempt to see into the future or to influence events or people was a common feature of the pagan cultures of the time, but it is always condemned in the Bible. God wants people to trust only him to meet all their needs.

Once again the Philistine army prepared to fight the Israelites. When Saul saw his old enemy paraded against him he was terrified.

Saul asked God to reveal to him what course of action he should take, but God would not speak to him.

In his desperation Saul said to his servants, "Find me a medium who will be able to tell me what I must do."

"There is such a woman in Endor," they told him. So Saul disguised himself and paid her a visit.

"I want you to call up the spirit of someone," Saul told her.

"But what about Saul?" she replied. "He has banished all mediums and spiritists. He would kill me if he found out."

Saul assured her that nothing would happen to her. "I promise you in God's name that you will not be harmed."

"Who do you want me to call up?" she asked nervously.

"Samuel," replied Saul.

Silently the woman began. When the spirit of Samuel appeared before her she screamed at the top of her voice, "Why have you deceived me? You are Saul!"

"Never mind that," said the king. "What can you see?"

"An old man in a robe."

"That's Samuel!" shouted Saul and he fell upon his knees.

"Why have you done this?" said Samuel sternly.

"The Philistines are about to attack us and so I asked God what we should do but he refuses to speak to me."

"If God will not talk to you why are you talking to me? You have disobeyed God and so what is happening now is merely the fulfilment of his word. David will become king after you. By this time tomorrow both you and your sons will be dead, just as I am."

Samuel disappeared and Saul collapsed on the ground in a heap. He was so frightened he couldn't get up. But the woman and his servants made him eat some meat and then he left.

The next day the Philistines attacked and there was a tremendous battle. One by one, Saul's soldiers were killed or deserted. Finally Saul himself died, just as the spirit of Samuel had predicted.

DAVID BECOMES KING OF ISRAEL

✤ 2 Samuel 2-5 ✤

After Saul's death, two people claimed the kingship. Some had chosen David while others wanted Ish-Bosheth, one of Saul's sons, to reign. Within a short period of time, the two groups were at war. It was a bitter struggle lasting a long time and many people on both sides were killed.

When Ish-Bosheth himself was treacherously murdered in his sleep, the Israelites knew that it was time for the bloodshed to end.

Representatives from all the tribes approached David at Hebron and said, "We are all part of the same nation. Let's put a stop to all this fighting. When you served Saul, God said that you would become our king. Now is the time. We want you to be king over us from now on."

David agreed to their request and so at the age of thirty they anointed him king.

Once David was established as king over all of Israel, he decided to make Jerusalem the new capital city. It was on top of a hill, and at that time was occupied by the Jebusites who had transformed it into an imposing fortress. David marched his army to the city walls.

The inhabitants were confident that their city could not be captured and so they taunted David and his men, "You'll never get inside! Even the blind and lame would have no trouble in keeping you out."

David issued a challenge to his soldiers: "The first soldier to kill a Jebusite will become the leader of the army."

Joab was the first to attack the city and so David gave him the reward he had promised, promoting him to commander-in-chief.

When he had captured the city, David enlarged it. He sent a message to his ally, the king of Tyre, asking for wood and stone to make a splendid palace. As he sat on his throne after many years of being an outlaw, he praised God for having made him king.

Jerusalem today
The modern city of Jerusalem is much larger than it was in David's time when you could have walked around it in about half an hour. Today it covers an area of about 107 km² and has a population of more than 425,000 people, made up of Jews, Muslims and Christians. Most of the population live and work in the western side of the city.

Carpenters at work
Hiram, the king of Tyre, sent skilled carpenters to help David construct the royal palace and build up the surrounding area. These drawings from Egyptian tombs illustrate the work carpenters did in splitting a beam, drilling, planing and polishing, sawing, and gluing wood together. Everything was done by hand.

Ruins of David's city
David made Jerusalem his royal city and the nation's capital. Its neutral location on the border between Judah and Benjamin enabled David to unite the kingdom. The city of David, or Zion, as it is also known, was about 12 acres in size, and had about 3,500 inhabitants. Built on the top of a hill with steep sides, the city was well fortified and almost impregnable.

THE ARK COMES TO JERUSALEM

✤ 2 Samuel 6-7 ✤

Acacia tree
The Tabernacle and the Ark of the Covenant were made of acacia wood, which is close-grained and hard and therefore excellent for cabinet-making. Few trees grow in the Sinai desert, but the acacia flourishes there.

David picked thirty thousand men to accompany him as he brought the Ark to Jerusalem from Kiriath Jearim. They carefully loaded it onto a cart and then set off, a long procession of joyful people, playing musical instruments and dancing with delight. Eventually they reached the city. At this point David was beside himself with joy and danced with everyone else. Michal, his wife, saw him behaving in what she considered an unseemly manner and was disgusted.

The Ark was put in position and David sacrificed offerings to God there. When he had completed the sacrifices he gave everyone food and sent them to their homes.

He then returned to Michal who, when she saw him, vented her feelings. "Why did you prance around in front of all those servant girls like some common man?"

David was incensed. "Why shouldn't I dance before God in a way that I think is suitable? I am the king and I can do as I please."

Later, when David had built himself a palace, he confided in the prophet Nathan, "It doesn't seem right that I should have this wonderful home and yet the Ark of the Covenant is kept in a tent. I would like to build a temple in God's honour."

Nathan was wondering how to reply when God came to him in the night. "Tell David that he will not be the one to build a house for me. Instead his son will do it. Indeed, it is I who will build a house for him, for I plucked him from obscurity and placed him in the position that he is in today. Without my help he would still be a humble shepherd. Under my guidance he will become the greatest king upon earth. I will establish an eternal kingdom for him and his children and he shall be like a son to me."

When Nathan reported the vision to David, the king was overcome with praise and gratitude. "May God do as he has promised and bless me and my family for ever."

Musical instruments
Music played an important part in the religious life of Israel. Singers and musicians led the temple worship, and on feast days music, singing and dancing were part of the festivities. The instruments shown here are (from top to bottom) the tambourine, cymbals and a bronze sistrum, a type of rattle. David was a gifted musician and is said to have invented a number of instruments, although we do not know precisely what they were.

MEPHIBOSHETH

✤ 2 Samuel 9 ✤

David enquired of his servants, "Out of respect for the memory of my dear friend Jonathan I would like to help any relatives of his who are still alive. Can anyone tell me if there is someone I could assist in any way?"

Ziba, who used to work for Saul, was summoned to the king's presence. David repeated his request, "Are there any relatives of Saul and Jonathan who need my help?"

"Yes, sir," he replied. "Do you remember Jonathan's son Mephibosheth, the one who is lame in both feet? He is still alive."

David leapt to his feet. "Where is he?" he asked excitedly.

"In the town of Lo Debar," came the answer.

Immediately David arranged to have Mephibosheth brought to Jerusalem. As Mephibosheth hobbled into the royal court he bowed low to mark his respect. "Don't be

frightened, Mephibosheth. For the sake of the memory of my friend, your father Jonathan, I am going to restore to you all your grand-father's land and you may come and eat with me whenever you wish."

Mephibosheth, overcome with emotion, bowed low and exclaimed, "Who am I that you should show such favour towards me?"

David then called Ziba and explained to him everything he had told Mephibosheth. "You and your servants are to work for Mephibosheth from now on. You will farm his land and harvest his crops for him."

Ziba replied, "Whatever you command, sir." He then left to arrange the transfer to Mephibosheth's new estates.

From that moment Mephibosheth lived in Jerusalem and he was always welcome at David's table.

DAVID TAKES ANOTHER MAN'S WIFE

✤ 2 Samuel 11-12 ✤

Myrtle
The myrtle shrub is a common plant in Palestine. The Bible often refers to it as a symbol of God's generosity. It has fragrant, glossy, evergreen leaves and clusters of star-shaped white flowers which were used to make perfume. It was also used in burial ceremonies.

Uriah the Hittite
Bathsheba's husband was a Hittite, one of several non-Israelites among David's mighty warriors. The Hittites were a warlike people from Anatolia (in modern Turkey) feared for their military skill. They were the first people to use chariots for warfare. They conquered Mesopotamia, Babylon and parts of Syria before being defeated in about 1200BC.

FOOD
In Old Testament times people's staple diet was based on grain and bread, with butter and cheese, washed down with water, milk, wine or beer. Meat (usually lamb, beef or game) was expensive and a rare luxury for most people. Grain, wine and olive oil were important as food, status symbols and trade goods. Nuts and honey were treats which could be used for entertaining or as gifts.

One spring, when kings were usually involved in military campaigns, David sent Joab and his army to besiege the town of Rabbah. David remained in Jerusalem and one day, while strolling on the palace roof, he saw an attractive woman having a bath. He found out that she was Bathsheba, wife of Uriah. He called her to the palace and made love to her. In the morning she returned home.

Later, she sent David a message, "I am expecting a child."

Immediately David ordered Joab, his commander, to send Uriah to Jerusalem. David quizzed him about the siege and then told him to go home and spend the night with his wife, so that he would think he was the father of the child. Instead he spent the night with David's servants.

"It would be wrong to enjoy the comforts of my home while my comrades are risking their lives fighting," he said.

David invited him to a meal and made him drunk, but still he did not go to his own house.

When David sent him back to the army, he ordered Joab to put Uriah in a dangerous situation and then withdraw the other soldiers, so leaving Uriah alone.

These cruel orders were carried out and Uriah was slain. After Bathsheba had mourned her husband, David married her and she gave birth to a child.

God was angry with David and sent his prophet Nathan to confront the king. Nathan told David a story. "One day a very rich man was entertaining a friend. Although he had many animals he helped himself to the only lamb of a poor man, killed it and gave it to his guest to eat."

David was enraged. "Such a harsh man deserves nothing but death."

Quietly but firmly, Nathan said, "You are that man, for you have done the same thing to Uriah. You have disobeyed God and he will bring upon you the same calamity that you brought upon Uriah."

David realized the truth of what Nathan said and was grief-stricken. "I have sinned against God," he confessed.

ABSALOM DIES IN AN OAK TREE

❖ **2 Samuel** 13-18 ❖

One of David's sons, Amnon, fell in love with his half-sister, Tamar. She did not love him, but despite her protests, he slept with her. Her brother Absalom was furious and vowed to take revenge. Two years later he invited Amnon to a banquet. While they were feasting Absalom ordered his men to kill Amnon for what he had done to Tamar. When the news reached David, he was sad, for he knew that this was the beginning of God's punishment for his murder of Uriah.

Absalom, fearing that David would kill him, fled. Later, when he felt it was safe, he returned to Jerusalem and was reunited with his father.

Despite this reconciliation, Absalom wanted to seize the throne for himself. He set about making himself popular with the people by listening to their concerns. Once he had won them over, he proclaimed himself king in Hebron.

Hearing this, David realized that Absalom was more popular than he was. David and his officials fled from Jerusalem, leaving his friend Hushai to spy on Absalom.

The oaks of Palestine
More than 20 different kinds of oak tree grew in Palestine, some reaching heights of 30 metres. The forest of Ephraim in Gilead, where Absalom was killed, was one of the many dense oak forests that grew in Palestine in Biblical times. The oak's hard wood was used for ship-building and carving. Trees like the oak symbolized stability and permanence.

Hushai persuaded Absalom that he no longer supported David, so the new king took his advice about defeating him. Hushai knew his plan would help David.

The two armies met in the forest of Ephraim and Absalom soon realized that his side would lose. As he fled, his long hair became tangled in the branches of an oak, trapping him. When Joab found him, he killed him where he hung.

When David heard the news that yet another of his sons was dead, he was inconsolable and wished that he had died instead of Absalom.

David mourns his son
David was distraught at the death of Absalom. Joab rebuked him for putting his personal grief first, and not showing his gratitude to the loyal men who had risked their lives to help him keep his throne.

WHO WILL BE THE NEXT KING?

✤ 1 Kings 1 ✤

Jerusalem – the holy city
This map shows the layout of Jerusalem in the time of David and Solomon. On the west of the Kidron Valley was the Gihon spring. A channel through the rock took water from the spring into the city. David and his men used this route to capture Jerusalem from the Jebusites. To do so they climbed an 11-metre high vertical shaft and followed the narrow water channel under the city's walls.

Solomon's palace
This is the floor plan of Solomon's palace, which he built when he finished the temple. The palace was magnificent. It was 45 metres long, 23 metres wide and 13 metres high, and took thirteen years to build. The walls were of stone and the roof was made of the finest cedar, specially brought from Lebanon, which is why it was called the Palace of the Forest of Lebanon.

David had now become very old and frail. Seeing how feeble his father was, his son Adonijah decided that he should become king. He made a series of sacrifices near En Rogel and invited his brothers and the royal court to the ceremony.

Then Nathan, who had not been invited, approached Bathsheba. "Have you heard that Adonijah has become king without David's knowledge or approval? You must go to David and alert him of this, reminding him that he has already chosen Solomon to take the throne."

So Bathsheba went in to see her husband and explained the matter to him. "Sir, surely you remember how you promised me that our son Solomon would be the next king? Instead, Adonijah has crowned himself king. The people are looking to you to see if you will approve this appointment."

As she was talking with David, Nathan entered and repeated exactly what Bathsheba had just said.

David then said to his wife, "I promise you by the living God that your son Solomon shall succeed to the throne after me."

Bathsheba was very relieved and bowed low before him.

David then sent Nathan and Zadok the priest to Gihon and told them to anoint Solomon as king.

When they arrived there, they did as the king had commanded.

At the end of the coronation a loud shout went up: "Long live King Solomon!"

Adonijah heard the noise and asked what was going on. When he was told that Solomon was the new king upon the express orders of David, he was alarmed.

He fled and took refuge in the Tabernacle because he was afraid that Solomon might wish to kill him.

When Solomon heard where Adonijah was, he sent some of his men to bring Adonijah into his presence and said, "As long as you do no evil then you will be safe, but if you sin then you will die. Now go to your home in peace."

CLEVER KING SOLOMON

✤ 1 Kings 3 ✤

One night God appeared to Solomon in a dream.

"I will give you whatever you quest," he said.

Solomon replied, "I am still young d have no experience of how to rule. erefore I ask that you will give me sdom so that I might govern your ople well."

His reply pleased God who then said, ince you have not asked for wealth or tories for your own selfish ends, I will nt your wish. But in addition I will give u those things which you have not asked – riches and glory, such that no other ng alive will be like you. And if you ey me as your father did, I will give u a long life too."

Soon Solomon was given an portunity to put his wisdom to the t. Two women came to him and e of them addressed him saying, r, we live in the same house. We ve both recently given birth to boys th only three days separating them. st night she rolled over onto her y and suffocated it. Then seeing at it was dead, she took my son ile I slept and replaced him with r lifeless son. When I woke up I ought my child was dead, but after ad checked I realized that it wasn't boy at all!"

The other woman interrupted, hat is not true! My boy is the ing one. It is yours that is dead."

The other one answered back d soon they were arguing bitterly in nt of Solomon.

"Silence!" he ordered. "Bring e a sword. Since you cannot decide tween you whose child it is, I shall t the living child into two and you n have half each." He motioned to s guard, "Cut the child!"

Then the boy's real mother fell her knees, trembling and crying, lease, sir, give her the child! hatever you do, don't kill him!"

The other woman, however, remained cool and calmly said, "Neither of us shall have him. Cut the thing in two!"

When he saw the reactions of the women, Solomon announced his judgement: "Do not kill the child. Give him to the first woman. Only the real mother would behave in such a way."

When news of the king's verdict became public knowledge, the people of Israel marvelled because they realized that such wisdom could only come from God.

Solomon's horses
Solomon was a great horse trader and breeder, importing horses from Egypt and Asia and exporting them to neighbouring states. He kept 12,000 horses in vast stables in the cities of Hazor, Megiddo and Gezer. In fact horses became so common in Jerusalem that the city had a special horse gate.

BUILDING THE GREAT TEMPLE

♣ **1 Kings 5-8** ♣

Solomon sent messengers to Hiram, king of neighbouring Tyre. "God has granted me peace and it is my intention to build the temple that my father David proposed. I require wood from your fine cedar and pine trees for which I will pay handsomely."

So Hiram's men felled trees and floated the logs in the sea to where Solomon's men could collect them and take them to the site of the temple which took seven years to build. No expense was spared – either on the imposing exterior or the elaborate interior.

When it was ready, Solomon brought the Ark of the Covenant and placed it in the inner sanctuary of the temple, the Most Holy Place. When the priests who had been carrying the Ark left the Most Holy Place, the cloud of God's presence filled the whole temple.

Solomon and the people were full of awe and wonder. The king turned to everyone there and prayed, "Most majestic God, there is no god like you. You have indeed kept the promise you made to my father David when he spoke to you of his desire to build a temple. You have helped us from beginning to end and here today we thank you for your continuing love towards us. Yet even the greatest temple in the world could never be the home of the Lord God who made the heavens and the earth. Nevertheless, this place is yours: when anyone prays in this temple, listen to them and answer their prayer and forgive their sins."

Then Solomon blessed the people. "May the Lord bless you as he blessed our fathers. May he make you always love, obey and serve him."

For two weeks the people celebrated, offering sacrifices to God and dedicating the temple. When it was time to leave, everyone was full of joy at having seen the temple, and grateful for what God had done for his people.

THE QUEEN OF SHEBA

❖ 1 Kings 10 ❖

Before long, Solomon's fame and his faith in God became known all over the whole world. The queen of Sheba heard the impressive reports of him and decided to go to Jerusalem to see if the rumours were true. She arrived at the head of a splendid caravan, her camels laden with spices, gold and jewellery. She lost no time in conversing with Solomon, testing his knowledge on a wide range of matters. He answered all her queries with ease, explaining everything she wanted to know.

Solomon entertained her lavishly, showing her all over his royal city and outlining the laws by which he governed the country. He took her to the temple and explained the history of the Israelites and the miraculous ways in which God had intervened throughout their long history.

When the queen realized how wise Solomon was and saw his palaces, his court and had tasted the delights of his royal kitchens, she was deeply impressed.

Overcome, she confessed to him, "All the reports that I had heard about you are completely true. In fact, to be honest, what I heard touched only the surface of the truth. Everything here is far better than I could ever have imagined. Your people are very fortunate to have you for their king. The credit and honour surely must go to the Lord your God who has placed you in your exalted position."

The queen gave Solomon the gifts that she had brought and, in exchange, he gave her everything that she asked for, before she finally left, content and full of admiration, to return to her own kingdom.

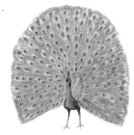

Peacock
Solomon's trade expeditions probably reached India and brought back peacocks. In the early Christian church the eyes of the peacock's tail represented the all-seeing eyes of God.

The Queen of Sheba's journey
The Queen of Sheba travelled from what is now Yemen in south-western Arabia, to Jerusalem, to see Solomon's wealth. Her journey was over 1600 kilometres and would have taken her through the Arabian desert and then along the main trade route from Arabia, the King's Highway.

Cedar of Lebanon
The cedar of Lebanon is a large coniferous tree. Its wood, valued for its strength and beauty, was always used for the temple's roof and wall panels.

SOLOMON TURNS AWAY FROM GOD

✢ 1 Kings 11 ✢

Earrings
Jewellery has been a valued possession from earliest times. These earrings show the variety of shapes and designs used in ancient times, ranging from the simplest brass hoop to the intricate workmanship of jewel-studded gold earrings. In the Bible earrings were often associated with idolatry, perhaps because the pagan cultures engraved their deities on them, and used them as lucky charms to ward off evil spirits.

Despite God's commands to the contrary, Solomon amassed for himself vast numbers of foreign wives. As he grew older, they gradually persuaded him to take an interest in their gods. As a result he did not follow God with all his heart. He even built an altar for Chemosh, the god of Moab, on a hill near Jerusalem.

So God became very angry with him and said, "You have rejected my commands and ways and so I will take the kingdom away from you and hand it over to one of your subjects. However, for the sake of your father David, I will not do this during your reign. When your son is king, I will wrench Israel from him, leaving him just one tribe."

God then raised up men who opposed Solomon and led groups of rebels against him. One such man was Jeroboam, whom Solomon had given the job of supervising the manual labourers.

As Jeroboam was leaving Jerusalem one day, he was approached by Ahijah the prophet, who grabbed Jeroboam's coat and ripped it up into twelve pieces.

Ahijah then prophesied, "You are to keep ten pieces, for God is going to rip the kingdom from Solomon's hand and give you ten tribes, leaving the others to Solomon's son. He will do this because of Solomon's wickedness in following after foreign gods. Now you must not fall into the same trap as Solomon. If you obey God's commands, then your kingdom will last for ever and Israel will be yours."

When Solomon heard what had happened, he tried to kill Jeroboam who fled to Egypt. He remained there until Solomon had died and his son Rehoboam took over the kingdom.

A DIVIDED LAND

♣ 1 Kings 12-13 ♣

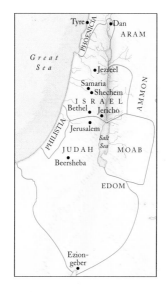

Scorpion
Many species of scorpion live in Palestine, but most of them are not deadly poisonous. The largest are up to 15 centimetres long, which is as big as a grown-man's hand. They spend the day under rocks or in holes, and at night hunt spiders and insects. They also hide in footwear, blankets and clothing. When Rehoboam threatened to beat the people with scorpions, he was probably referring to a whip with many tails and hooked knobs of metal which was known as a scorpion.

REHOBOAM
Rehoboam was the last king of the united Israel after the death of his father, Solomon, and the first king of the southern kingdom of Judah. He was so unpopular because of the heavy burden of taxation he tried to inflict on the northern kingdom, that he was stoned to death.

Rehoboam was in Shechem where the Israelites were waiting to crown him king. When Jeroboam heard about this, he returned from his exile in Egypt. With the backing of the whole people Jeroboam went to Rehoboam and asked, "Your father worked us hard, will you now make life easier for us?"

Rehoboam replied, "Come back in three days and I will give you an answer." He then consulted the advisers of his father who told him, "If you give the people what you want, they will serve you for ever."

He then asked his friends and acquaintances what they suggested. "Tell the people that the burdens Solomon placed upon their backs will seem as light as a feather compared to the burden that you are going to give them."

Three days later Rehoboam informed the people of his decision. "My father made you work using whips; I will beat you with scorpions."

The assembly was dismayed and cried out, "We will have nothing to do with this descendant of David. Everyone to their own home!" And, disgruntled, they trooped home.

Soon afterwards, a rebellion began. The Israelites proclaimed Jeroboam king, leaving only the tribe of Judah faithful to Rehoboam.

Both sides began preparing for war, but God spoke to his people through Shemaiah the prophet saying, "No one is to fight against his brother. This split in the kingdom is the work of God."

So peace was preserved and the warring factions both returned home.

Jeroboam feared that if the Israelites had to go to Jerusalem in order to make sacrifices, they would come under the influence of Rehoboam once more and revert to him. So he decided to build altars at Bethel and Dan. He also built shrines in the mountains and appointed priests who were not from the tribe of Levi.

In many different ways he broke God's commands. Even when God sent prophets to warn him of his disobedience, he did not stop. He continued making people priests whether they were Levites or not. It was this sin, more than any other, that led to his eventual downfall.

The division of the kingdom
Because Solomon had not followed God wholeheartedly, his kingdom was divided in two, leaving his son Rehoboam with only the two southern tribes of Judah and Benjamin. Jeroboam, an official in Solomon's court, ruled over the ten northern tribes of Israel.

ELIJAH SAVES THE WIDOW AND HER SON

✤ 1 Kings 17 ✤

Quail
Quails were the smallest and tastiest of the game birds hunted in biblical times. They migrate in large flocks flying only a metre or two above the ground. Quails were the meat which God gave to the Israelites when they were hungry in the desert.

BIRDS OF THE BIBLE
There is a rich variety of bird life in the Middle East, both because it has a wide range of habitats and because it lies on one of the main migration routes.
Pigeons and doves are the most familiar and important of all birds mentioned in the Bible. Owls, storks, game birds, such as partridge and quail, and birds of prey, such as eagles, kites and hawks, are all familiar to us today, as are the ravens which took bread and meat to Elijah. Although ravens are often associated with evil, the Bible uses them as illustrations of God's goodness.

A prophet named Elijah prophesied to King Ahab of Israel, "As surely as the Lord God reigns in the heavens, there will be no more rain in the land except at my command."

Under God's guidance, Elijah then went to a hiding place in a ravine near the river Jordan. Here, he drank from a brook and ravens brought him bread and meat every morning and evening.

Eventually, even the brook dried up, so God said to Elijah, "Go to Zarephath where I have ordered a widow to provide you with food."

As Elijah arrived outside the town he came across a woman gathering firewood.

He called to her, "Could you please bring me a little water so that I may drink?" As she set off to fetch it he added,

"Please may I have some bread, too?"

She turned and looked him in the eye. "I don't have any bread. All I have is a small amount of flour in a jar and some oil. I was collecting these sticks to light a fire to cook a final meal for myself and my son before we starve to death."

Elijah said, "Don't worry. Return home and do what you had planned, but before you do, bake a cake and bring it back to me, then go and eat. God has told me to tell you that neither your jar of flour nor your jug of oil will run out until rain falls upon Israel again."

The woman left and obeyed Elijah. Everything that he had predicted came true. Every day there was enough food for the woman, her family and Elijah.

After some time, the woman's son fell ill. His condition got worse and he died.

His mother blamed Elijah. "What have I done to you to deserve this?" she cried.

"Give me your child," Elijah said, and he carried the boy upstairs to his room and placed him on the bed. He then prayed to God, "Why have you brought this sadness upon this kind widow?" He stretched out over the boy three times and cried out, "May life return to this boy!"

God heard Elijah's prayer and the boy came back to life. Elijah carried him back downstairs to his waiting mother who, with tear-filled eyes, thanked Elijah. "Now I understand that you are a man of God who only speaks the truth from God," she said.

A desolate region
In fleeing from Jezebel, Elijah covered some 320 kilometres from Mount Carmel to Mount Horeb, crossing a barren wilderness, which would have looked then much as it does now. The wild, empty landscape was punctuated with a few small oases of sparse vegetation around seasonal wadis. Where permanent streams exist, as here at Wadi Feiran in Sinai, the vegetation is more lush.

GOD'S ALTAR BURSTS INTO FLAMES

✤ 1 Kings 18 ✤

After three years' drought, God said to Elijah, "Go and tell King Ahab that I am about to send rain on the land."

When Ahab saw Elijah he exclaimed, "Is that really you, the cause of all Israel's troubles?"

Elijah replied, "I am not the one who has caused problems for the country. It is you and your family who have brought disaster upon us by your wickedness in following the gods of Baal. Gather the people on Mount Carmel, together with the prophets of Baal."

Ahab did as Elijah requested. When the crowd had assembled, Elijah addressed them: "How much longer will you dither between two options? If the Lord is God, follow him, but if Baal is God, follow him."

An embarrassed hush fell over the throng – no one dared speak a word.

Elijah continued, "I am the only prophet of the Lord, but beside me are four hundred and fifty prophets of Baal. Fetch two bulls. They can choose one for sacrifice. Then we will both prepare altars and place the bulls on them without setting fire to them. Then we will call upon our gods. Whichever one sends fire from heaven will be the true god."

The people agreed this was a good idea and so preparations began.

The prophets of Baal slaughtered their bull, built the altar and danced around it calling to Baal. "Answer with fire," they shouted all morning.

At midday Elijah taunted them, "Perhaps he is asleep!"

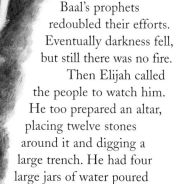

Baal's prophets redoubled their efforts. Eventually darkness fell, but still there was no fire.

Then Elijah called the people to watch him. He too prepared an altar, placing twelve stones around it and digging a large trench. He had four large jars of water poured over everything. This was done three times, soaking the altar and filling the trench.

Then Elijah prayed, "Lord God of Abraham, Isaac and Jacob, show that you are the God of Israel and that I am your servant. Show these people who you are, so that they will return to you again."

Then fire engulfed the altar, setting the water in the trench alight. The people cried out, "The Lord is God!"

"Seize the false prophets," ordered Elijah, and the people caught and killed them.

Amid the confusion a small cloud appeared far out to sea. Gradually it grew bigger until rain was lashing down on everyone. God had ended Israel's drought just as he had promised.

Baal, god of rain
It was Jezebel who sought to establish the worship of Baal, god of rain, as the religion of Israel. Showers marked the start of the winter rains, softening the ground baked hard during the hot dry summer. If the rains did not come, ploughing and sowing the new season's crops were impossible, bringing the fear of hunger and starvation the following winter.

Contest on Mount Carmel
Baal was worshipped on Mount Carmel. When Elijah brought this forbidden worship to an end, the three-year drought also came to an end.

91 ✤

NABOTH'S VINEYARD

♣ 1 Kings 21 ♣

Vines and vineyards
In biblical times vineyards were often surrounded by a high wall. The vines were trained on supports to keep the grapes off the ground. Grapes, raisins and wine were so important to the economy and diet of the Israelites that people who helped harvest grapes did not have to serve in the army.

Jezebel the wicked
As punishment for having Naboth killed, Jezebel was later thrown from a window in the palace at Jezreel and trampled under horses' hooves. As someone of royal birth she should have had a proper burial, but this was impossible because dogs had eaten most of her body. Her violent death fulfilled Elijah's prophecy.

A man called Naboth owned a vineyard in Jezreel next to the palace of Ahab, king of Samaria. Ahab wanted the vineyard, so he approached Naboth, "I would like to have your vineyard and turn it into a vegetable garden. I will give you money for it, or find you another one in exchange, whichever you prefer."

But Naboth replied, "The land has been in my family for generations, and I have no intention of parting with it."

Ahab left, angry at Naboth's refusal. He went to his bedroom without eating, closed the door and sulked.

Jezebel, his wife, asked him what the matter was. "Why are you so moody? Why have you lost your appetite?"

"Because Naboth has refused to give me his vineyard, even though I offered him the chance to get a better one or to take money for it," came the reply.

"This is no way for the king of Israel to behave! Are you the king or aren't you? Get up and have something to eat. Don't worry, I will get you the vineyard," laughed his wife.

Then Jezebel wrote in Ahab's name to the leaders of Jezreel. In these letters she instructed the leaders to arrange a special banquet and seat Naboth in an important place. Two rogues were to be placed either side of him and they were to testify that he had spoken against God and the king. Naboth was then to be taken out and executed. These orders were carried out ruthlessly and soon Jezebel received a message announcing the death of Naboth.

Jezebel immediately informed her husband, who then seized the vineyard that he had set his heart upon.

But God sent Elijah to prophesy against Ahab, "As you have murdered a man and plundered his land, God says that in the place where Naboth was stoned to death dogs will lick the blood from your dead corpse!"

When Ahab heard what Elijah said, he repented. God saw his change and declared, "As you have admitted your sin, I will not destroy you as I promised."

Dogs
Dogs were useful scavengers. They roamed in packs around the city walls waiting for rubbish to be thrown down. When Ahab was killed in battle his body was brought to Samaria where dogs lapped up his blood – as Elijah had foretold.

TAKEN UP TO HEAVEN

✦ 2 Kings 2 ✦

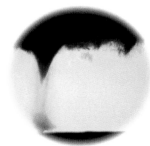

Whirlwind
Whirlwinds start in storm clouds as warm air spins upward at high speed. They include cyclones, hurricanes and tornadoes and are quite common in the Middle East. In the Bible they are often seen as a sign from God.

It was almost time for God to take Elijah up to heaven in a whirlwind.

"God is sending me to Bethel, but you must remain here," he told Elisha, his successor.

"No, I'm coming with you," replied Elisha. So they travelled on together.

At Bethel the resident prophets said to Elisha, "Do you realize that God is going to take Elijah away from you soon?"

"Yes," he replied, "don't remind me."

Again Elijah said to Elisha, "Stay here while I go to Jericho."

"No, wherever you go, I will go as well," came Elisha's reply.

So Elisha followed Elijah, first to Jericho, then to the river Jordan. Fifty prophets from Jericho followed them to see what they would do.

When they reached the river, Elijah removed his coat, rolled it up and hit the water with it. As he did so, the river divided, so they could cross to the far side.

"Now I must leave you, Elisha. Is there anything I can do for you before I go?"

"Let a double measure of your spirit fall upon me," he replied. "What you ask is very difficult. If you see me when I go, you will receive what you wanted. If you do not, then you will not have it."

As he spoke, a chariot and horses of fire appeared and Elijah was taken up to heaven in a whirlwind. As Elisha saw it, he cried out, "My father! The chariots and horsemen of Israel!" Then Elijah disappeared for ever.

Elisha picked up Elijah's cloak, walked back to the river and hit the water with the cloak. It parted for him, just as it had for Elijah. The prophets on the far bank saw everything. When Elisha reached them, they bowed to him, saying, "The spirit of Elijah has come upon you."

Then Elisha knew his last request had been granted.

Golden chariot
This gold model of a chariot pulled by four horses dates from about 500BC. The armies of Israel used chariots in battle, but they were also used as transport for important people. The chariot and horses of fire, which carried Elijah up to heaven in the whirlwind, symbolize the power of the heavenly host which had accompanied Elijah's ministry.

SAVE MY SON!

✤ 2 Kings 4 ✤

Biblical home
Inside an average home, a raised area would have separated the living accommodation from where the animals were kept at night and the family's business was carried on by day. The Shunammite was fairly well-to-do, so this area may have been walled off. The annexe, or extension, she and her husband built for Elisha was on the roof.

Hasidic boy
The Hasidim are Jewish mystics whose worship is very joyful. Sons were important in Bible times because they continued the family line when their fathers died, and they could earn a living for their widowed mothers and unmarried sisters.

View from Mount Carmel
In Hebrew, "Carmel" means "vineyard" or "garden of God". In the Bible, the area was famous for its beauty and lush vegetation. The slopes were densely wooded with forests of oak trees, groves of olives and vineyards. Today much of the area is protected as a nature reserve.

Once when he was in Shunem, Elisha was invited to eat at the home of a rich lady. They became friends and whenever he was in the town they had a meal.

After a while she said to her husband, "Let's build an annexe onto our house so that when Elisha passes through he can be our guest."

Once, when Elisha was lodging with her, he asked if there was anything he could do to repay her kindness. She said she was perfectly content, but it would be nice to have a son. He promised her, "Within a year you will give birth to a boy."

She thought he was mocking her and begged him not to be so cruel, but sure enough, she gave birth to a boy, just as Elisha had predicted.

When the boy was older he was out with his father in the fields when he suddenly doubled up in pain, screaming that his head hurt. They rushed him home to his mother but in a few hours he lay dead on her lap. She took his body up to Elisha's room and laid him on the bed. She wanted to tell Elisha of the tragedy and rushed off to see him at Mount Carmel. As soon as he saw her he realized something was wrong.

"When you told me that I was going to have a child, didn't I tell you not to make fun of me? Now he is dead, struck down by a strange illness," cried the woman.

Elisha told his servant to go to the house and lay his staff on the boy. He did as he was told but nothing happened, so he returned to his master who was travelling behind with the boy's mother. At the house, Elisha went to see the boy alone and prayed to God. He then stretched himself out on top of the boy whose body began to get warm. Elisha got up, walked around the room and lay on him again. The boy gave seven big sneezes and opened his eyes.

"Fetch his mother," Elisha called and she burst in, joyfully embracing the child.

"Take your son," Elisha whispered quietly and the two of them left the prophet alone in the room.

NAAMAN IS HEALED

✤ 2 Kings 5 ✤

Naaman, the commander-in-chief of the victorious army of the king of Aram, was afflicted with leprosy, a skin disease. His wife had a servant girl, an Israelite, who had been captured in one of the raids on Israel.

"There is a prophet in my country who could cure him," she told her mistress. So Naaman asked permission from his king to go to Israel to seek a cure. The king gave his approval and sent him to the king of Israel.

The king of Israel suspected a trap. "Do you think I can cure leprosy? This is a trick to make trouble between our countries!" he screamed.

When Elisha heard of the king's reaction he sent him a message: "Send him to me and then he will know that there is a prophet in Israel."

So Naaman went to see Elisha. But Elisha sent a message saying, "Bathe seven times in the river Jordan and you will be healed."

This made Naaman angry. "I expected him to meet me, pray to his God and then heal me. We have rivers in Damascus. Why couldn't I wash myself in one of them?"

His servants tried to calm him. "If he had asked you to do something complicated you'd have done it. So why not do this simple thing?"

Naaman accepted this and did as Elisha said. When he came out of the water a seventh time his skin was like a child's. He returned to Elisha saying, "Now I know your God is the only God. From now on I will only make sacrifices to him."

Elisha blessed Naaman who returned to his own country.

ISRAEL'S FINAL DEFEAT

✤ 2 Kings 17 ✤

Assyrian household god
Many Assyrian homes had little figures of household gods like this. The Israelites also had them, despite God's repeated warnings against worshipping other gods. Known in Hebrew as "teraphim", these little idols were small enough for their owners to carry with them when travelling.

THE FALL OF ISRAEL
The fall of Israel, the northern kingdom, is seen as a result of the people's failure to worship God alone. Israel was conquered by Assyria and sent into exile. The people of Israel had ignored the messages that God spoke through his prophets Elijah, Elisha, Hosea and Amos, calling them back to himself.

The Assyrian empire
Assyria was a major world power for 250 years. At its largest, its empire stretched from Egypt in the west to the Persian Gulf in the east. Shalmaneser deported the Israelites to Assyria in about 722BC when he attacked Hoshea for refusing to pay him tribute and forming an alliance with the king of Egypt instead.

From the time that God had delivered the people of Israel from the land of Egypt, they disobeyed him again and again. They worshipped other gods and copied the religions of the people who lived in the Promised Land. They built altars and monuments to all kinds of gods, scattering the land with idols of wood and stone.

God warned them repeatedly through prophets whose message was always the same: "Stop your evil ways. Obey my precious law that I gave to you through the mouths of my servants."

But it made no difference; each new generation was as proud and arrogant as the one before. They rejected anything to do with God, preferring the ways of the nations around them. They worshipped Baal; they bowed down to the stars in the evening sky; they sacrificed their children in fire; they used witchcraft and indulged in all kinds of wickedness.

Despite his great patience and willingness to forgive, God became increasingly angry with them and he split the nation in two. Yet even then, the man he had chosen as king of Israel, Jeroboam refused to acknowledge God. Both he and his descendants committed sins without thought for the God who loved them.

Finally it all came to an end and G[od] carried out his threat to exile the people t[o] a far-off land. Hoshea was on the throne and instead of paying respect to the king [of] Assyria he formed an alliance with the ki[ng] of Egypt. For his treachery Shalmaneser, king of Assyria, attacked him and capture[d] him, placing him under lock and key in o[ne] of his prisons.

Then Shalmaneser deported the whole nation to Assyria where they settle[d] on the banks of the river Habor. So Hoshea was the last wicked king of the rebellious nation of Israel. Never again di[d] the people return to the land that God ha[d] given to their ancestors centuries earlier.

JUDAH'S NOBLE KINGS

✤ 2 Kings 18-23 ✤

Most of the kings of Judah were wicked and did not follow God as required by his commands and laws. One exception to this was Hezekiah. He ordered the destruction of all the idols, shrines and altars that had been dedicated to other gods. He even broke his alliance with the king of Assyria and relied solely on the power and protection of God. When Sennacherib, the Assyrian king, heard of Hezekiah's defiance, he sent his forces to Jerusalem to besiege it.

His commander sent a message to Hezekiah: "Do not trust in God. My king, Sennacherib, is the only one who can protect you. Let us inside the city walls and we will shower you with fine horses and other presents. If you do not pay attention to my words you will all be killed."

Hezekiah sought the advice of Isaiah the prophet. Isaiah's reply was simple but firm: "Don't listen to the Assyrians. God will keep you safe."

Isaiah then prophesied against the Assyrians: "I am God and I will make you go back from where you have come. You will not capture Jerusalem."

Sure enough, that very night, an angel from God destroyed the Assyrian army, leaving only a few survivors to return home and tell of the disaster.

Another good king was Josiah, who became king when he was eight years old.

After he had reigned for eighteen years he issued a royal command: "Go and rebuild the temple." Soon the workmen discovered something very precious.

"We have found the book of the Law!" they informed the king.

"Read it to me," commanded Josiah. When they did so, he realized how far the people had strayed from God's ways. Josiah was extremely upset.

"Find out what God wants us to do," he ordered. His servants spoke to Huldah, the prophetess, who told them what to do.

"Because you were sorry when you learnt how you had forgotten God he has promised to protect you," she said.

Josiah then called the people together and they listened very carefully to God's word. Afterwards, they renewed their covenant with God, promising to follow his ways once more.

The Book of the Law
The Book of the Law which was rediscovered during the reign of King Josiah could have been a copy of the first five books of the Old Testament or part or all of the book of Deuteronomy. It was originally written down by Moses to remind the Israelites of their obligations and covenant with God. It was written in narrow columns on a papyrus scroll, and read from right to left.

Wall relief
Sennacherib made Nineveh the capital of the Assyrian empire. He built new city walls and gates and vastly improved the city's water supply. Archaeologists have discovered many treasures at Nineveh. This wall relief from Sennacherib's royal palace shows the king wearing his royal crown and riding out victorious in his chariot. After he failed to defeat Hezekiah, Sennacherib returned home only to be murdered by two of his sons.

DAVID WORSHIPS GOD

♣ 1 Chronicles 16 ♣

Singing psalms
There are 150 psalms in the Bible. As the picture (from an illuminated Bible) shows, they are used by both Jews and Christians in worship. Sometimes they express praise to God, but they can be laments of grief and even anger. All human emotion can be expressed prayerfully to God.

W hen David brought the Ark of the Covenant to Jerusalem, he sacrificed offerings to God. He distributed bread, dates and raisins to all the participants at the ceremony. Then he chose Levites to serve before the Ark, to pray, give thanks and praise God with lyres, harps, cymbals and trumpets.

David himself wrote a psalm of praise to God:

All praise be to God;
let all the world hear of what he has done.
May he fill all those who look to him
with joy and strength.
God is the Lord of all the earth,
who never forgets his covenant,
the promise he made to our father Abraham
concerning his desire to give us the land
of Canaan for ever.
Although there were not many of them,
God protected our ancestors;
they wandered from country to country.
Declare the glory of God!
He is to be honoured before all other gods;
they are merely lifeless idols.
The Lord God alone created the world
in its glorious beauty and awesome power.
Bring offerings to God;
come and bow down before his holy name,
worship him, for he is holy and pure.
By his word he set the earth firmly in place -
nothing can move it from its position.
Let the swirling seas, the gentle fields,
and the trees of the spreading forests
sing with one voice to God.
God is good, for his love lasts for ever.
Save us from all those that hate us,
so that we might praise you
with every breath that we have until the end of time.

Date clusters
Dates are a fruit rarely mentioned in the Bible but they must have been grown and enjoyed. When the crowds welcomed Jesus into Jerusalem, they waved date-palm branches like flags. Dates are usually pressed into "cakes" or slabs.

God's majesty
The writers of psalms, like poets in many periods, often see God's greatness mirrored in the wonders and beauty of creation – as in the psalm on this page. Bible writers stress that God is bigger than creation; he is not part of it, and creation is not to be worshipped.

When they heard this song of praise, the people shoute
"Amen. Praise God!" Then, leaving the priests to continue their dutie
David dismissed the Israelites and everyone returned to their home

PRAISES WIN THE VICTORY

♣ 2 Chronicles 20 ♣

The Moabites and their allies joined together to attack Jehoshaphat, king [of] Judah. When Jehoshaphat heard of their [in]tentions, he ordered the people to fast [an]d to seek guidance from God.

Jehoshaphat stood up in front of [th]em all and prayed, "O Lord, you are king [ov]er all the nations and no one is able to [op]pose you. In the past you alone drove [aw]ay the former inhabitants of the land, [giv]ing it to us. In your honour we have [bu]ilt this temple believing that whenever [o]ur people call to you from within its [wa]lls, you will hear and answer their prayer. [Bu]t even now our enemies are waiting to [in]vade us, even though we have done them [no] harm. Therefore protect us for we are [no]t able to oppose them as there are so few [of] us. We do not know what to do, but we [ar]e looking to you for help."

As the people were standing there, [G]od's Spirit fell upon Jahaziel who [pro]claimed, "God says, 'Do not be afraid. [Th]e battle belongs to God. Tomorrow, [alt]hough you will march out to face them, [yo]u will not have to fight to gain the [vic]tory. Only maintain your positions and [yo]u will see the power of God.'"

Jehoshaphat and the people fell on [th]eir knees in thanksgiving for this.

Early the next morning they set off. Jehoshaphat appointed men to lead the people with singing as they walked. As they began to sing, God made the Moabites and their allies fight among themselves. They turned on each other until not a single soldier was left alive. When the army of Judah arrived, all they saw were bodies on the ground. For three days they plundered the corpses. Then they returned to Jerusalem rejoicing at the victory that God had won for them.

THE POWER OF PRAISING GOD
Jehoshaphat's praise of God made him strong and allowed God to work on his behalf. Instead of worrying about failing at something, it is better to praise God for the talents he has given us and to ask for his blessing to help us succeed. Praise shows God we are depending on his help.

Old city of Jerusalem
From Old Testament times, Jerusalem has been continuously inhabited so it is difficult for archaeologists to be sure of the city's exact history. But excavations in the Old City have revealed some of the different occupation layers. In Jehoshaphat's time, the city probably remained much as it was in Solomon's time.

THE BOY JOASH IS CROWNED KING

✣ 2 Chronicles 22-24 ✣

Tax chest
People placed their contributions for the restoration of the temple into a money chest which was placed at the temple gate. Funds for the repairs would have come from voluntary offerings as well as the temple tax that was levied by Joash. Court and temple officials administered the revenues, and in this way enough was collected to complete the repairs and furnish the interior.

Weighing scales
An official coinage was not in use in Israel before the reign of the Persian king Darius I. Instead, the value of things was determined by weighing out precious metals like silver and gold. Standard weights like the talent and the shekel were the currency of the time, and these were only gradually replaced by standard coins. Dishonesty in weights and measures was widespread, even though it was forbidden.

THE KINGDOM OF JUDAH
When Solomon died, the kingdom was split in two: Israel in the north and Judah in the south. The kings of Judah were the descendants of King David and they ruled in its capital, Jerusalem, until the Babylonians invaded and exiled the southern tribes to Babylon in 586BC. The fall of Judah was seen as a punishment by God for their disobedience in not keeping his laws. After the exile in Babylon the land of Judah was left destroyed and depopulated. It was from these days that the exiled people from Judah become known as "Jews".

W hen King Ahaziah of Judah died, his mother Athaliah set about murdering the entire royal family of Judah. But Ahaziah's half-sister, Jehosheba, took her nephew Joash and hid him in the temple for six long years.

At the end of that time Jehoiada, the priest who was the husband of Jehosheba, vowed his allegiance to the young prince in front of the people at the temple.

Jehoiada declared, "Joash is next in line to the throne and will indeed become king as God intends. Let us guard him with our life. Anyone who attempts to break into the temple will be killed."

So three companies of men were stationed around the temple protecting the boy.

Then Jehoiada and his sons crowned Joash king and they anointed him, shouting, "Long live the king!"

When Athaliah heard the commotion, she entered the temple only to see Joash standing there with the crown on his head.

"Treason!" she screamed, but Jehoiada ordered her arrest.

"Execute her outside the temple," he commanded. So some of the guards grabbed her and put her to death.

Until Joash was old enough to rule, Jehoiada acted as his regent. He directed the royal affairs with dignity, observing all of God's commands.

Later Joash himself decided to repair the temple. He commanded the Levites to raise taxes for its restoration. They put a chest at the entrance to the temple where people could place their money. Enough money was collected to complete the repairs and furnish the temple interior.

While Jehoiada lived, the people obeyed God. When he died, they stopped going to the temple and began to follow other gods again. God sent prophets urging the people to obey him, but they did not listen to them.

Even Joash neglected God. So God sent the army of Aram to attack and plunder Jerusalem. Joash was left mortally wounded and murdered.

RAISING THE TEMPLE FROM ITS RUINS

♣ Ezra 1-6 ♣

Within the first year of his coming to power, Cyrus king of Persia [iss]ued a royal proclamation throughout his [kin]gdom: "God has made me king over all [the] earth and has chosen me to rebuild his [tem]ple in Jerusalem. Therefore any of his [peo]ple may, if they wish, return to their [cap]ital to perform this holy task."

Over 40,000 Israelites made the [ret]urn journey. When they had resettled, [th]ey met in Jerusalem to begin the work.

When the first stone was laid, the [wh]ole people praised God, saying, "He is [G]od, his love of Israel will last for ever."

Some of the older priests who still [rem]embered the first temple wept in [sad]ness while others wept for joy. Their [eye]s mingled into one so it was impossible [to] tell the difference between the two.

Seeing this, opponents of the [b]uilding approached the leader Zerubbabel, but he told them, "You shall have nothing to do with our programme. We shall build it as the king has commanded."

However, Judah's enemies continued to hassle the builders, so that they gave up the work in frustration. For sixteen years nothing was done until the prophet Haggai encouraged the people to start again.

As soon as they did, their opponents wrote to the new king, Darius, saying that the Jews were planning to rebel. But the king looked up his records, and found that the Jews did have permission to rebuild their temple.

"Stop hassling them," he ordered. "Instead, make sure they have everything they need." The work started again, and soon the temple was finished. It was dedicated to God with great joy.

Cyrus Cylinder
The Cyrus Cylinder is a baked clay barrel inscribed with cuneiform writing which was found in excavations at Babylon. It records how Cyrus captured Babylon without a battle, and allowed exiled peoples to return to their homeland and reinstate their gods. This action gained him people's loyalty and helped to keep the peace.

The Persian empire
The policy of the Babylonian kings had been to deport the peoples they conquered, but when Babylon fell to Persia, the Persian king Cyrus reversed this policy. The Jewish exiles were allowed to return to Judah with the captured temple treasures. This map shows the size of the Persian empire and gives us some idea of the distance people travelled back to Jerusalem – on foot!

Oxen
Oxen (which are castrated bulls) were used in Bible times to pull ploughs and carts and to work big grinding wheels or olive presses. They were very strong. Cows were kept for milk, and calves were eaten on special occasions, but beef does not seem to have been part of most people's diet.

The walls of Jerusalem
The walls of Jerusalem played an essential part in ensuring the security of the city, and were repeatedly rebuilt and altered. They were made from huge blocks of stone to protect the city from attack. Today, the Old City in East Jerusalem is built on the site of ancient Jerusalem. The Old City is still surrounded by stone walls which are almost 12 metres high and 4 kilometres long. Although most of these walls were built during the 16th century, parts date back to biblical times.

JERUSALEM, A PILE OF RUBBLE

✤ Nehemiah 1-2 ✤

Hanani, who had just returned from Judah, visited Nehemiah, the royal butler at the court of Babylon, with news of the Jews living there.

"The survivors of the exile are struggling to live. The walls of Jerusalem are in ruins and the gates are charred remains."

Nehemiah was heartbroken and wept bitterly. After a few days he said, "Great God of heaven who keeps his covenant of love to those who love and obey you, hear my prayer on behalf of your people. We have disobeyed you, neglecting the laws you gave us through your servant Moses. Yet you promised that if, after a period of unfaithfulness, we turned back to you, you would gather your people from the ends of the earth and take them back to Jerusalem – the city you chose for us. Please hear my prayer and the prayers of all those who

revere you. Give me success when I talk to my master the king about what is in my heart."

As Nehemiah was serving King Artaxerxes, the king noticed that he looked sad and said, "Tell me why you are looking so downcast."

Nervously, Nehemiah replied, "Sir, the city in which my ancestors are buried lies in ruins."

"Can I help you?" the king enquired.

Silently Nehemiah prayed to God and answered, "With your permission I would like to return to Jerusalem and rebuild it."

After questioning Nehemiah further, the king gave him permission to go. He also gave him official papers which allowed him to travel safely to Jerusalem and ask for timber and materials for the work. Armed with these documents, Nehemiah set off to Jerusalem to put his plan of restoration into practice.

THE WALLS MADE STRONG AGAIN

✤ Nehemiah 2-7 ✤

Three days after his arrival in Jerusalem, Nehemiah set out secretly night to survey the state of the walls. ccompanied by a handful of trusted men quietly picked his way through the bble, examining what remained of the lls and the burnt gates.

The next day he addressed the city's ders: "Let us rebuild the walls of the city and remove the disgrace we feel. God has blessed me in my dealings with the king and he will help us to accomplish this task."

Everyone was delighted and agreed enthusiastically, except Sanballat and a few of his supporters.

Nehemiah assigned different groups to different sections of the wall. Some of these groups were families, others were professional groups such as priests or servants.

Sanballat, governor of Samaria, became incensed at the progress and began to make fun of the rebuilding. "Those pathetic Jews haven't a hope of ever rebuilding the walls. They're simply wasting their time!" he mocked.

But the people ignored these remarks and before long the wall was half completed. This made Sanballat and the others even angrier and they planned to halt the work by attacking the city.

Nehemiah responded to this threat by stationing guards at strategic points along the wall. Half the people carried on building and the other half watched and waited for the enemy attack. If anyone saw their opponents arrive, they were to sound the alarm and the soldiers would rally to their defence.

When Sanballat saw that Nehemiah was ready for a surprise attack, he tried to trick him into attending a meeting in the country. He sent a series of messages to him asking him to meet him outside the city. Each time Nehemiah refused, because he knew he was simply trying to kill him. His enemies tried to intimidate him in other ways too, but his courage never failed him and he continued to encourage the builders day by day. After only fifty-two days the walls were rebuilt. Sanballat and the others realized that the work had been carried out with God's help and they gave Nehemiah no further trouble.

Nehemiah's dream, which had started far away in the palace of King Artaxerxes, was fulfilled at last.

Persian drinking cup
This gold Persian drinking cup dates from the time that Nehemiah was rebuilding the walls of Jerusalem. It is just one of the many magnificent objects dating from this period found by archaeologists. They show just how powerful and wealthy the Persian kings were.

Rebuilding the temple
Nebuchadnezzar destroyed the temple in 586BC. When the exiles returned, they began to rebuild it, but progress was slow. Urged on by the prophets Zechariah and Haggai, the temple was finished c.515BC and the Jews could again keep the Passover in Jerusalem.

Mason's float
Almost nothing remains of the tools used by the stonemasons who helped rebuild the walls of Jerusalem. This mason's float is Egyptian. The stonemasons hammered wooden pegs into holes in the rock and then wet them so that the wood swelled and split the stone. The blocks were then sawn and trimmed into shape.

GOD'S PEOPLE SAY SORRY

✦ Nehemiah 8 - 9 ✦

The Tabernacle
The Tabernacle was like a large tent, 13 metres long, 4 metres wide and 4 metres high. It was made of animal skins laid over an acacia wood frame. Inside the Tabernacle was the Holy Place with the gold table for the bread of the Presence, the gold lamp-stand and the altar of incense. A curtain separated this area from the Most Holy Place in which the Ark of the Covenant was kept.

The Dung Gate, Jerusalem
Jerusalem had many gates in its strong defensive walls because many roads converged on the city. As well as the Dung Gate, there was also the Water Gate, the Valley Gate and the Fish Gate. Every night the city's gates were closed to protect it from a surprise attack during the hours of darkness.

An Orthodox Jew
There are about 13 million Jews in the world today, of whom about 6 million live in the USA and about 4 million live in Israel. They trace their ancestry back to Abraham who founded the Hebrew race. Their Hebrew Bible became a cornerstone of two other major world religions, Christianity and Islam.

After the city walls of Jerusalem had been rebuilt, the people returned to their home towns. Later they travelled to Jerusalem and assembled in the square by the Water Gate.

"Bring out Moses' book of the Law," they said to Ezra the scribe. So, at day-break, Ezra climbed a wooden platform above the crowd, opened the book and began to read it aloud to the people.

As Ezra began, everyone bowed down and worshipped God. Ezra read until midday. As he read, some Levites explained what the words meant so that everyone could understand what Ezra was saying. Many in the crowd began to cry, but Nehemiah interrupted them saying, "Don't cry. Today is a holy day."

Sensing that they were tired, Nehemiah said, "Go and have a good meal. Share it with those who have nothing. Today is God's holy day! The joy that God gives you will make you strong."

So the people went to eat and drink, their hearts full of gladness because they understood God's word.

The next day the people returned to hear Ezra read again. A he spoke, they discovered that it was th month of the Feast of Tabernacles, when God wanted them to live in small tents. they went out and returned with branche cut from trees, and soon the whole city w dotted with tiny green tents.

For a month, Ezra read the book of the Law to the people, with the Levites explaining it to them.

Towards the end of the month the people met together to fast. Each one of them wore sackcloth, a sign of repentanc and sprinkled dust in their hair.

Together they confessed their sins. "Despite all the good things you have do for us, our deliverance from Egypt, your care in the desert and your gift of the lan we have continually disobeyed you. Now we are back in Jerusalem, yet we still live slaves to foreigners. You are still punishin us for our sins. Come in your mercy and relieve our suffering, as you have done in the past, even though we do not deserve i If you do so, then we will serve you for ev and obey your commands to the letter."

The people wrote these words in ar agreement and all their leaders signed it their behalf. Then everyone returned hom once more.

ESTHER FOILS A PLOT

✤ **Esther 1-10** ✤

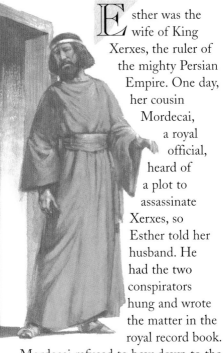

Esther was the wife of King Xerxes, the ruler of the mighty Persian Empire. One day, her cousin Mordecai, a royal official, heard of a plot to assassinate Xerxes, so Esther told her husband. He had the two conspirators hung and wrote the matter in the royal record book.

Mordecai refused to bow down to the ew prime minister, Haman, because Jews ill only honour God, so Haman swore ngrily to kill not only Mordecai but every w in the Persian empire.

"The Jews refuse to obey you," the evious Haman told the king. "You would e wise to command their destruction."

When Mordecai heard the king's rders, he was extremely distressed. He rged Queen Esther to plead with the king o spare their people. "Perhaps God has put you in this influential position for just such a desperate situation as this," he said.

Prayerfully, Esther went to King Xerxes, and when he kindly offered her anything she wanted, she held a banquet for the proud and boastful Haman, who greatly enjoyed himself.

That night, the king could not sleep and began reading about Mordecai's success in foiling the murder plot, as written in the royal record book. "What reward has this loyal man received?" he asked. He commanded the horrified Haman to lead Mordecai through the streets to be honoured.

At a second banquet for Haman, Esther bravely asked Xerxes to save the Jews from their murderous enemy. "Who is this enemy?" the king demanded, angrily. When Esther pointed to Haman, the king ordered him to be hung on the gallows that Haman had had built to hang Mordecai.

So Mordecai replaced Haman as the most powerful official in the kingdom. The king allowed the Jews to defendthemselves against attack, and they celebrated God's deliverance of them through Queen Esther.

Persian bracelet
Perhaps Esther wore jewellery like this gold bracelet with horned griffins when she went to plead with King Xerxes. She needed to make a grand entrance, because to approach the king without his permission was an offence punishable by death.

The scroll of Esther
The Jewish festival of Purim commemorates the story of Esther. The scroll of Esther is read out on the evening before the feast, and every time Haman's name is mentioned the people boo and hiss. It is a joyful and noisy occasion.

JOB TRUSTS HIS GOD

✤ **Job** 1-42 ✤

His friends came to sympathize, but only made things worse. "God is punishing you for some hidden sin," they suggested. "Say sorry, and he will end your suffering."

Even though Job knew he was innocent, he started to question God's fairness to him. "Why don't you heal me? I'd rather die than suffer this pain in my body!" he groaned.

Then, as a storm raged across the sky, God revealed his power and majesty to Job. "Would the sun obey you, if you told it to rise?" God asked him. "Are you so clever that you can argue with someone as powerful as me?"

Job still didn't understand why God had allowed him to suffer so much, but now he realized that God was a wise friend who could always be trusted. Eventually, God healed Job's sores, and gave him twice the riches that he had before, including many more sons and daughters.

The sufferings of Job
The book of Job asks why God allows people to suffer. In Job's day people assumed that if you were good, God would look after you: people who did wrong were "punished" by some kind of suffering. Job knew that he didn't deserve what happened, but discovered that there is no simple answer. He realised that no one – not even him – is as good as God wants them to be, and that God is fair. Elsewhere in the Bible God promises to support people who suffer, and to end all suffering in heaven.

Although Job was a good man, Satan, the evil accuser, suggested that Job only loved God because he was blessed with great wealth.

"Take away Job's possessions, then see if he still worships you!" Satan sneered at God.

God knew that was untrue, so he allowed Satan to test Job. "Very well, take what you like from him, but don't harm the man himself."

Several messengers came rushing to Job with the shocking news that all his animals had been stolen or killed, and his servants slaughtered. Then came the worst news of all. "All your beloved sons and daughters have been killed in a terrible storm!"

Job sank to his knees with sorrow, yet he said, "Almighty God, I cannot be angry, because you gave me everything that I owned, and you have the right to take it all away. I will still praise your name." Job had passed the first test.

"But what if you struck Job with a horrible illness?" Satan continued. "Surely then he would curse you to your face!"

So God allowed Satan to cause painful sores to erupt all over Job's body. Job was miserable, but knowing that life has both blessings and troubles, he still respected God, whatever happened to him.

THE WAY OF HAPPINESS

♣ Psalms ♣

The Psalms are a collection of songs that came together over a long period in the history of the people of Israel – from the time of David until after the exile in Babylon. The Psalms express the response of the people of Israel to God in a variety of circumstances. These are some of the ideas expressed in the Psalms.

Medieval book of psalms
Christians have used psalms in worship since New Testament times. Today some are sung to "plainsong" chants, others are rewritten metrically like hymns. We do not know what music was used in biblical times.

GOD SHOWS US THE WAY OF HAPPINESS
People know great happiness,
when they ignore what wicked people tell them,
and don't join in with those who do evil by rejecting God's ways.
Instead, they love God's law and ponder it day and night.
(Psalm 1:1-2)

GOD IS CREATOR OF EVERYTHING
"The world and all that is in it belong to the Lord;
the world and all people who live on it are his."
(Psalm 24:1)

GOD LOOKS AFTER HIS PEOPLE
"The Lord God cares for me like a shepherd,
so I will never lack anything."
(Psalm 23:1)

GOD IS KIND AND FORGIVING
"The Lord is merciful, kind, and patient.
He never stops loving. He doesn't punish us as our sins deserve."
(Psalm 103:8,10)

GOD IS FAIR AND JUST
"Lord, you punish wrong. Show what you are really like and
punish those who do evil. How long will the wicked get away
with it? Pay back the proud for what they have done."
(Psalm 94:1-3)

GOD GUIDES HIS PEOPLE THROUGH THE SCRIPTURES
"Your word is like a lamp so I can see where I'm going.
Your words throw light on my dark path."
(Psalm 119:105)

ONE DAY GOD WILL REIGN OVER THE WHOLE WORLD
"The Lord is coming to rule the earth.
He will judge the people honestly and fairly,
and all the trees will sing with joy."
(Psalm 96:13)

Rabbi teaching the Torah
The Torah is the basic teaching of the Jewish faith, especially that contained in the laws of Moses. In Psalm 119, the author says God's law is good and guides him through life. If he follows it, he cannot go wrong.

The creation of people
Several psalms praise God for the beauty of the world and the value which God gives to people. The writers said that they owed their lives to God, and called on everyone to worship and serve him.

THE LORD IS MY SHEPHERD

✤ Psalm 23 ✤

Wolf
In New Testament times wolves were common enough to be a danger to livestock like sheep and cattle. The wolf of Palestine is smaller than that found in Central and Northern Europe. Jesus said his followers were like sheep among wolves; people would want to stop them sharing God's love, and might even attack them.

This psalm shows that God cares for his people. He is like a loving shepherd looking after his sheep, leading and guiding them to pastures where they can feed, and to waters where they can be refreshed as they drink. God protects them – he guards them from wild beasts.

The Lord God cares for me like a shepherd,
so I will never lack anything.
He brings me to rest in fields of lush green grass,
he leads me by streams of calm waters,
he refreshes me deep in my innermost being.
He guides me along right paths
so that I bring honour to his name.
Even when I walk through valleys where there is a deathly darkness
I will not be afraid,
because you are there with me,
and your shepherd's crook makes me feel secure.
You give me a feast of food
in front of my enemies.
You welcome me as your special guest,
making me feel honoured,
and you give me so much more than I need.
I am sure that your friendship and loving goodness will be with me every
day for the rest of my life,
and that I will stay by your side for ever, Lord.

WHERE WILL I FIND HELP?

✤ Psalm 121 ✤

Psalm 121 is one of fifteen psalms that are called "Songs of Ascent". They are probably so-called because they were sung as the people of Israel made their way on a pilgrimage up to Jerusalem to worship. It was the highest city geographically in Palestine, on top of a steep hill.

Succoth celebration
This is another name for the feast of Tabernacles or Booths. It was one of the three main pilgrim feasts held in Jerusalem to which people walked long distances each year. On the last day, prayers are said for a good harvest in the coming year. The other two pilgrim festivals are Unleavened Bread (or Passover) and the harvest (or Pentecost).

*I look up at the hills,
and wonder where I will find help.
My help comes from you, Lord,
who made heaven and earth.*

*You will not let me stumble,
you will not doze off while you shelter me;
you watch over Israel
and never doze off or fall asleep.*

*The Lord watches over you,
he is right there at your side, giving you shade
so that the sun won't burn you during the day,
nor the moon harm you at night.*

*The Lord will save you from all trouble,
he will guard your whole life;
the Lord will watch over you as you go about all your business,
now and always.*

EVERYBODY PRAISE GOD

✤ Psalm 150 ✤

Praising the Lord
Music is an important part of all religious worship. Christians in different countries have adapted biblical psalms and written Christian songs and hymns to fit their varied musical styles. Although not every musical style appeals to every person, worship takes place when the person singing means the words they are using.

Psalm 150 exhorts us to praise God with all the instruments of the orchestra: the wind instruments (trumpets and flutes); the stringed instruments (harps and lyres) and the percussion section (tambourines and cymbals). Music was an integral part of Israel's social and religious life. Musical instruments were employed on any and every occasion – after a victorious battle, at national feasts and festivals, at marriages and funerals.

MUSIC
The language of music is universal and can be understood and enjoyed by all. Evidence from Old Testament times shows us that music was greatly appreciated. A musician was a highly respected member of the community and was in great demand for his services. David was well known as a skilled musician and is famous for his harp playing. His music soothed King Saul's temper, just as music can help people calm down today.

Praise God!
Worship him in his temple,
worship him under all his skies.
Applaud him for the powerful things he does,
and admire him for being so great and wonderful.

Praise him with the trumpet,
and praise him with the harp and lyre.
Bang your tambourines and dance before him.
and praise him with stringed instruments and the flute.
Praise him with a booming clash of cymbals.

Let every living creature adore God.
Praise the Lord!

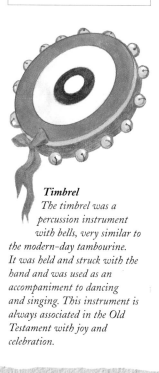

Timbrel
The timbrel was a percussion instrument with bells, very similar to the modern-day tambourine. It was held and struck with the hand and was used as an accompaniment to dancing and singing. This instrument is always associated in the Old Testament with joy and celebration.

WISE SAYINGS

✣ Proverbs 1-31 ✣

The book of Proverbs is a collection of wise sayings about the best way to live. For the writers of Proverbs, the key to life and the beginning of wisdom was a God-centred life. The wisdom of Proverbs is distilled into concise expressions, lively contrasts, and graphic descriptions of everyday life. Wisdom is to be applied at home and work, in words and attitudes, in family relationships, and with friends.

Families and friends
Families were large in Bible times, with grandparents, uncles and aunts all living close to each other and helping each other. The book of Proverbs encourages families to help each other, and also praises the value of having good friends who will tell us the truth and help us when we are in need.

WISDOM AND FOLLY

Reverence for God is the starting point of all knowledge,
but fools reject wisdom and training.
It is far better to own only a little, and respect God,
than to be extremely rich and live in confusion.
If you are proud, it will destroy you;
being big-headed will lead to your downfall.

FRIENDS AND NEIGHBOURS

If you forgive what is wrong, then love will increase,
but repeating a sin divides good friends.
A true friend is loving all the time,
and relatives are born to share our troubles.
Someone who looks after the poor is like lending to God;
he will reward them for their kindness.

SPEAKING AND LISTENING

A person who gossips betrays someone's trust,
but a real friend keeps a secret.
Wild words cut to the heart like a sword,
but the words of the wise are healing.

HONESTY AND DISHONESTY

Using dishonest scales and dishonest measures –
God hates them both.
The food you get by cheating will taste delicious at first,
but it soon turns to gravel in your mouth.

DISCIPLINE AND LAZINESS

A person with lazy hands is always poor,
but someone who works hard will grow rich.
Employing a lazy worker is as irritating as
having a mouth full of vinegar, or smoke in your eyes.
Train children to behave well,
and as adults they will still know right from wrong.

King Solomon
It is commonly thought that King Solomon is the writer of most of the book of Proverbs. God gave Solomon a dream in which he could choose any gift he wanted. He chose wisdom above fame, power, wealth or glory.

Working hard
"Go and watch the ant!" says the writer of Proverbs. "She works hard all day. That's what you should do, otherwise you'll end up poor and despised by people." That is an example of the practical common sense in the book. The whole Bible encourages people not to be lazy.

LIFE HAS A MEANING?

✦ Ecclesiastes 1-12 ✦

As an old man, the writer looked back on his life to see what lessons he had learned.

"I built myself sumptuous palaces, filled them with treasures, and enjoyed women and laughter and song," he said, "but in the end, pleasure for its own sake doesn't mean anything. Nothing lasts for ever, only how much I know of God."

"I studied hard to be knowledgeable but discovered that, without God's answers, it didn't help me to live a better life. It's good to work hard, have fun, and be content with what God gives you, but hoping to hold on to wealth is as useless as trying to chase after the wind."

He knew that God had planned his life and that at the right time, everything had fallen into place. He couldn't predict the future, but as long as he lived honestly according to God's rules, helped others, and made the most of every opportunity, then life had a sense of purpose.

The world was imperfect and sometimes life seemed unfair. But as long as he respected God and kept his commandments, he could lead a fulfilled life.

Everything has its season
Traditionally it has been thought that the author of the book of Ecclesiastes was King Solomon. Ecclesiastes is about the meaning of life. It teaches us that there is a right time for everything, that there is a season for every activity. For example, there is a time to sow and a time to reap, a time to be born and a time to die.

Gold
In the Old Testament, wealth was measured by possession of animals, like sheep and cattle, and precious metals, like gold and silver. Gold was often carried as thin bars or ingots, or else made into jewellery. Pouches were used for carrying small pieces of precious metal on a journey.

HOW BEAUTIFUL YOU ARE!

❖ **Song of Songs** 1-8 ❖

When King Solomon met a Shulammite peasant woman as she was tending the vines in his royal vineyard, he could not forget her outstanding beauty. He returned and set about winning her love until she agreed to become his wife.

"You are shy, like a dove hiding in the rocks," King Solomon told her. "Please show me your lovely face and let me hear the sweetness of your voice. You have stolen my heart. Come with me so I may smell the scent of your perfume and kiss your scarlet ribbon lips."

The woman replied tenderly, "How handsome you are, like a young deer running in the hills. You have showered me with a feast of love, and when you hold me, I faint with love for you, too."

So the two fell in love with each other, and they prepared to be married. The woman's friends were curious and asked her to describe King Solomon.

"My lover is so attractive, with hair as black as a raven, eyes sparkling like jewels, and lips like lilies dripping with myrrh," she told them, believing that he was the most wonderful man in the world. "His body is like polished ivory decorated with sapphires and his arms are like rods of gold."

So King Solomon and the Shulammite woman married, and loved each other deeply. Their love was so strong, the woman said, that it burned like a blazing fire that water couldn't put out, nor rivers wash away.

Myrrh
Myrrh is a sticky substance which comes from cut stems or branches of a low shrubby tree. This gum oozes from the incisions as "tears", which harden to make an oily yellowish-brown or reddish resin. Myrrh was used in cosmetic preparation, as an ingredient in holy anointing oil, and was valued for its fragrance.

The wealth of King Solomon
With no wars to wage, Solomon concentrated his efforts on trade and wealth. He saw the strategic importance of Israel, lying between Egypt and Asia, and set out to exploit his position. He opened up new trade routes to unfamiliar lands. He sent fleets of ships to faraway countries, loaded with copper from his mines. They returned laden with gold, silver, jewels, hardwood and ivory.

Cosmetics
Women coloured their eyelashes with black powder mixed with oil or vinegar to achieve an effect like mascara. They coloured their cheeks and lips red with iron oxide. A green stone called malachite was used for making a green eye paint.

GOD CALLS ISAIAH TO BE A PROPHET

✤ Isaiah 6 ✤

King Uzziah's tombstone
On the tombstone of Uzziah, the tenth king of Judah, are the words: "Hither were brought the bones of Uzziah, king of Judah. Not to be opened."

The prophet Isaiah
Prophets were people who spoke God's word. They made sure God's people obeyed his laws. They often predicted punishment when people turned away from God. Isaiah was from an aristocratic family. He prophesied in Judah from about 740BC and foretold the destruction of Israel by the Assyrians.

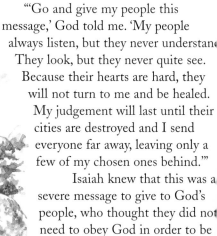

God chose Isaiah to be one of his greatest prophets, to warn and encourage the nation of Judah to return to obeying his ways. One day, he gave Isaiah an amazing vision.

"In the year that King Uzziah died, I saw God sitting on his throne in all his might and majesty," Isaiah explained with wonder. "Angels flew above him, covering their faces and feet with their wings, and shaking the building with their powerful voices as they called out, 'Holy, holy, holy are you, Lord God Almighty! Your glory fills the whole earth.'

"I felt overwhelmed at the utter holiness of my God, the one who is perfect and pure. So I cried out, 'I am a sinner, Lord, not clean enough to stand in your presence!' An angel flew over to me with a glowing, hot coal in his hand, taken from the holy altar. As he touched my lips with

it, he said, to my relief, 'Now your guilt is taken away and your sins are forgiven.'

"Then God himself asked, 'Who is willing to be my messenger?'

"I replied, 'Here I am, Lord. Send me!'

"'Go and give my people this message,' God told me. 'My people always listen, but they never understand. They look, but they never quite see. Because their hearts are hard, they will not turn to me and be healed. My judgement will last until their cities are destroyed and I send everyone far away, leaving only a few of my chosen ones behind.'"

Isaiah knew that this was a severe message to give to God's people, who thought they did not need to obey God in order to be blessed by him. But Isaiah was willing to do as he was commanded by God.

The vision of Isaiah
The type of angel mentioned in the story is a seraph. This is the only occasion in the Bible that seraphs are mentioned. When they appeared before God they covered their faces and feet as a sign of reverence, humility and awe.

HEZEKIAH CRIES FOR HEALING

✣ **Isaiah 38** ✣

At the very time that King Hezekiah needed to be a strong leader to fight the Assyrians who were threatening to attack Jerusalem, he became gravely ill. A boil erupted on his skin and spread infection all over his body until he was almost dying.

The prophet Isaiah went to see him and told him, "God says you won't recover from this illness, so you must hurry and put your affairs in order before you die."

Hezekiah's heart sank with despair. With tears streaming down his face, he turned his face to the wall and prayed, "Lord God, please remember that I have loved you sincerely and always tried to do good. Must the best years of my life be cut short like this? Listen to my cries, O God, and help me!"

God gave Isaiah another message for the sick king.

"Tell Hezekiah that I have heard his tearful prayer and will give him another fifteen years to live. And by the strength of my hand, I will defend Jerusalem from her Assyrian attackers. Watch and see! As a sign that my promise will come true, I will make the shadow cast by the sundial move back ten paces."

Then Isaiah told the king to take a thick mixture of figs, and to apply it as medicine to the boil. Hezekiah did this and was healed completely, and he watched in awe as indeed the sundial's shadow moved back ten paces.

"I praise you, loving God, for saving me from death," Hezekiah joyfully wrote afterwards. "My suffering has made me humble and I will spend the rest of my days singing about your faithfulness."

Assyrian stone carving
The Assyrians established a line of fierce warrior-kings and conquered a great empire. They decorated their palaces with stone carvings of huge winged monsters, with the bodies of bulls or lions, and bearded human faces. Lion hunting was the sport of the kings of Assyria and the animal was regarded as a royal beast. In the time of Isaiah, Judah was the only nation the Assyrians did not conquer, although it had to pay the Assyrians an annual tribute of goods and crops.

GOD COMFORTS HIS PEOPLE

✣ Isaiah 40 ✣

Eagle
The eagle's strength and the speed with which it swoops on its prey are used in the Bible to picture powerful nations attacking Israel. Ezekiel described King Nebuchadnezzar as an eagle. Isaiah said that people who trust God will be like eagles, rising above their problems.

Babylonian weights
The Babylonians made many important discoveries and had a sophisticated culture. They were skilled in mathematics and astronomy, and are believed to be the first to use a system of weights. These lion weights date from about 2600BC. The lion was a popular symbol of royal power.

Babylonian map
This clay tablet dates back to about 2300BC. It shows the world as a circle surrounded by water with Babylon at its centre. This is the oldest known "map" of the world discovered so far. People in ancient times did not know that the earth was round, like a ball. They thought it was more like a flat disc.

Isaiah gave a prophecy concerning the Judean exiles in Babylonia. This prophecy was full of encouragement that God was looking after his people and, one day, would give them the peace and prosperity that they longed for.

There is a voice calling out,
"Make a straight road through the wilderness for God.
Raise every valley, flatten every mountain, and smooth the rough ground. Then God's glory will appear before everyone."

"We are all like grass and flowers, which wither away to nothing. But every single word spoken by God will last for ever."

Tell Jerusalem and all the towns of Judah the good news,
"Your God is here!"
Look, he will come to rule with mighty power!
Tenderly, he cares for his people, just like a shepherd who carries his lambs in his arms, close to the warmth of his heart.

God is so mighty, that he measured the oceans and the heavens with his hands. No one could possibly teach him wisdom or knowledge. Whole countries seem like drops of water in a bucket to him, their islands like grains of sand.
Who can be compared with God?
Certainly, no idol made from gold, silver, or special wood.
Almighty God rules the whole world, while its people seem like tiny grasshoppers. He takes away the power of rulers, until they are nothing. They take root like a plant, but then God blows them away like straw in the wind.

"Who is as mighty as I am?" asks God.
Look up at the stars, he knows each one by name.
By his power, none ever go missing.

Why do the people of Israel complain?
"God doesn't see how we are suffering!" you say.
Do you not realize that God never grows tired? He strengthens the weary, and makes the weak powerful.
Even young people become tired, and stumble and fall.
But those who trust in God will be given new strength.
Like eagles soaring in the sky, they will run, and not become weary.

THE SUFFERING SERVANT

✣ **Isaiah** 52-53 ✣

The prophecy of Isaiah contains four "Servant songs" in which the servant is the coming Saviour who brings salvation not only to Israel but also to the whole world. He will be opposed and will suffer for doing this.

King Nebuchadnezzar
He was already a successful army commander when his father died in 605BC and he inherited the empire. He is mentioned often in the Bible because he attacked Judah several times and conquered Jerusalem in 586BC. He was famous for his buildings which include the "hanging (roof) gardens" in Babylon.

My servant will achieve what I have planned,
and be respected and highly praised.
Many were horrified because
he was hurt until he no longer looked human.
He will purify many nations, bringing kings to silence before him.
He was not handsome,
nor did he look anything like a king.
Nothing about him was attractive.
People hated and rejected him,
causing him to suffer much sadness and pain.
We turned away from him,
hating him, because we believed that he was no one special.
But he experienced the suffering that should have been ours,
he willingly took all our weaknesses and misery.
Yet we thought that God himself had struck him with evil.
The truth is that he was wounded and broken for our sins,
and his punishment has brought us peace.
Like sheep, we have all wandered away,
following our own path,
but our punishment was given to him instead.
Though he was roughly mistreated,
he made no protest.
Like a lamb being sheared or going to be slaughtered,
he remained silent.
He was falsely accused and sentenced to death,
because of the sins of my people.
He had never been violent or dishonest,
yet he was buried alongside the wicked.
Remember that it was God's decision to let him suffer,
to make him a sacrifice to take away the sins of us all.
God will richly reward him,
by giving him a position of greatness and power.
People thought he was a wicked man,
but he took away our sins, and prayed for us to be forgiven.

The people mourn the destruction of Jerusalem
King Nebuchadnezzar conquered Judah and destroyed Jerusalem in 586BC. The city was burned and plundered and the people deported to Babylon.

Taken captive
A captured king – the most prized trophy of war – was subject to the most cruel torture. Prisoners were led by a ring through their lips before being blinded, tortured and humiliated. This was followed by a cruel death or a life of slavery as a blind cripple. King Zedekiah of Judah was captured and blinded as shown in this picture.

117 ✣

THE POTTER SHAPES THE CLAY

✢ Jeremiah 18-20 ✢

A potter at work
The way potters shape their clay has changed little since the potter's hand-wheel was invented by the ancient Egyptians about four thousand years ago. This potter uses a foot-wheel which was probably introduced around 300BC. Clay is a common material and potters' workshops made pots quickly and cheaply.

Pottery and archaeology
Pottery is vital in the study of ancient civilizations. Everyone used it, it was cheap to make and almost indestructible. From the shape, decoration and style of a piece, archaeologists can tell its date, where it came from and sometimes even the quarry from which the clay came.

Potter's wheel
The first potters were women who made pots from coils of clay. The invention of the potter's wheel led to the craft becoming an exclusively male profession. The oldest wheels were made of two stones. The upper one was turned by hand as it pivoted in a recess cut in the lower stone.

One day, God sent Jeremiah to the potter's workshop to show the prophet the message he had for the people. As Jeremiah watched the potter skilfully moulding the clay on his wheel, the pot suddenly went out of shape and was spoilt. So the potter squashed the clay back into a ball and began making a new pot that was smooth and perfect.

"Tell my people that I am like a potter, shaping Israel into a strong nation I can be proud of," God said to Jeremiah. "Warn them that they must stop doing evil otherwise, like clay in my hands, I will crush what does not please me."

Then God told Jeremiah to buy a p and take some of the elders and priests to the city rubbish dump where he would gi them another important message. There, Jeremiah stood before them and bravely said what God wanted them to hear.

"Here in this valley you have disobeyed God by worshipping false gods and committing many murders. Now Go will punish you. He will smash this natio just as I am going to smash this pot."

Then Jeremiah threw the pot on the ground where it cracked into so many pieces that it was impossible to repair.

When the people heard him repeating the same uncomfortable messag in the temple, they were angry and demanded that he should be punished. So Jeremiah was beaten and chained up until the following morning.

THE GOOD AND BAD FIGS

✤ Jeremiah 24 ✤

Jeremiah's grave warnings to the people of Judah soon came true when the king of Babylon, Nebuchadnezzar, defeated them and won control of the city of Jerusalem. When Nebuchadnezzar returned home to Babylon with stolen treasures and some of Jerusalem's cleverest and most skilled citizens, those left behind felt relieved at first. At least they hadn't been captured and taken away from their homes. But they were proud people who mistakenly thought that they didn't need to respect God, and this was to be their downfall.

To explain what would happen to them, God showed Jeremiah a vision of two baskets of figs in front of the temple, and asked him to describe what he saw.

"One basket is full of ripe, tasty-looking figs, while the other basket is full of rotting figs that no one would want to eat," Jeremiah replied, wondering what God was trying to say.

"The good figs stand for those people whom I have sent into exile to Babylon, who have hearts that will learn to listen to me," God explained. "I will look after them and once they have learnt their lesson and are sorry, I will bring them back here and they will obey me. The rotten figs stand for the new king of Judah, Zedekiah, and all those who were not taken to Babylon. Their hard hearts will never love me so I will curse them with hunger and disease until they completely disappear. Like rotten figs, they will never do any good."

A much-valued tree
The fig tree is highly valued for both its fruit and the shade it gives. In the Bible it is often associated with prosperity and well-being, along with the vine and the olive. Today the tree is a familiar sight in the Middle East. Fig trees form conspicuous features in the landscape, whether they are planted in private gardens, in the corner of a vineyard or are growing wild beside a well. Figs are also grown commercially in orchards.

JEREMIAH REWRITES THE SCROLL

♣ Jeremiah 36 ♣

Baruch writes the prophecies
Jeremiah dictated his words to his scribe, Baruch. Baruch wrote onto a parchment scroll, which he then read aloud to all the people assembled in the temple.

Scribes
In Bible times, most people, including the king, could not read or write. Scribes worked as professional secretaries, to keep public accounts and records, or to write letters. It took between 15 and 20 years for a man to train to become a scribe.

Papyrus plant
Most writing was done on sheets of papyrus, which came from the papyrus plants that grew beside the river Nile. While the Egyptians had used papyrus for more than 2,000 years, it was relatively new for the Israelites who had used clay tablets until then. Papyrus plants, also known as bulrushes, grow 4–5 metres high and up to 8 centimetres thick.

During the fourth year of King Jehoiakim's rule over Judah, God told Jeremiah to write down on a scroll all the prophecies he had ever made. "Perhaps then my people will fear the disasters I am promising to inflict on them, and turn away from their sin so I can forgive them," God said.

Jeremiah asked his secretary and friend Baruch to write down his words as he dictated them, then to read the scroll to the people who had gathered in the temple from the towns of Judah for a day of fasting. Jeremiah knew how great God's anger was against them, and hoped fervently that they would listen.

When the king's officials heard of this, they asked Baruch to repeat the reading specially for them. They looked at each other with shock, knowing that such powerful words could threaten the king's rule. "You and Jeremiah must hide while we show him this," they said.

King Jehoiakim was sitting in his apartment, warming himself by the winter fire, when his official entered with the scroll. As the official read a few columns, the hard-hearted king took knife, cut off that section and threw into the fire, showing no fear at God's stern warnings. Again and again, he cut and burnt the scroll, until nothing was left.

"Arrest Jeremiah and Baruch!" the king commanded, but they were safely hidden.

The king thought that he had totally destroyed the worrying words that spoke about the king Babylon conquering his land, but he was wrong.

"Take another scroll," God commanded Jeremiah, "and write on it all the words that were on th first scroll, and even more. Tell the king that because no one has listene to me, they will be ruined."

GOD'S WORD CANNOT BE DESTROYED
King Jehoiakim wrongly thought that h country could avoid God's judgement simply by cutting and burning the scrol which contained Jeremiah's prophecies. B every word that God says is true and las for ever, and no one can force God to change his mind just by destroying the paper that it's written on.
People today may reject the Bible – God word – but they cannot destroy it. The may laugh at what the Bible teaches, bu if our opinion agrees with God's then we won't go wrong.

THROWN INTO THE WELL

✤ Jeremiah 37-38 ✤

King Nebuchadnezzar made Zedekiah king of Judah. Zedekiah and his officials never paid much attention to the messages that God gave Jeremiah. Nonetheless, Zedekiah did ask Jeremiah to pray for him.

"Tell the king that the Babylonian army may have left to fight with the Egyptians, but they will be back to burn down Jerusalem," God told Jeremiah.

Jeremiah had annoyed the city leaders with his prophecies for many years. So when the captain of the guard saw him leaving the city, he was arrested, thrown into a dungeon, and falsely accused of deserting to the Babylonian army.

"I am innocent!" Jeremiah protested to Zedekiah. "Why should I be punished when I am right to tell the people that only those who surrender to the Babylonians will be saved?"

The king's officials were disturbed when they heard Jeremiah's words. "This man constantly encourages the soldiers and the people to give up fighting!" they told the king. "He must be killed."

"Do as you wish," replied Zedekiah. So Jeremiah was taken to the guard's courtyard and lowered down by ropes into a dried-up well. Jeremiah wondered what would happen to him, as a chilling darkness closed around him and his feet sank into the mud at the bottom.

But soon, God sent someone to help him. Ebed-Melech, a royal official, bravely rushed to the king to protest. "Jeremiah has been wrongly treated and will soon starve to death."

So the king changed his mind and ordered his release. Ebed-Melech hoisted the grateful Jeremiah out of the well, and he was confined to the guard's courtyard.

One day Zedekiah asked Jeremiah to tell him God's truth, promising not to kill him. Zedekiah listened quietly, but did not tell his officials what Jeremiah said. Later, God's words came true, and the city of Jerusalem was overrun by the king of Babylon.

Well
This well is constructed from specially built and shaped kiln-fired bricks, and has been sunk to a depth of 25 metres. It is shaped to be narrower at the top, so that a cover can be placed over the opening. A ladder gives access. Jeremiah was lowered by ropes into a similar well-shaft, which was used as a dungeon. Although the well was dry, the bottom would have been muddy and dark.

PURPLE CLOTHING
Under Nebuchadnezzar, Babylon had a rich and sophisticated culture. The height of luxury in the clothing of the period was seen by their colour. Purple clothing was the status symbol of the wealthy and important. Purple dye had to be extracted by hand from the glandular secretion of a shellfish found in the Mediterranean Sea. As this was slow and therefore costly to produce, purple cloth was a very rare and expensive luxury.

Zedekiah orders his soldiers
Zedekiah was the last king of Judah, the southern kingdom. He had been made king by the Babylonian invader Nebuchadnezzar. Zedekiah was a weak king who rebelled against Babylon even though Jeremiah told him not to. Nebuchadnezzar captured him, killed his sons and then blinded him.

GOD'S PEOPLE IN EXILE

Ezekiel warns the people

Sennacherib

Sennacherib was king of Assyria between 705 and 681BC. He was a great warrior and did much to strengthen the position of the Assyrian empire by sending his armies to subject rebel nations. When Hezekiah refused to pay him tax, his army surrounded Jerusalem but failed to capture it because they were diverted to the south to deal with the Egyptians. Sennacherib returned to Nineveh and was murdered by two of his sons.

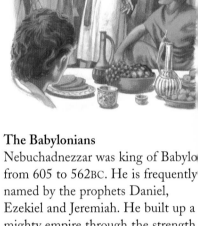

Daniel in the court of Nebuchadnezzar

The prophets warned God's people that his judgement would come if they refused to listen to him and obey him. The people rejected the warnings, however, and the northern kingdom of Israel collapsed in 722BC and the southern kingdom of Judah in 586BC, with their inhabitants taken to Assyria and Babylonia respectively.

Charioteer from wall relief of Sennacherib's palace, Nineveh

The Babylonians

Nebuchadnezzar was king of Babylon from 605 to 562BC. He is frequently named by the prophets Daniel, Ezekiel and Jeremiah. He built up a mighty empire through the strength of his army. In 586BC he beseiged Jerusalem. The city was destroyed, the temple was burnt and all its treasures were taken to Babylon, and the people deported to his kingdom.

The Assyrians

Like most of the peoples in the ancient world, the Assyrians worshipped many different gods and goddesses. Although Ashur was the national god, each city had a temple where its own particular god was worshipped; for instance, Ishtar, the goddess of love and war, was worshipped at Nineveh. The gods were thought to control everything, and on feast days their idols were taken from the temples and paraded through the streets.

The Assyrians levied taxes and demanded tribute. King Hoshea of Israel refused to pay and the Assyrian king Shalmaneser V began a three-year siege of Samaria, the capital of the northern kingdom of Israel. The Assyrian army was highly trained and well-equipped with a force of chariots, siege-engineers, bowmen, slingers and spearmen. Samaria fell in 722BC and the people were taken prisoner and exiled to Assyria.

The Assyrian army besiege Samaria

...dah in exile: the birth of Judaism

...hile in exile in Babylonia, the ...ople of Judah had the freedom to ...aintain their own culture and to ...actise their own religion. Some ... the people, like Daniel, were ...tegrated into the court of ...ebuchadnezzar, while others, like ...zekiel, settled in various parts of the ...untryside. In order to survive as a ...tion in exile, however, they had to ...odify their religion, and it was ...ring this period that Judaism was ...rn. The exile became for these ...ws a time of waiting, longing ... restoration and ...e rebuilding of ...e temple.

Daniel is thrown to the lions

...syrian, Babylonian and Persian empires

... ordinary people, the change of ruler from Assyrian to Babylonian to Persian would not have made ...ch difference to daily life. The conquered peoples were allowed to follow their own customs and religion.

Persian soldier

Persians

We know of Persia from about 650BC as a nation living east of the Persian Gulf. It was under Cyrus the Great that the Persians began to expand their borders and gained control of lands as far west as modern-day Turkey, and as far east as India. He conquered the Babylonian empire in 539BC and unified his huge empire by making Aramaic the official language and maintaining control through a wise system of administration. He created great wealth and his court was famous for its luxury and artistic splendour.

The Promised Land

The return to the Promised Land

Cyrus reversed the policies of his predecessors and repatriated all foreign exiles to their homeland. The Jews returned in 538BC together with all the objects originally plundered from the temple, and with royal permission to rebuild their temple in Jerusalem.

The exile was an opportunity for national cleansing and renewal, in which God's people could turn back to him. The return of the exiles to Jerusalem saw the restoration of Jerusalem's religious life and customs under the leadership of Ezra and Nehemiah, and the rebuilding of the temple, with the encouragement of the prophets Haggai and Zechariah.

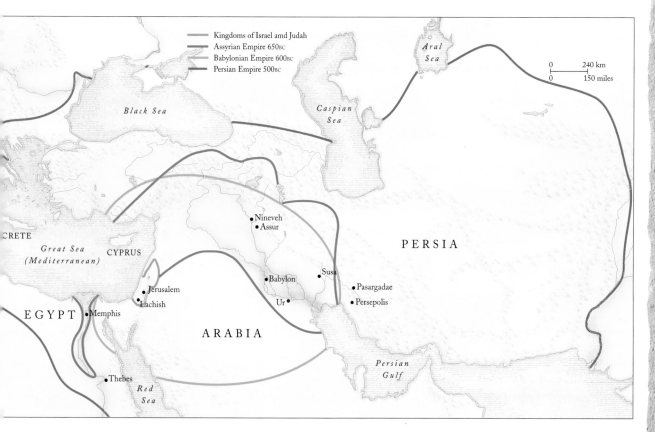

Kingdoms of Israel amd Judah
Assyrian Empire 650BC
Babylonian Empire 600BC
Persian Empire 500BC

0   240 km
0   150 miles

Aral Sea

Black Sea

Caspian Sea

• Nineveh
• Assur

PERSIA

*Great Sea
(Mediterranean)*   CYPRUS

CRETE

• Susa

• Babylon   • Pasargadae

Jerusalem •   Ur •   • Persepolis

Lachish •

EGYPT   • Memphis

ARABIA

• Thebes

Red Sea

Persian Gulf

EZEKIEL WARNS OF GOD'S ANGER

✤ Ezekiel 4-5 ✤

The Ishtar Gate
The Ishtar Gate, named after the Babylonian goddess of love and war, was Babylon's northern gate. It was decorated with bright blue tiles on which were bulls and dragons – symbols of the god Marduk. The double gateway was 12 metres high and spanned the Processional Way, which linked the temple of Marduk in the city with an important religious site outside the city's walls.

Ezekiel
Ezekiel was training to be a priest in the temple at Jerusalem when he was taken into exile in Babylon. But there, five years later, on the banks of the Kebar River, God called him to serve as a prophet to the exiles. The call was accompanied by a vision of God which coloured Ezekiel's entire ministry.

Ruins inside Jerusalem's walls
Jerusalem's origins go back more than 4,000 years. Its historical importance began when King David captured the city from the Jebusites in about 1000BC, and made it the capital of the united tribes of Israel.

God wanted to warn the exiles in Babylon about the hard times that lay ahead for the people of Jerusalem. But instead of telling his prophet to speak his message, God told Ezekiel to use actions so that only those paying attention would understand what he was trying to say.

Ezekiel sat where the crowds gathered and drew a picture of Jerusalem on a brick, then formed small mounds of earth around it to look like enemy camps.

Then he put an iron pan on its side between him and the brick to symbolize a wall. God told Ezekiel to bake a small loaf and allow himself only a little water to drink, so that when the crowd saw his poor diet they would understand that Jerusalem would be cut off by their attackers and they would all be desperately hungry.

As another warning, Ezekiel took a sharp sword and shaved off his hair and beard. He then divided the hair into three equal piles and burnt one pile on the brick. Next, he chopped up the second pile and let it fall all round the brick. Finally he threw the third pile into the air.

Then God explained that some of the people would be killed, some would die of starvation and others would be sent away. Ezekiel managed to find a few stray hairs that had escaped and tucked them away in his clothes, showing that a few of the people of Jerusalem would be saved.

The bones of the dead
*After ten years in captivity, and
with Jerusalem destroyed, the
exiles had given up all hope. But
in a vision, Ezekiel saw a valley
of dry bones become a great army.
This vision was God's way of
encouraging his people with hope
for the future.*

DRY BONES COME TO LIFE

✤ Ezekiel 37 ✤

The captives in Babylon had received stern warnings from God about the difficult times that faced them in the future, but now he wanted to encourage them to have a little more hope. In a vision God took his prophet, Ezekiel, to a valley full of piles of dried-up human bones. Where once there had been life, there was now a dead emptiness, just like God's people who had cut themselves off from his goodness.

"Could these bones come to life again?" God asked Ezekiel, but the prophet wasn't sure. "Tell these bones I am going to make them live again, so that they will know how powerful I am," God declared.

Ezekiel had hardly finished speaking when he heard an extraordinary rattling sound and watched in amazement as the bones started coming together. First the bones were covered with muscles, and then skin, until the skeletons looked like ordinary people again. But still they were dead.

"Now, Ezekiel," God said, "tell the winds to blow from every direction and breathe life into these dead bodies."

Ezekiel commanded the winds to blow, and immediately the bodies began to stand up, until there were so many that it looked like an enormous army.

"Tell my people that just as I have breathed life into this valley of dry bones, so I will breathe new life into them," God said, as he explained his plan for Israel to Ezekiel. "I will bring them home and care for them like a shepherd, and they will become powerful and live in peace."

TRAINED FOR THE KING'S SERVICE

✤ Daniel 1 ✤

Fanning the fire
This wooden model from Egypt shows a man fanning a charcoal fire, which was probably used for cooking. Food was normally boiled in a pot over an open fire. To bake bread, large, flat stones were heated in the fire. When the dough was ready, the hot stones were taken out of the fire and the dough was placed on them to cook.

Spices
Like other ancient peoples, the Babylonians used spices to flavour their foods. One of the most commonly used spices was the herb cumin. It was grown for its aromatic seeds, which were ground up and used in place of pepper.

A diet of vegetables
The diet of vegetables that Daniel requested would have been fairly limited. Many vegetables, such as cucumbers, were eaten raw. Others, such as lentils, beans and leeks, were boiled in water or oil. Seasoning with garlic or cumin helped to give some flavour to what was otherwise a rather boring diet.

When the Babylonians captured Jerusalem, they selected a group of Israelites who had useful skills and took them back to Babylon. One of these men was called Daniel.

The Babylonian king, Nebuchadnezzar, ordered his chief official to select the very best of these young men. They were to be trained to help him rule his kingdom.

Daniel was willing to work hard for the king, but he also wanted to remain faithful to God.

When he realized that he would have to eat the same food and wine as the king, including foods forbidden by his faith, Daniel asked the chief official if he could eat a plainer diet.

"I am sorry, Daniel," the official said, sympathetically, "but the king has ordered you to eat his food. If you do not eat it

and become weaker than the others, he w[ill] execute me!"

So instead, Daniel appealed to his guard. "Feed my three friends and me on[ly] vegetables and water for ten days. Then s[ee] whether we suffer or not."

The guard agreed. At the end of th[e] ten days of their new diet, Daniel and hi[s] friends looked fitter and healthier than t[he] Israelites who had eaten the royal food, s[o] they were allowed to continue.

As Daniel followed his training, G[od] gave him great knowledge and wisdom, and the gift of understanding dreams and visions. At the end of three years, the ki[ng] questioned Daniel and found that he wa[s] much cleverer than his magicians. So Daniel became the king's servant.

DANIEL EXPLAINS THE KING'S DREAM

✤ Daniel 2 ✤

King Nebuchadnezzar was tormented by a troubling nightmare that he could not understand, so he summoned all his wise men.

"You should be able to tell me exactly what was in my dream and what it means, without me giving you any details!" he insisted. "Unless you answer, I will have you executed!"

"But only the gods can reveal such things," the wise men protested. At this, the furious king ordered that they should all be put to death, including Daniel and his friends.

Wisely, Daniel asked the king for more time. Then he went home and prayed that God would spare their lives by showing him what the dream meant. To Daniel's relief, God revealed the mystery to him in a vision.

"No man, including me, is clever enough to explain your dream," Daniel humbly told the king the next day, "but there is a God in heaven who can reveal all mysteries." Daniel explained that the dream foretold what would happen in the future.

"You saw an enormous and terrifying statue of a man," he told the king. "It had a gold head, a silver body, and bronze legs. As you were watching, a rock smashed the statue's feet which were made of iron mixed with clay.

"Then every part of the statue was smashed into tiny pieces that were blown away by the wind, leaving no trace. But the rock itself became a huge mountain which covered the whole world.

"Your Majesty, the gold represents your mighty kingdom, and the other parts of the statue represent other, less great kingdoms. And the rock that destroyed them all is God's eternal kingdom that, one day, will cover the whole world."

The king realized that Daniel was speaking the truth, and showed his appreciation by making him the ruler of the whole province of Babylon.

Babylonian boundary stone
The Babylonians kept records on clay tablets or stones. Sometimes records of who owned the land were made public and the stones would be set up in the field or temple to which the agreement related. Boundary stones like this one were marked with the symbols of the gods and goddesses who were believed to have witnessed the contract.

The Babylonian empire
The Babylonians reached the height of their power in about 600BC, during the reign of King Nebuchadnezzar. At this time, they controlled a huge empire, stretching from the Mediterranean Sea in the west to the Persian Gulf in the east. The story of Daniel takes place just after the Babylonians had conquered Jerusalem, in 586BC.

SIGNS OF THE ZODIAC
Astrologers believe that the stars and planets exert a decisive influence on a person's character and destiny. Astrology flourished in Babylon under the influence of the priests. The zodiac and its twelve signs are thought to have originated there. The Bible rejects beliefs such as astrology, because God alone has control over the universe which he created.

THE FIERY FURNACE

✣ Daniel 3 ✣

The ruins of Babylon
Babylon was on the river Euphrates, about 80 km south of modern Baghdad in Iraq. It was the capital of the huge empire of Babylonia which it took over from Assyria. Under King Nebuchadnezzar the city was rebuilt and enjoyed fame and prosperity. Its "hanging" roof gardens were one of the seven wonders of the world.

Clay cylinder of King Nebuchadnezzar
This cylinder proclaims the rebuilding of the sun-god temple. Under King Nebuchadnezzar, many great structures were built. Their bricks were made from mud and clay mixed with straw. They were shaped into 30-cm squares, about 10 cm thick. Bricks were often inscribed with the name of the reigning king.

Musicians
These Assyrian-Babylonian musicians are playing (from left to right) the bagpipes, flute and harp. Musical instruments were made from many materials, including wood, leather, gut, ivory, shell, gold and silver. Music has been an important element of religious worship in every culture. Everyone had to bow down to Nebuchadnezzar's statue when the music began.

King Nebuchadnezzar decided to build a gigantic gold statue that all his subjects would worship. It was twenty-seven metres high and nearly three metres wide.

"As soon as you hear the music," the king's herald announced, "kneel down and worship it. Anyone who disobeys will be thrown into a fiery furnace."

When Nebuchadnezzar was told th[at] Shadrach, Meshach and Abednego had refused, because as Jews they worshipped only God, he erupted with anger. "You have one last chance," he told them, "bef[ore] I throw you into the furnace. What God [of] yours could save you then?"

The three stood bravely before the king. "Our God can save us from the flames," they replied, "but even if he doesn't, we still won't worship your gods."

The king's fury increased even furth[er] and he ordered the furnace to be made seven times hotter. So fierce were the flames that the soldiers who threw Shadrach, Meshach and Abednego into t[he] furnace died immediately.

The king expected to see the three quickly burnt to a cinder, but his eyes widened with amazemen[t.] "Look! I can see not three, but four men walking in the fire. Come out, servants of the Most High God!"

Shadrach, Mesha[ch] and Abednego walked out. Their bodies and clothe[s] had not been burned at all. The[y] didn't even smell of smoke.

"Everyone shou[ld] praise the God o[f] Shadrach, Mesha[ch] and Abednego!" Nebuchadnezzar declared. "They we[re] willing to die rather than worship any go[d] except their own, but God sent an angel to save them."

The king was so impresse[d] that he promoted them to higher jobs in his kingdom.

THE WRITING ON THE WALL

✤ Daniel 5 ✤

One evening, as King Belshazzar and a thousand of his most important officials were feasting, he issued a royal command. "Let us drink wine from the sacred gold and silver cups my father stole from the temple in Jerusalem!" he declared. After a while they all got drunk and started worshipping their idols.

Daniel
God gave Daniel great wisdom, so that he could interpret the strange dreams of King Nebuchadnezzar. Now the new king Belshazzar needs him to explain the meaning of the writing that has appeared on the wall of his palace.

The writing on the wall
Archaeological excavations of the site of the Babylonian palace have revealed a throne room that was built in Nebuchadnezzar's reign. One wall is decorated with glazed blue bricks, while the others are of white plaster. On one of these walls Belshazzar saw human fingers writing the words MENE, MENE, TEKEL and PARSIN. The three words written in the Aramaic script of the 6th-5th centuries BC mean numbered, weighed, and divided.

Suddenly, in the light of the lamp, the king saw human fingers writing on the palace wall. His face turned white with fear, and his knees started shaking. The message was written in a language he couldn't understand, so he called his wise men together.

"Tell me what this means!" he demanded, but when none of them could explain, he grew even more afraid. The queen reassured him and told him that Daniel could help him solve the riddle.

"I have been told that God has given you wisdom to understand everything," the king told Daniel. "Now, if you can tell me what this writing means, I will make you powerful in my kingdom."

"I don't want any reward," Daniel replied modestly, as he simply wanted to serve God. "God says that because you have used sacred cups for your partying and have worshipped false gods, he has shortened your reign. He has weighed you on his scales and decided that you are not good enough to be king. So your kingdom is divided amongst the Medes and the Persians."

Despite the bad news, Belshazzar kept his promise and gave Daniel a purple robe and gold chain and made him a powerful governor.

That same night, God's message came true. An invading army killed King Belshazzar, and Darius took over his kingdom.

WORSHIPPING IDOLS
Idols are statues of animals and super-humans made from metal, wood or stone. God forbids the worship of idols. He wants us to worship only him. We can still worship idols today, because an idol is anything we put in the place of God, such as money, football, pop singers, even our friends. There is nothing wrong with any of these things, as long as they are not more important to us than loving God.

Bull from the Ishtar Gate
Marduk, the chief deity of the Babylonians, was sometimes represented as a bull. Although we can't be sure what Nebuchadnezzar's 27-metre image of gold looked like, it was probably some kind of idol of Marduk. Marduk was honoured each spring at a festival where all the other gods came before him to supposedly determine the course of people's lives for the coming year.

129 ✣

DANIEL IN THE LIONS' DEN

✤ **Daniel 6** ✤

Daniel governed so well that King Darius wanted to put him in charge of the whole of Babylon. But the other officials were jealous of Daniel's success. They searched for something wrong with Daniel's work so that they could get him into trouble.

But Daniel was so honest that they failed. So instead, they tricked the king into making a law. For thirty days, it said, people could pray only to the king. No one was allowed to pray to any other god, and anyone who disobeyed the law would be thrown to the lions as punishment.

Daniel knew that the new law was wrong and decided that he would carry on praying to God. At home, Daniel got down on his knees three times each day, as usual, and thanked God for his goodness.

But the wicked officials were spying on Daniel

and one day they caught him praying and asking God for help. They rushed off to the king and told him, gleefully, "Daniel has disobeyed your new law by praying to his God. He must be punished."

Darius was horrified because Daniel was a wise ruler, but he could not change the law. So, reluctantly, he ordered his guards to throw Daniel into the den of snarling, hungry lions. Then the king lay awake all night, praying that somehow Daniel would escape.

The next morning, he ran to the den and shouted, "Daniel! Did your God save

Lion earrings
Lions symbolized power and authority. They were a popular motif in jewellery and art. An Asian species of lion once lived along the marshy riverbanks of the Tigris and Euphrates, and lion hunting was a favourite sport. In royal cities, lions were often kept in captivity, and could be used to execute prisoners.

Median nobles
Median influence was so strong in the Persian empire that Medes and Persians are often depicted side by side. This wall relief from Persepolis shows a noble couple dressed in typical Median clothes. The men's rounded hats and short tunics made them easy to distinguish from the Persians.

The Babylonian world
This picture shows the Babylonian view of how the world fitted together. At the top were the heavens, next came the air, whilst underneath and surrounding the earth were the oceans. Each of these three layers had its own gods: Anu was the god of the heavens, Enlil god of the air, and Ea "lord of the deep oceans". The king reigned as the representative of the gods on earth and was thought to be especially blessed by them.

u from the lions?" and waited anxiously
r an answer.

Then he heard Daniel call out, "My
od knew that I was innocent, and he sent
angel to stop the lions from eating me."
aniel's trust in God had saved him.

King Darius breathed a sigh of relief
d commanded that Daniel should be set
e. Then he ordered the wicked officials
be thrown to the
ns instead.

COURAGE TO OBEY GOD
*Daniel knew the king's law was wrong
and he was prepared to disobey it, even if
it cost him his life. Sticking to what you
believe, even when this makes life difficult,
shows that you are a courageous person.
Sometimes this is hard, especially if it
means going against what all your friends
are doing. But obeying your conscience –
the part of you that tells you right from
wrong – helps you do the right thing.*

Ruins of Babylon
*The Persian king, Cyrus, captured
Babylon without a battle. The
Greek historians Herodotus and
Xenophon record that the Persian
invaders made their way into the
city along the old dried-up bed of
the river Euphrates. Then they
launched a surprise attack while
King Belshazzar and his nobles
were feasting.*

Darius the Mede
*The Medes lived in the
mountainous area of modern-day
Azerbaijan and Kurdistan. In
about 550BC they were defeated
by Cyrus the Great and became
allies of the Persians. When the
Persians captured Babylon, they
installed Darius the Mede as the
city's ruler. Although the Bible
calls him a king, he was actually
appointed as a governor by
King Cyrus.*

The Persian empire
*The death of king Belshazzar in
539BC brought the Babylonian empire to an end,
and marked the rise of the mighty Persian empire.
The Persian kings extended their borders even
further than the earlier empires had done. Persian
control extended from Turkey and Egypt in the
west, to India in the east.*

GOD WILL POUR OUT HIS SPIRIT

✤ **Joel 1-2** ✤

We do not know much about Joel. He may have lived in Jerusalem. He saw a plague of locusts and a drought which devastated Judah as judgement from God. He called on all the people to turn back to God. After repentance and judgement would come salvation and blessing. Joel looks forward to the time when all believers, of whatever age or status, would receive the outpouring of God's Spirit.

Locust
Locusts are mentioned more than fifty times in the Bible. Locusts destroyed crops and a huge swarm of them would blot out the light of the sun, but they were also eaten as a useful source of protein. Locusts are a kind of grasshopper and the word may be used to describe both.

Wheat field
Excavations of Jericho have shown that Palestine was one of the earliest agricultural centres yet discovered, with irrigation methods being used in the Jordan valley. Wheat was the main and most valuable grain crop grown in the region.

Desert landscape
The most common Hebrew term for desert denotes empty wastes of rock and sand, inhabited by wild animals, and with no settled population. The Bible compares God's ability to renew life with the transformation of a desert into a productive garden.

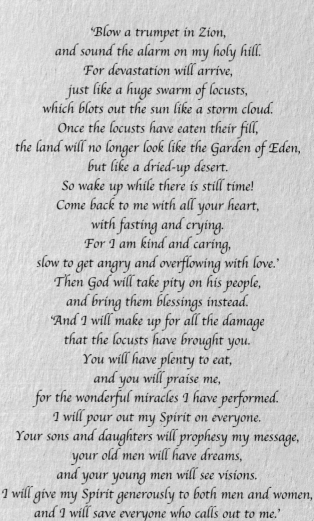

'Blow a trumpet in Zion,
and sound the alarm on my holy hill.
For devastation will arrive,
just like a huge swarm of locusts,
which blots out the sun like a storm cloud.
Once the locusts have eaten their fill,
the land will no longer look like the Garden of Eden,
but like a dried-up desert.
So wake up while there is still time!
Come back to me with all your heart,
with fasting and crying.
For I am kind and caring,
slow to get angry and overflowing with love.'
Then God will take pity on his people,
and bring them blessings instead.
'And I will make up for all the damage
that the locusts have brought you.
You will have plenty to eat,
and you will praise me,
for the wonderful miracles I have performed.
I will pour out my Spirit on everyone.
Your sons and daughters will prophesy my message,
your old men will have dreams,
and your young men will see visions.
I will give my Spirit generously to both men and women,
and I will save everyone who calls out to me.'

BE FAIR TO MY PEOPLE!

✣ Amos 1-9 ✣

Amos lived a simple life as a shepherd in Judea, looking after his sheep and tending fig trees. As God's prophet, could see that the wealth and peace that the Israelites were joying under King Jeroboam II had made them selfish. If ey truly loved God, then they would stop being greedy and at the poor kindly. "This is God's message to you," nos announced.

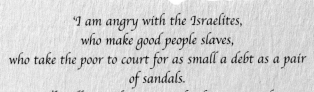

'I am angry with the Israelites,
who make good people slaves,
who take the poor to court for as small a debt as a pair
of sandals.
They flatten the poor on the dusty ground,
and treat the weak unfairly.
Violently, they steal their wealth,
no longer knowing right from wrong.
Many times, I warned you about my anger,' says God,
'by sending diseases on your crops,
but you still haven't turned back to me.
You take from the poor levies of grain.
You take bribes, and swindle the poor in court.
You cheat, using dishonest scales,
to measure out your wheat, charging high prices,
even though you mix dust in with the grain.

I hate to see you pretending to love me
during your worship and religious ceremonies.
Even though you are generous with your offerings to me,
I will ignore them.
I don't want to hear your empty music and praise.
What is important to me is to see justice and fairness
flowing like a never-ending river.

At the moment, you feel comfortable and relaxed,
as you lie on your couches, eating succulent meals of lamb.
You drink wine by the bowlful,
not caring that your behaviour
will bring your country to ruin.
I warn you that you will be the first to be attacked,
and dragged off to a foreign land.
Then your partying will come to an end.
But after your punishment, I will restore the house of David.'
I will rebuild your ruined cities, and make you prosperous again.

Star of David
The six-pointed star of David is a symbol of Judaism today, but it was probably not used in biblical times. It had appeared in Jewish architecture by the 3rd century AD, and in 14th-century AD Jewish literature it is referred to as "the seal of Solomon".

Amos
Amos kept sheep and tended fig trees at Tekoa, a hill village in Judah. Amos warned the people of the judgement and exile that would come if they failed to repent. He spoke out against injustice, indulgence and dishonesty and defended the poor and the oppressed.

133 ♣

A MIGHTY FISH SWALLOWS JONAH

✦ Jonah 1-2 ✦

Sperm whale
At about 18 metres in length, the sperm whale is one of the world's largest living creatures. Sperm whales are sometimes found in the waters of the eastern Mediterranean Sea, and their mouths are certainly wide enough to swallow a person whole. However, the enormous fish which swallowed Jonah need not necessarily have been a whale. Whatever it was, it certainly caused him to change his mind and go to Nineveh.

Jonah's journey
Jonah's mission took him on a journey of over 800 kilometres. God told him to go to Nineveh, but he boarded a ship for Tarshish - in exactly the opposite direction. Tarshish is thought to have been Tartessus, a port in south-west Spain. The fish left Jonah on a beach somewhere further up the coast of Canaan. From there he would have travelled overland to Nineveh.

Nineveh
The city of Nineveh is first mentioned in Genesis. It lay on the east bank of the Tigris river in modern-day Iraq. In Jonah's time, Nineveh was a royal city of the Assyrian kings. It later became the capital of their empire. Nineveh was surrounded by a brick wall over 11 kilometres long. It had fifteen gates, each guarded by enormous stone bulls. The wall in this photograph is a reconstruction of the city wall, made from old stone and bricks.

God told the prophet Jonah to go to Nineveh and warn the people about their wickedness. But Jonah was reluctant to go. He did not think that the people there deserved to be forgiven for their terrible crimes. Why shouldn't they suffer God's punishment?

So instead of obeying God, Jonah ran off to Joppa and got on a boat heading for Tarshish. But while Jonah was sleeping peacefully below deck, God made a strong wind blow and the boat was rocked by huge waves.

The captain of the boat was frightened and woke Jonah. "How can you sleep when we are in danger of being shipwrecked?" he asked. "You must pray to your God to save us all from drowning!"

As the storm continued to rage, the sailors cast lots to find out who was bringing this trouble on them. They discovered it was Jonah. "Yes, I must be th[e] cause of the storm because I am running away from God," Jonah agreed. "The only way to stop it is to throw me overboard."

The sailors tried to control the ship with their oars, but the storm just got worse. So, reluctantly, they lowered Jonah over the side of the boat, knowing that he would probably drown.

Jonah sank under the crashing wave[s] and got tangled in seaweed. Surely this w[as] the end of his life, he thought miserably. But God had other plans. An enormous fish swam by, opened its mouth and swallowed Jonah alive.

For three days and nights Jonah stayed in the stomach of the fish, praising God for saving him. Then God told the fish to land Jonah safely onto the beach.

GOD FORGIVES NINEVEH

✤ Jonah 3-4 ✤

Once more, God told Jonah to go to Nineveh and tell the people to stop being wicked. This time, after his terrifying adventure at sea, Jonah was willing to obey.

Jonah walked through the streets, crying out, "People of Nineveh, in forty days' time, unless you turn to God, he will destroy your city!"

Everywhere he went, people took notice of Jonah's message and began to change their ways. The king of Nineveh ordered everyone to give up eating their fine food and to dress in sackcloth as a sign that they were truly sorry and wanted God's forgiveness.

God was glad that he did not have to punish Nineveh after all. But Jonah felt angry, and prayed, "Dear Lord, I knew from the beginning that you would be kind to these people, even though they are our enemies. I would rather have seen them all destroyed! I am so disappointed that I feel like dying."

Jonah went off and sat under a shelter he had made to watch the city, just in case God changed his mind about punishing the people. To protect Jonah from the fiercely hot sun, God made a leafy vine grow over the shelter to provide more shade.

But early the next morning, God sent a worm to chew through the vine so that it wilted and died. So Jonah was left miserable and uncomfortable in the scorching hot winds and sunshine, and he wished that he was dead.

"You should not be angry that I am kind to the people of Nineveh," God said to him. "You are unhappy about losing this vine. But you did not even plant it or care for it. Why shouldn't I be concerned for the many people who live in this city, and show that I love them?"

Castor oil plant
There is some dispute over exactly which type of plant provided shelter for Jonah. The Bible calls it a vine, but it could quite possibly have been a castor oil plant. This plant grows very quickly and has huge umbrella-like leaves which provide a lot of shade. The castor oil plant often grows in waste places near water, and is said to wither if it is handled even slightly.

REBUILD MY TEMPLE

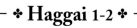

✦ Haggai 1-2 ✦

Ruins from the time of Solomon
Stone was so widely available that it was the commonest building material in ancient Israel. It was used for all kinds of buildings: from the huge defensive walls which surrounded every city to the simplest of animal pens. Houses were also built of stone. The joints were filled with mud which dried hard in the sun and bonded the stones together. Inside the house the walls were finished with a mud plaster.

When God's people returned to Jerusalem from exile in Babylon, God told them to rebuild the temple that had been destroyed many years earlier. The people began enthusiastically, but their enemies soon made the work difficult, so they gave up and became busy with their own affairs.

Haggai gave Zerubbabel, the governor, and Joshua, the high priest, a warning from God. "Do you think it is right for the people to build themselves luxurious houses to live in, while my holy house is still a ruin? No wonder the people never seem to have enough food to eat, clothes to wear, or money to spend. Their harvests won't make them rich until they learn to honour me first."

Zerubbabel and Joshua listened carefully, then immediately began obeying God's command. They respected God and didn't want any more punishment to fall on the people of Jerusalem. So the people resumed work on the temple again.

Some older people remembered the first temple built by King Solomon and felt sad that the new one wouldn't be as beautiful. "Let me encourage you all to work hard," God reassured them through Haggai. "The new temple will be so full of my presence that it will be even more glorious than King Solomon's temple."

As soon as the people of Jerusalem relaid the temple's foundation stones, God began to shower his blessings on their harvests and to make them wealthy.

WALK IN MY WAYS

✤ Zechariah 1-6 ✤

Despite their sins, God had not forgotten his promise to those returning to Jerusalem that they were his specially chosen people. To encourage them, he showed Zechariah, his prophet, several visions explaining what would happen in the future.

"I saw God's messengers on horseback bringing back reports that Judah had been punished by her enemies much more harshly than he wanted," said Zechariah. "Now God will show his love for Jerusalem by angrily crushing those enemies. Next, I saw a man measuring the new, prosperous Jerusalem, teeming with God's people gathered from many nations. Almighty God himself will be the only protective wall the city will ever need.

"I saw the high priest, Joshua, dressed in filthy clothes just as Judah was dirty with sin.

God will generously forgive the past, and give Joshua clean, priestly clothes so that Satan has no right to accuse his people. And God said, 'If you walk in my ways, I will put you in charge of the temple.' And God showed me a woman inside a large basket who stood for all the crimes that my country had ever committed. He took her away to Babylon, leaving Judah pure and holy.

"Then God gave me an important message for Zerubbabel, the governor. God declares, 'Not by might, nor by power, but only by my Spirit.' Although he must work hard and build a strong army, it is only with God's help that he can succeed in rebuilding the temple."

Zechariah knew from all these visions that God's loving kindness and forgiveness would make Jerusalem great once more.

Zechariah's vision
In a vision Zechariah saw four chariots coming from between two bronze mountains. The first chariot was drawn by red horses, the second by black, the third by white and the fourth by dappled. This vision was to encourage God's people: to show them that God was in control, that he would conquer his enemies and that his agents were already riding out to bring divine judgement on them.

WHY DON'T YOU HONOUR ME?

♣ Malachi 1-3 ♣

Dome of the Rock
The Dome of the Rock in Jerusalem occupies the area known as Mount Moriah. The Muslim mosque was built in AD691 and stands on the site of Solomon's temple. The great rock inside the mosque is thought to be the place where Abraham was prepared to sacrifice Isaac.

Cattle
Sheep and cows were valuable animals and were offered in sacrificial worship as a mark of respect to God. The best calf was kept and fattened up for special occasions. Malachi complains because God's people were not offering the best of their animals in sacrifice.

Worship at the Wailing Wall
This is now the holiest place in the world to modern Jews, and they come here to pray. The huge stones are all that remain of the western wall on which Herod's temple was built. The temple was destroyed by the Romans in AD70 after a Jewish rebellion.

one who rules over you, would certainly n[ot] be pleased with them, so why do you thin[k] you can cheat me? Only the purest offerings are worthy of my holy name.

"A priest speaks on my behalf, so everyone looks to you for sound knowledg[e] and instruction. But your weak teaching

At long last, God's people had returned from Babylon and had rebuilt the temple in Jerusalem. But all was not well. It was hard work reconstructing a prosperous life, and the nation was missing out on God's full blessing because they were not following his laws wholeheartedly. Malachi brought God's word of encouragement to his dispirited people.

"I have loved you dearly, Israel, yet you question my love when you see how hard your lives are. This is the problem," God told them. "A son honours his father, and a servant his master, but look at your behaviour! Why don't you honour me? As leaders, you priests ought to know better than to allow offerings of diseased and injured animals in my temple, instead of the best of the flock. Your governor, the

has made many stumble in their lives and you have not applied the law equally to everyone. So now I will make everyone despise you.

"My people, it's no use weeping and wailing when you realize that I won't accept your offerings or bless you. What d[o] you expect when you heartlessly divorce your wives for women who worship idols? I'm tired of hearing you lie, 'Those who d[o] evil are good', and question, 'Where is the God of justice?'

"Listen, one day I will send a powerful messenger who will suddenly appear in my temple. With the searing he[at] of a refiner's fire, he will burn away the impurities in people's hearts, leaving thos[e] who will once more make honest offering[s] to me."

RETURNING TO GOD

✤ Malachi 3-4 ✤

"I will protect your crops from pests and make your grapevines heavy with fruit. Foreigners will see your rich harvests and say that you are greatly blessed by me.

"So stop saying, 'It's pointless to serve God and obey his laws. Evil people become rich so easily, and even those who proudly challenge God seem to get away without punishment.'

"Don't be mistaken. One day, my fierce judgement will burn them up like straw in a field, and they will be like mere ashes under the feet of my treasured children, those who love and respect me. Then my power will shine on you like the healing rays of the sun and your faithfulness will be well rewarded. Just remember to obey the laws that I gave to Moses."

"How are we to return to God?" asked the people of Israel, who longed to receive God's blessings after so many generations in exile, but who didn't understand why life was still difficult.

"I have never changed," God explained. "I still offer you my forgiveness, only you will stop stealing what belongs to me. Your whole nation is cursed by me because you don't fill the temple storehouse with the right offerings. If you give a tenth of your income back to me, then I will make sure that you have plenty of food. Watch me open heaven and pour out such a flood of blessing that you won't have room to store it!

The chosen people

The Israelites thought of themselves as God's 'chosen people' who were called to bear witness to his love and purposes for the world. Even though they often rebelled against him, he always preserved a remnant to continue his work. In the New Testament Peter says Christians are God's new chosen people, called to take the message of Jesus into the world.

MALACHI

Malachi was the last of the Old Testament prophets. The name Malachi means "my messenger". The prophet Malachi spoke of one coming who would prepare the way for the coming of the Lord. Such a one would come to purify and restore the true worship of God. The New Testament understands this reference to speak of the coming of John the Baptist, who made the way ready for the coming of the Messiah, believed by Christians to be Jesus.

Barley

Wheat and barley were the staple cereal crops in ancient Israel. Barley, pictured here, ripens before wheat and is harvested in early summer. It makes a flour and bread that is inferior to wheat, but because it was cheaper to produce, barley was often fed to animals and was the common food of the poor. Barley loaves came to symbolize poverty and worthlessness.

THE NEW TESTAMENT

Here we read about Jesus, about his
miraculous healings and teachings.
The New Testament tells of his love
and how he died, but overcame death
so that we might be free. We read of the
changed lives of the first disciples and
how they told others about Jesus and
formed the Christian church.

*I have come that they may have life and that they
may have life in all its fullness.*

(John 10:10)

THE NEW TESTAMENT

The *New Testament* contains 27 books: four books that describe the life and message of Jesus Christ, the story of the first Christians, letters written by the apostles to give teaching and encouragement to Christians and a prophetic book of visions.

The Gospels and Acts

The word *gospel* means "good news". Nearly half of the *New Testament* consists of four accounts of Jesus Christ's life and the good news that he brought to the world. The Gospels particularly emphasize the events of the last week of Jesus' life, his death and his resurrection.

Each of the Gospels has its own emphasis. *Matthew* shows an interest in Jewish Christians: Jesus is the Messiah long expected by the Jews. *Mark* is a brief, action-packed, account of Jesus' life and work. The Gospel of *Luke* and the *Acts of the Apostles* are two parts of one work. Luke emphasizes Jesus as the Saviour of all different kinds of people, especially the poor and needy. The Gospel of *John* is different from the other three: seven signs (miracles) and seven sayings point to Jesus as the Son of God.

The *Acts of the Apostles* takes the story on from Jesus' ascension into heaven, the gift of the Holy Spirit at Pentecost and the birth of the church. Peter and later, Paul, became leaders, and the message of Jesus spread rapidly from Jerusalem throughout the eastern Roman Empire.

The Letters

The Church was helped in its early years by apostles who wrote letters teaching about God and the gospel, with instructions on practical aspects of the Christian life.

The letters can be grouped in this way: *Romans, 1 and 2 Corinthian* and *Galatians* emphasize the nature of the gospel preached by Paul. *Ephesians, Philippians, Colossians* and *Philemon*, all written while Paul was a prisoner in Rome, contain teaching on what it means to be a Christian. Paul's two letters to the *Thessalonians* were probably his earliest letters and are especially concerned about Christ second coming. The two letters to *Timothy* and *Titus* contain practical advice on church organization.

Hebrews shows that Jesus was better than the *Old Testament* priesthood and system of sacrifices, and the perfect fulfilment of all that they had stood for. *James* is a letter about practical Christianity; *1 Peter a*

NEW TESTAMENT TIMELINE

BC | AD

30 | 20 | 10 | 0 | 10 | 20 | 30

- *c.* 30 Herod made puppet King of Judea by Romans
- *c.* 19 Herod begins building Jerusalem temple
- *c.* 4 Jesus born
- *c.* 4 Herod's "kingdom" divided between his three sons
- *c.* 5 Jesus in temple at age 12
- *c.* 26 John the Baptist begins ministry, Jesus baptized, Jesus begins ministry
- *c.* 27/28 John the Baptist imprisoned
- *c.* 28/29 John the Baptist dies
- *c.* 30 Jesus crucified, resurrected and the Ascension

ROMAN EMPERORS

27BC–AD14
Augustus

14-37
Tiberius

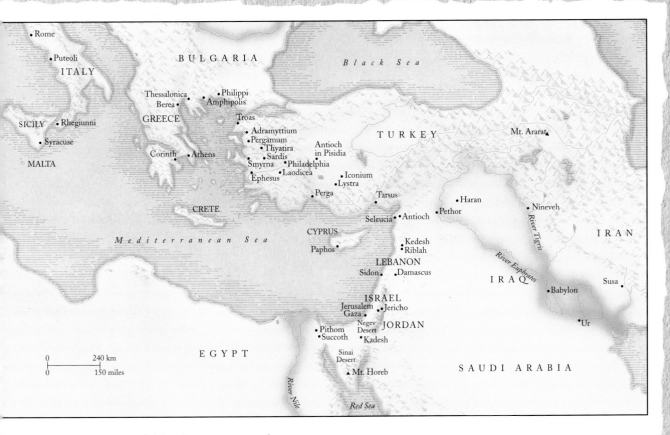

The world of the New Testament (with modern country names)
The Roman empire covered the whole area around the Mediterranean Sea. The network of roads and freedom from war gave Christians the opportunity to travel and spread their message. Some Christians were forced to migrate out of Judea because they were persecuted.

etter to Christians who were persecuted for their faith; *2 Peter* and *Jude* warn against false teachers. *1 John* was written to help Christians be sure of their faith; the very brief *2 and 3 John* show some of the implications of the life of love and truth.

Revelation

The final book in the Bible is *Revelation*, a prophetic book of visions and symbols, written at a time when Christians were being persecuted. Its author is believed to be the apostle John. It opens with a vision of Christ in glory; then come letters to seven churches. Visions of judgement and victory follow, showing God's sovereignty and his ultimate triumph over evil through Christ. The book closes with an inspiring picture of a new heaven and a new earth.

30
- c. 30 Pentecost
- c. 35 Stephen martyred
- c. 35 Paul converted to Christianity

40
- c. 40 Gentile "Pentecost" at Caesarea
- c. 44 James martyred and Peter imprisioned
- c. 46-48 Paul's first missionary journey
- c. 49/50 Jerusalem Council

50
- c. 50-52 Paul's second missionary journey
- c. 51 Paul's letters to the Thessalonians
- c. 52-56 Paul's letters to the Corinthians
- c. 53-57 Paul's third missionary journey

60
- c. 59-61/62 Paul imprisoned in Rome; writes letters to the Ephesians, Colossians and Philippians
- c. 64 Christians blamed by Nero for fire of Rome
- c. 65-67 Paul's letters to Timothy and Titus
- c. 65-80 The four Gospels begin to circulate

70
- c. 67/68 Paul dies
- c. 70 Jeruselem destroyed

80
- c. 81 Emperor Domitian persecutes Christians
- c. 85 John's three letters written

90
- c. 90-95 John exiled on Patmos

37-41	41-54	54-68	69	69-79	79-81	81-96
Caligula	Claudius	Nero	Galba, Otho, Vitellius	Vespasian	Titus	Domitian

143 ✤

ZECHARIAH IS PROMISED A SON

✤ Luke 1 ✤

The angel Gabriel
The angel Gabriel was sent to give Zechariah the news of John the Baptist's birth. Gabriel was God's special messenger, and his name means either "God is my hero" or "Mighty man of God". Gabriel and Michael are the only angels in the Bible to be mentioned by name.

Incense altar
A gold incense altar stood before the Most Holy Place in the temple. A priest had to keep the incense burning on the altar and make sure there was a fresh supply before the morning sacrifice and after the evening sacrifice. This was a great honour and priests were chosen by lot. Zechariah was chosen in this way.

Galbanum
One of the ingredients used in the sacred incense burnt on the altar was galbanum, an aromatic resin from a plant related to fennel which grew in Syria and Persia. The other ingredients for the sacred incense were gum resin, onycha (which came from mollusc shells) and frankincense.

Zechariah was a priest during the reign of King Herod. Both he and his wife, Elizabeth, were humble followers of God, obeying all his commands. They were now old and their lives were sad because they did not have any children.

One day, as part of his priestly duties, Zechariah was chosen to burn incense on the altar. As he was going about his task, an angel came and stood next to the altar.

TRUSTING WHAT GOD SAYS
Sometimes it seems impossible to believe what God says to us. Like Zechariah, we may be full of doubts that God's will for us can come true. By taking one step at a time, we can ask God how he's going to make our dreams happen, and then watch him provide what we need.

Zechariah was terrified, but the angel calmed him saying, "Don't be afraid. After all these years your prayers have been answered. Elizabeth will have a son called John. Not only will he give you much happiness, but his birth will bring great joy to many people. He will be filled with the Lord's Spirit from birth and will persuade many Israelites to return to God. Above all else, he is destined to prepare the way for the coming of the Lord himself."

"How can I know that what you are saying is true?" stammered Zechariah. "Surely Elizabeth and I are too old to have a child now?"

"I, Gabriel, have come from the very presence of the Lord to bring you this wonderful message. But because you have doubted me, you will be unable to speak until the day that the child is born," the angel answered before disappearing.

Outside, the crowds were wondering why Zechariah was taking so long. When he finally emerged, they knew that he had seen a vision because he was unable to talk to them.

Elizabeth became pregnant, just as the angel had said, and in due course she gave birth to the promised child. All her relatives were overjoyed for her sake.

When they took the baby to be circumcised they were ready to call him Zechariah, but Elizabeth intervened, "No, we want to call him John."

Everyone was surprised because there was nobody in the family with such a name, so they asked Zechariah what the boy should be called. They handed him a writing slate and were amazed when in clear, bold letters he wrote the name "John". No sooner had he done so than he was able to speak once more and gave praise to the Lord.

Everybody who heard what had happened was intrigued and began to wonder about the special future that lay ahead of the boy.

AN ANGEL BRINGS NEWS FOR MARY

✣ Luke 1 ✣

Six months into Elizabeth's pregnancy God sent Gabriel to Nazareth in Galilee where Mary lived. She was engaged to Joseph who could trace his family tree back to King David.

"Greetings, chosen one of God. God with you," the angel said. Poor Mary was frightened by this introduction and trembled with fear.

"Don't be alarmed, Mary. God is pleased to bless you. You are going to have a child called Jesus. He will be called the Son of the Most High God. God will give him David's kingdom and establish him as king over the house of Jacob for ever."

"How is this possible?" Mary queried. "I am not yet married to Joseph."

Gabriel replied, "The power of the Holy Spirit will rest upon you. So the child that is to be born will be called the Son of God. Even your cousin Elizabeth is expecting a son in her old age. Nothing is beyond the power of God."

Mary was speechless. All she could say before the angel left was, "May everything that you have spoken to God's humble servant come true."

Mary soon packed her belongings and paid a visit to Elizabeth. When they met, the child in Elizabeth's womb leapt for joy, and speaking with the inspiration of the Holy Spirit, Elizabeth proclaimed, "You are blessed among all women and the child you are carrying is blessed too. To what do I owe this honour that the mother of my Lord has come to see me? When I heard you speak, my child danced inside my body. You will indeed be blessed because you have believed the words of the Lord!"

When Mary heard what Elizabeth said, she declared, "May my soul give glory to God, for he has looked upon his humble servant. From this day onwards everyone shall call me blessed because the all-powerful God has done something remarkable for me. He always shows mercy to those who honour him and he humbles the self-confident. He dethrones kings and exalts the humble. He satisfies the hungry and sends the rich away empty-handed. He has not forgotten his people Israel but has remembered the promise he made to our father Abraham."

Mary remained with Elizabeth for three months and then she went home to Nazareth.

The Church of the Annunciation
The Church of the Annunciation in Nazareth marks the site where Christians believe the angel told Mary about the birth of Jesus.

Gabriel brings news to Mary
The angel Gabriel was active in the preparations for the birth of Jesus. First sent by God to Zechariah, he then went to Mary to announce to her that she would become the mother of the Messiah, God's promised Saviour. This is called the Annunciation, and is a popular subject in religious art. Although Christians often refer to Gabriel as an archangel, the term is not used in the Bible.

NAZARETH
The village of Nazareth, which was the home of Mary and Joseph, lay in the Roman province of Galilee. It is 32 kilo-metres from the Mediterranean coast, 24 kilometres west of the Sea of Galilee and about 112 kilometres north of Jerusalem. Although close to a number of important trade routes, it was a small and isolated village.
Archaeological remains suggest that ancient Nazareth was higher up the hill than the present village.

GOD REASSURES JOSEPH

✤ **Matthew 1** ✤

Then Joseph realized that Mary was expecting a baby before they were married, he was terribly upset. She had always seemed so pure and lovely, he never imagined she would be unfaithful to him with another man. Sadly, Joseph knew that he could not marry her, but being kind, he decided to break their engagement quietly, so that she would not suffer too much public shame and disgrace.

Joseph was still thinking about his disappointment, when God's angel appeared to him in a dream with a reassuring message. "Don't be upset, Joseph," the angel said. "Go ahead and marry Mary, because it is God himself who has conceived the child by the power of the Holy Spirit. And when the boy is born, you are to name him Jesus, because he will save his people from their sins."

When Joseph woke up, he felt relieved that, after all, Mary had not sinned with another man. And he was proud and excited that as a descendant of the mighty King David, it would be through his family that the eagerly awaited Messiah would be born.

Being a righteous man who trusted God, Joseph obeyed and quickly married Mary as they had planned. But he did not sleep with her until after she gave birth to her son, Jesus.

Joseph
The Roman Catholic, Eastern Orthodox and Episcopal churches honour Joseph as a saint. We know little about his life after he and his family settled in Nazareth, but we are told that he was a craftsman or carpenter. Early Christian legends portrayed him as an aging widower with children of his own when he married Mary, but marriage customs of the day make it much more likely that he was in his mid-teens when they married.

BORN IN A STABLE

✤ Luke 2 ✤

Not long before Mary was due to give birth, the Roman emperor, Augustus, ordered everyone to register in their home towns so they could be counted in order to work out how much tax to collect. So Joseph loaded his donkey with a few possessions and took Mary on the long journey south from Nazareth to Bethlehem, which was the town of his ancestor, David.

When they arrived, Mary and Joseph were exhausted and looked forward to a good night's sleep in one of the town's inns. But Bethlehem was so full of visitors that there wasn't an empty room anywhere. Joseph was worried because it was nearly time for Mary to have her baby. Eventually, they found a stable and decided that they would rest there.

When Mary gave birth to her son, she wrapped him snugly in strips of cloth to keep him warm and secure, then laid him gently in a manger full of hay where the animals fed, so he could sleep comfortably.

Joseph and Mary were delighted with their new baby son and called him Jesus, just as the angel had told them to.

Madonna and child
Over the centuries the virgin Mary, the Madonna, has been a popular subject for works of art. According to legend, Luke was the first to paint a picture of the Madonna, although the oldest known pictures of her are in the catacombs of the early Christians just outside Rome. The Madonna and child together have also been an important source of inspiration for artists.

Coins of Caesar Augustus
Caesar Augustus was the first, and perhaps the greatest, Roman emperor. Augustus means "exalted" – a title which the Roman Senate awarded him in 27BC. His rule (31BC–AD14) was a golden age in Roman literature and architecture. In addition he expanded the Roman empire to include the whole of the Mediterranean world.

The Church of the Nativity
The Church of the Nativity in Bethlehem is said to be the oldest Christian church in existence. Built in AD325, it has been added to over the centuries. The low 'Door of Humility' stopped people riding into the church. Today, Roman Catholic, Greek Orthodox and Armenian Christians share the church.

THE SHEPHERDS AND THE WISE MEN

✦ Matthew 2; Luke 2 ✦

In the fields nearby, some shepherds were keeping an eye on their sheep. Suddenly an angel appeared to them and their eyes were dazzled by the glory of God.

The shepherds were overcome with fear, but the angel reassured them. "Do not be afraid. I come to you with a message of great happiness for everyone. This very night, in the quiet back streets of Bethlehem, the Saviour has been born.

You will know that what I have told you is true when you discover the child, neatly wrapped in strips of cloth and lying in a manger."

As soon as the angel had finished speaking, the dark night sky was filled with a huge crowd of angels, all praising God. "Glory to God and peace to all the peoples of the earth," they sang.

When the angels disappeared, the shepherds raced off to Bethlehem and

found Jesus, exactly as the angel had told them. After paying their respects to Joseph and Mary, they told everyone they met about the unique baby boy.

Soon, other visitors came looking for Jesus. Wise men from a distant eastern country arrived in Jerusalem and began making inquiries about the presence of a new king.

"For many days we have followed a star that will lead us to him. We want to worship the new king and present him with gifts," they said.

When King Herod learnt of their arrival, he was alarmed and quizzed his advisors about the possible birthplace of the long-awaited Saviour. They told him about one prophecy which predicted that the Saviour would be born in Bethlehem.

Then, unknown to anyone else, Herod spoke to the wise men and discovered how long they had been following the star. He directed them to Bethlehem saying, "When you discover the child, let me know, so that I can come and worship him as well."

So the wise men set off for Bethlehem, following the star until it came to a halt above where Jesus was staying. They entered the house, their hearts pounding with joy at the thought that their long journey was at an end.

When they saw Jesus, they fell on their knees and worshipped him. Then they opened their bags to reveal the precious presents that they had brought: gold, frankincense and myrrh.

When they left, the wise men did not go to see King Herod because they had been warned in a dream to return home without going back to Jerusalem.

The wise men's journey
The Bible says that the wise men, or magi, had travelled from the east. They could have come from Persia, Babylonia, or southern Arabia. We do not know how many wise men there were, although it is often assumed that there were three of them, because they brought three gifts.

GREAT REJOICING!

✤ Luke 2 ✤

When Jesus was just a few weeks old, Mary and Joseph took him to the temple in Jerusalem to present him to God, as the law required. They offered two young birds as a sacrifice of thanks for the gift of a child.

There was a devout man in Jerusalem, called Simeon. God had promised him that he would not die before he had seen the Christ, the anointed one of God.

Led by the Holy Spirit, Simeon entered the temple while Jesus and his parents were there. Shaking with excitement, Simeon asked if he could hold the baby in his arms.

As he cradled Jesus close to his chest, Simeon praised God: "Lord of all, now I can die in peace, for you have kept your promise to me. With my own eyes I can see the child who will bring your salvation. He will bring glory to Israel and be a light to the Gentiles."

Mary and Joseph were astounded as they listened to his words. Then Simeon turned to them and whispered to Mary, "Your child will bring joy to many people. But he will also provoke anger in the hearts of many in this land and will cause you great pain, too."

Scarcely had Simeon finished speaking, than they were approached by another stranger. She was an elderly prophet, called Anna, who was continually in the temple fasting and praying.

When she saw Jesus, Anna too gave thanks to God. She talked endlessly about Jesus to everyone who was longing for the time when God would come and set Jerusalem free.

When Joseph and Mary had carried out their obligations, they returned to their home in Nazareth. As the years passed, Jesus grew into a child full of God's grace and wisdom.

Offering a sacrifice
Forty days after the birth of a child, the Jewish law required a mother to go to the temple to offer a sacrifice of thanksgiving. The normal sacrifice was a lamb and a pigeon, or dove, but poor people were allowed to present two pigeons or doves instead.

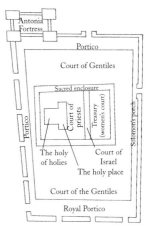

Presentation in the temple
The law stipulated that the firstborn child was to be dedicated to serve in the temple. In a ceremony, parents paid money to the priests who served there in place of the firstborn son.

Courts of the temple
This floor plan shows the layout of the temple courtyards in Herod's day. Anyone was permitted to enter the Court of the Gentiles, but only Jews were allowed to go into the Inner Court. Mary would have been able to enter the Treasury or Women's Court, while men could go into the Court of Israel. Only the high priest could enter the Holy of Holies.

ESCAPE FROM HEROD

✤ Matthew 2 ✤

beside himself with rage.

He summoned his soldiers and, shaking with anger, he commanded, "Go straightaway to Bethlehem, and hunt dow every baby boy under the age of two. The kill every one of them! You must show no mercy and make no exceptions."

So the soldiers went to Bethlehem, where they carried out their grim task,

After the wise men had left Bethlehem, an angel appeared to Joseph one night in a dream.

"Quick!" the angel said, "you must leave here as soon as possible. Take Jesus and Mary with you and flee to Egypt. You must stay there until I tell you that it is safe to return. You are in great danger here, because King Herod has decided to kill the child, and will leave no stone unturned in his search for him."

So, that very same night, Joseph woke Mary and Jesus. Gathering up all that they had, they set off in great haste on the long journey to Egypt.

Meanwhile, King Herod was anxiously waiting for news from the wise men. They had promised to come back and tell him where he could find Jesus. When Herod finally realized that the wise men had tricked him and that they had no intention of returning to see him, he was

Travel by donkey
In paintings like this one, the holy family are shown travelling to Egypt on a donkey. These animals have been used for centuries, both for riding and as pack animals. In Bible times, if a married couple had only one donkey, the husband usually walked alongside while the wife rode. The saddle was only a covering tied onto the donkey's back, and a simple halter served as a bridle.

leaving a trail of bloodshed behind them. Day after day, the air was pierced by the screams of the mothers of the young boys.

Soon after this awful event, King Herod died. Once more, an angel appeare to Joseph in a dream. "Take your family with you and return to Israel. You will be safe, because the people who were trying t kill Jesus are all dead."

So Joseph, Mary and Jesus left Egyp and travelled back to Israel.

When they arrived, they heard that Herod's son, Archelaus, was now the ruler of Judea, so they were afraid to go there. Instead, they travelled further north and settled in the town of Nazareth, in the region of Galilee.

IN MY FATHER'S HOUSE

✤ Luke 2 ✤

Each year, Jesus' parents went to Jerusalem for the Passover feast. When Jesus was twelve, he travelled there with them.

When the feast had finished, his parents set off for home, travelling in a large group of family and friends. They thought that Jesus was somewhere in the group, and were completely unaware that he had stayed behind in Jerusalem.

After a day, as they settled down to rest, Mary and Joseph were alarmed to discover that they could not find Jesus. They questioned all their relatives and friends, but no one had seen Jesus since they had left the city.

So his parents hurried back to Jerusalem and began looking everywhere for a sign of him. For three agonizing days, they searched high and low, but they could not find Jesus anywhere.

Eventually, they went to the temple, and there they found him. Jesus was sitting among the teachers of the law, listening to them and challenging them with all manner of questions. Everyone who heard him was amazed by his understanding and his answers.

But his mother and father were less impressed. "Jesus, how could you have treated us in this way? We have been beside ourselves with worry ever since we realized you were not with us," they chorused.

"Why were you looking for me?" he replied. "Didn't you know that I would be here, in my Father's house?"

But they did not understand the significance of his answer.

Relieved to be reunited with their son, they left Jerusalem and returned to Nazareth together. Jesus continued to grow in wisdom. He obeyed his parents in everything and was a delight both to God and to all the people who knew him.

Mary and Joseph's journeys
Mary and Joseph travelled first to Bethlehem, then fled to Egypt, and finally returned to Nazareth. Archelaus, the new ruler of Judea and Samaria, was a cruel tyrant, so Mary and Joseph decided to avoid his territory and settled in Galilee, to the north.

Boys in Mea Shearin
The Mea Shearin district of Jerusalem is a very orthodox Jewish area of the city. Many synagogues include a school where children study Jewish history, the Hebrew language, and Judaism. Judaism is the world's oldest major religion and the first to teach the belief in one God.

Jesus and the teachers of the law
The teachers in the temple would have been Pharisees and other experts in the Jewish law. These men based their studies on the Torah – the first five books of the Old Testament. They would have met in the courtyards of the Temple to teach and discuss the Jewish law.

JOHN BAPTIZES JESUS

✤ Matthew 3; Mark 1; John 1 ✤

John the Baptist
John the Baptist was Jesus' cousin. He prepared people for Jesus' ministry by saying they needed to turn away from their sins and receive God's forgiveness. He preached in the desert of Judea, and many people came a long way to confess their sins and to be baptized in the river Jordan.

John the Baptist preached an important message from God in the Judean desert. Crowds flocked to hear him. He dressed in camel skins and ate locusts and wild honey.

"Tell God that you are sorry for your sins, and he will forgive you!" the prophet cried, preparing people for Jesus the Messiah. John baptized people in the river Jordan, to show that they had turned away from their old life of sin and now wanted to serve God.

John knew that the religious leaders would never change their ways. "You nest of snakes," he said, "pretending to be good when your evil actions speak louder than any words! Simply being Jewish won't save you from God's judgement."

"Someone is coming who is far more important than me," John told the crowds "someone whose sandals I am not worthy to untie. He will baptize you with the powerful Holy Spirit."

That man was Jesus himself, who asked John to baptize him. John bowed

River Jordan
This river flows from Mount Hermon north of Galilee down to the Dead Sea. It passes through the Jordan Valley which is the lowest rift valley in the world. In biblical times the valley was heavily forested and wild animals roamed there. The river is difficult to cross towards its southern end because it flows very quickly. There were no bridges across it in biblical times.

Sandals
The sandals of Jesus which John said that he was unworthy to untie might have looked something like the ones pictured here. They were generally made of leather and consisted of a sole with thongs attached, which were laced around the ankle or leg. When he compared himself with Jesus, John felt unfit to perform even the duties that a servant would have carried out.

THE DEVIL TEMPTS JESUS

✤ Matthew 4 ✤

After his baptism, the Holy Spirit led Jesus into the desert so that God could allow his enemy, the devil, to test him.

For forty days Jesus ate nothing, and by the end he was extremely hungry. The devil tried to get him to do wrong by saying, "If you are really God's Son, why don't you use your power to turn these stones into tasty bread?"

Firmly, Jesus replied, "Scripture says that people need more than bread to live on. They need to obey every word that God has spoken."

Then the devil took Jesus to the highest part of the temple in Jerusalem and again tried to tempt him. "Jump off and see if God saves you! Doesn't Scripture say that God's angels will catch you?" But Jesus answered, "God also says that we must not play games and test him."

Finally, the devil took Jesus to a high mountain so he could see all the world. "I will give you power over it all, if you will worship me as your master."

But nothing would stop Jesus in his mission. "Go away, Satan!" he said. "The only person I will ever serve is the Lord my God."

The devil realized that he could not tempt Jesus, so left him alone. Then God sent his angels to help Jesus recover.

umbly before him. "Master, should it ot be you who baptizes me?"

But Jesus insisted that this was hat God wanted. As Jesus rose out of he water, the Holy Spirit came upon im like a dove, and a voice cried from eaven, "This is my own dear Son and am very pleased with him."

The devil
The devil is a spiritual being who opposes God's purposes by tempting people to disobey God. The temptations that Jesus resisted were very real, but because he remained faithful to God in the face of them, he is the model for all Christians when they are tempted.

THE MINISTRY OF JESUS

John the Baptist's ministry made way for the coming of Jesus Christ. Jesus Christ began his public ministry in Galilee. Opposition to his miracles and teaching grew, as Jesus made his way to Jerusalem.

Jesus

It is thought that Jesus was born in about 4BC. Miraculous events surrounded his conception and birth in the stable at Bethlehem. His parents then fled with him to Egypt to escape Herod, and when they returned they settled in Nazareth, an obscure village in Galilee. Jesus had a very ordinary upbringing. He was probably apprenticed to the trade of Joseph as a carpenter, and lived in a simple home with several younger brothers and sisters. Because Joseph isn't mentioned much in the Bible, it is thought that he died while Jesus was young. Jesus' public ministry began when he was about thirty years old and lasted for roughly three years.

The Sermon on the Mount

Political situation

Jesus was born in the time of the Roman emperor Augustus, when Palestine was under Roman occupation. Augustus had unified the whole of the Mediterranean world under one peaceful government, and each province paid him regular taxes. When he died in AD14, he was succeeded by Tiberius.

Mary and Joseph escape

The Romans ruled through a succession of Jewish Herodian kings; it was Herod Antipas who built the city of Tiberias on the Lake of Galilee, who had John the Baptist executed, and who was involved in the judging of Jesus. The Romans were careful to respect the customs and beliefs of their subjects, but they found the religion and nationalism of the Jews difficult to handle.

The teachings of Jesus

Jesus' teaching is based very firmly on the Old Testament and his teaching method is very similar to that used by traditional Jewish rabbis; for example, his use of arguments from the scriptures, or his use of parables. What made his teachings different from anything that had gone before, however, was that he vividly brought to life the formalized teachings of the Old Testament law. He taught using examples from personal experience and simple stories from everyday life, to illustrate religious truths or moral lessons. The illustrations he used were familiar to his listeners, and his teaching, far from

being for the privileged few, was accessible to everyone.

The Pharisees were violently opposed to Jesus because they saw that his teaching compromised their interpretation of the law. Until now they had studied and interpreted the scriptures for the people – most of whom were illiterate – and had demanded strict adherence to the ritual law and to the established traditions. Jesus criticized the Pharisees because he saw they had distorted the original intention of God's law; it had become a heavy, dry burden for most people, so that following God was hard for them.

The kingdom of God

When Jesus spoke about the kingdom of God, he wasn't referring to a place. He meant 'God's reign' – his rule. He was not referring to something political – he had not come to deliver the Jews from their Roman overlords. For Jesus, God's kingdom meant God's rule in the human heart. When he spoke about it it was to invite people to acknowledge God's rule and humbly to submit themselves to it.

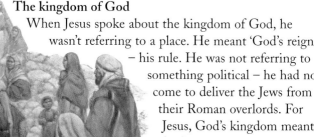

AESAR
aesar was the title of several different
oman emperors from Augustus to Nero.

ugustus (27BC-AD14)
e issued a decree that a census should
e taken of the Roman world. This meant
at Joseph returned to Bethlehem, his
ome town.

berius (AD14-37)
ohn the Baptist began his ministry during
e fifteenth year of his reign.

audius (AD41-54)
 severe famine struck the Roman world
uring his reign. He also ordered all the
ws to be expelled from Rome.

ero (AD54-68)
e undertook the first official Roman
ersecution of Christians.

he location of Jesus' ministry

ost of Jesus' public ministry took
ace in the Galilee area of Palestine.
s first miracle was at Cana in
alilee where he turned water into
ne at a wedding feast. The Sea of
alilee is where he called his first
ciples and is the setting for many

Cana in Galilee

miracles. He based himself at
Capernaum, a thriving commercial
fishing village on the lakeshore. Here
he taught in the synagogue, and on
the hillside above the lake preached
his Sermon on the Mount and fed the
five thousand. Jesus went from village
to village healing and teaching people.
At Nain he raised a widow's son to
life, at Bethsaida a blind man was
healed, and in Capernaum he healed a
paralysed man.

THE TWELVE APOSTLES

Simon Peter: originally called Simon, he was a fisherman who became one of Jesus' closest disciples. Jesus renamed him Peter, which means "rock" in Aramaic. He denied Jesus three times, but was commissioned again after Jesus' resurrection.

Andrew: Simon Peter's brother who, like Peter, was a fisherman. He is known for his role in introducing people to Jesus.

James: son of Zebedee and brother of John who with Peter and John was one of Jesus' closest disciples. He was the first of the apostles to die for his faith.

John: son of Zebedee and brother of James. He was the only apostle present at the crucifixion and the first to see the empty tomb.

Philip: he came from Bethsaida and introduced Nathanael to Jesus.

Bartholomew: also called Nathanael.

Matthew: also called Levi. Originally a tax collector employed by the Roman government.

Thomas: a twin, who at first doubted Jesus' resurrection.

James: son of Alphaeus, probably "James the younger" to distinguish him from James, son of Zebedee.

Simon the Zealot: a member of a group who stirred up rebellion against the Roman government.

Judas: son of James, also known as Thaddaeus.

Judas Iscariot: a Jewish zealot and the treasurer for the disciples. He betrayed Jesus for thirty silver pieces, but later, filled with remorse, committed suicide.

e ministry of Jesus

*Roman times, Galilee was the northenmost part of Palestine, lying between the Mediterranean Sea
the west and the river Jordan and Sea of Galilee on the east. Today the region is part of Israel.*

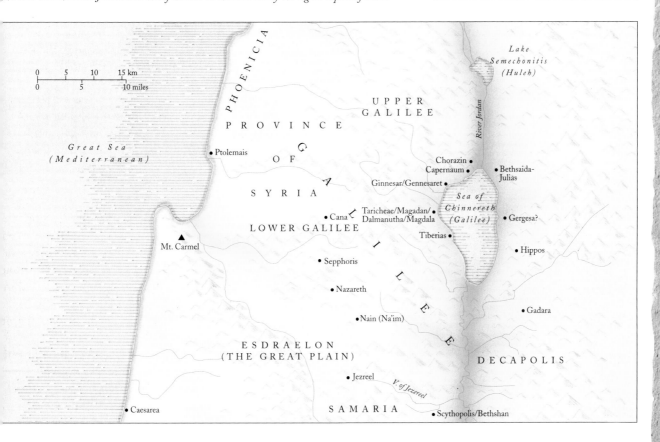

THE SPIRIT OF GOD IS ON ME

✦ Luke 4 ✦

Dove
The dove has been used as a symbol of peace ever since one brought an olive twig back to Noah after the flood. The dove resting on Jesus was a sign that he had been filled with God's love and that his mission had started. There were several kinds of dove and pigeon in Palestine.

Olive
Olives were eaten fresh, and pressed to make oil. Olive oil was sometimes poured over someone's head to 'anoint' them as a sign that they had been called by God to do a special work. Jesus said that he had been 'anointed' by God's Holy Spirit.

Jesus reading in the synagogue
Jesus went to the synagogue every week. He would have read from the scroll of Isaiah in Hebrew, and then he, or someone else, would have paraphrased verse by verse what was read in Aramaic, the common language of the day. People stood when they read from the Scriptures, but sat while teaching.

News about Jesus circulated quickly throughout the towns and the villages of Galilee. As he taught under the guidance of the Holy Spirit, everyone who heard his preaching in the synagogues marvelled at him.

One Sabbath day while in his home town of Nazareth he went as usual to the synagogue. He was handed the scroll containing the words of the prophet Isaiah. The passage which he selected began:

"The Spirit of God is on me because he has anointed me to teach good news to the poor. I have been sent to pronounce freedom to all prisoners and recovery of vision for the blind, to liberate all the downtrodden, and to declare the time of God's kindness."

He rolled up the scroll and returned it to the man who had given it to him and sat down. The whole congregation fixed their eyes on him in anticipation of what he would say.

Then he said, "This very day t[he] words of this prophecy have come true."

Everyone thought well of him and said, "Can this really be Joseph's son?"

Jesus continued, "Are you all expecting me to do a miracle of the sort you have heard I did in Capernaum?"

No one uttered a word so he spoke again, "The truth is that no prophets are eve[r] welcome in their own home towns. In the tim[e] of Elijah when there wa[s] drought and famine for over three years the grea[t] prophet did not go to hi[s] own people, but to a foreign widow in the region of Sidon. Do you suppose there were no lepers in the time of Elisha? Yet only the Syrian Naaman went to him for healing."

When the people in the synagogue heard these words they were livid. Angril[y] they pushed him out of the synagogue an[d] forced him through the winding streets u[p] onto the top of the hill on which the tow[n] stood. They were so outraged at what he had said that they intended to hurl him over the cliff's edge, but just as all seeme[d] lost he simply walked through the mob unopposed and left them standing there bewildered and confused.

FOLLOW ME

✤ Luke 5-6 ✤

ne morning Jesus was teaching the word of God on the shore of e sea of Galilee. Nearby were two pty boats.

Jesus boarded the boat that belonged Simon Peter and told him to push it a le way into the water. From here he s able to continue teaching without ing crushed.

When Jesus had finished speaking, turned to Simon and said, "Go to a ep part of the lake and cast your nets."

Simon protested, "But we have been hing all night and haven't caught a single h. Nevertheless, if you insist, I will let e nets down one more time."

To Simon's enormous surprise, the nets were full to breaking point with fish. They quickly hailed their colleagues, James and John, who came to help in another boat. But there were so many fish that both boats began to sink.

Simon realized that Jesus had performed a miracle. He fell on his knees and cried, "Don't come near me, Lord, I am a sinful person."

Jesus smiled gently. "Don't worry. From this day onwards you will catch people, not fish."

So they left all that they had, and followed Jesus wherever he went.

Gradually Jesus assembled a large group of followers. He spent one night in prayer, high on a mountain. When he came back he selected twelve of his disciples to be his special messengers, called apostles. They were: Simon Peter, Andrew, James, John, Philip, Bartholomew, Matthew, Thomas, James son of Alphaeus, Simon the Zealot, Judas son of James, and Judas Iscariot.

Sea of Galilee
The Sea of Galilee is also known as "the lake of Gennesaret" or "the sea of Tiberias" in the New Testament. It is approximately 21 kilometres long, up to 11 kilometres wide, and lies at 211 metres below sea level. Unlike the Dead Sea however, its waters are sweet and abundant with marine life. Its fisheries were famous in New Testament times and produced a flourishing export trade throughout the Roman Empire.

Fish symbol
The fish was an early Christian symbol, and still enjoys widespread use among Christians today. Persecuted Christians in Roman times originally used the sign of the fish to identify one another. The Greek word for fish, ichthus, is made up of the initial letters of the words in the phrase "Jesus Christ, God's Son, Saviour." In the Bible, the fish symbolizes God's abundant provision.

WATER BECOMES WINE

✤ John 2 ✤

Grapes

The climate and soil in Israel are perfect for growing grapes, and their production has been important since ancient times. Besides being eaten fresh, they are dried for raisins or fermented to make wine. Wine in New Testament times was sometimes mixed with other ingredients. The Bible warns against getting drunk and recommends moderation when drinking wine.

water," and he pointed to six stone water jars, of the sort used in ritual washing that had been lying in a secluded corner. They were very large – each one could hold about a hundred litres.

The servants did as he told them and when they reported back to him he said, "Pour out a little and give it to the master of the banquet to taste."

So the servants took some to the master of the banquet and asked him to

WATER JARS

Water vessels were sometimes made from gold, silver or ivory. But by far the most common and practical way of carrying and storing water was in large jars made from stone or pottery. The porous earthenware would absorb some of the liquid, which helped to stop it evaporating and kept it cool. The largest jars could hold over 100 litres of water.

The Law required Jews to cleanse themselves ritually, especially before a meal or religious ceremony, and so several water jars would have been needed at the wedding for the ritual washing of hands and utensils. The wine would have been drawn from these jars and served from jugs.

On one occasion Jesus, his mother Mary and his disciples were guests at a wedding in the Galilean town of Cana.

During the feast, the wine ran out, so Mary told her son, "The wine has run out; there is none left to drink."

Jesus replied, "Why are you telling me about this? It is not my responsibility. It is not the right time for me to act."

Nevertheless, Mary attracted the attention of some of the servants and, nodding in Jesus' direction, she whispered, "Do whatever that man tells you."

They approached Jesus and told him what his mother had said. Jesus looked at Mary (who was busy avoiding his glance) and said to them, "Fill those jars with

taste it. He had no idea where the drink had come from, but sipped some, letting it linger in his mouth before swallowing it. It was delicious. Privately he congratulated the bridegroom. "Normally the best wine served first so that by the time it has run out and only inferior wine is left, the guests have drunk too much to notice the difference. You, however, have kept the best wine until last!"

This was the first miracle that Jesus performed and in so doing he showed the first glimpse of his glory, and his disciples put their trust in him.

JESUS HEALS THE LEPERS

✤ Mark 1; Luke 17 ✤

Many of the people who came to Jesus suffered from leprosy. One day a leper approached Jesus and fell on his knees in front of him, crying out in his desperation, "If you want to, you have the power to make me well again!"

Jesus felt sorry for the man and stretched out his hand and touched him gently. "Of course I want to," Jesus said. "Be healed!"

As he spoke, the man was cured of his leprosy.

Jesus sent the man on his way, but as he did so he told him, "You must not tell anyone what has happened to you. Instead go to the priests and make the offerings as instructed in the book of Moses."

But the man paid no attention to what Jesus had said. As soon as Jesus had gone, the man began to explain to everyone what Jesus had done for him.

Another time, as Jesus was travelling to Jerusalem, he was met by ten lepers on the outskirts of their village.

When they recognized him, they shouted out, "Take pity on us, Jesus!"

As he came near to them, he could see that they were suffering from leprosy, so he said to them, "Go to the priests, so they can examine you." While they were on their way there, they were cured.

Realizing that he had become well again, one of them, a Samaritan, returned to Jesus and flung himself onto the dusty road at his feet.

"Thank you, Jesus!" he cried.

"But weren't there ten of you altogether?" asked Jesus. "What has happened to the others? Was the only one who was grateful enough to come back and thank God a foreigner?"

Jesus then looked at the man and said, "Get up and be on your way. You have been healed because you trusted in me."

Cana of Galilee
Israel rises gently from the Mediterranean coast to about 1000 metres above sea-level and then drops sharply down to the Jordan rift valley. There are great variations in temperature, but in general the country has warm wet winters and hot dry summers.

Leprosy
The Greek word in the Bible which has been translated as "leprosy" was used to describe many skin conditions, not necessarily leprosy as we understand it today. Lepers were confined to isolated colonies to prevent the spread of the infection. They had to wear torn clothing and call out "Unclean, unclean" so that no one came near them. Today leprosy can be treated, but in the time of Jesus there was no known cure.

Jesus heals a leper
Jesus was not afraid to touch any leper who came to him for healing. His attitude was in marked contrast to that of other religious leaders of the time, some of whom would even throw stones at lepers to keep them away. Jesus told the man to go to the priest to be certified ritually clean so that he could become a member of society again.

159 ✤

THE CENTURION'S SERVANT

✤ Matthew 8; Luke 7 ✤

One day, while Jesus was in the town of Capernaum, a centurion came to him and said, "Please, Lord, you must help me. My servant is very sick. He is at home, lying helpless in terrible pain."

The centurion was upset because the servant was one of his very best and he did not want to lose him.

Immediately, Jesus replied, "I will gladly go with you to your home and heal him."

But the centurion did not think that was necessary. He knew that Jesus had the power to heal without having to be with the servant.

"Lord, you are far too important to come into my house," the centurion said, humbly. "I know that just a single word of command from you will heal my servant without you being

there, because I understand that you have great authority. I myself am in the army, and when my commanding officer gives me orders, I obey him, just as those soldiers below me do exactly as I tell them."

When Jesus heard the centurion's words, he was amazed. "I have not found anyone, even in Israel, with so much faith," he told the listening crowd.

Then, turning to the centurion, he said, "Go home now, and you will find that your servant is already healed."

And when the centurion arrived home, he was delighted to find that his servant had got out of bed and was completely well again. He had been healed at the very moment that Jesus had spoken.

Roman centurion

A centurion was an officer in the Roman army. He was in charge of a group of a hundred soldiers, called a century. Centurions commanded a lot of authority because they were the working officers in direct contact with the men. They were often ordinary soldiers who had worked their way up through the ranks. The centurion who came to see Jesus may have been an officer in the army of Herod Antipas.

JESUS FORGIVES SINS

✤ Matthew 9; Mark 2; Luke 5 ✤

By now, large crowds followed Jesus everywhere he went, wanting to hear his message about God's forgiveness and to witness his power to heal the sick.

One day, Jesus was teaching in a house in Capernaum. A huge crowd of people had squeezed into the house to listen to him.

Four men arrived, carrying a sick friend on a mat because he could not walk. They wanted to ask Jesus to heal him, but they could not get into the house to talk to him. Looking around for another way in, they climbed onto the roof and made a hole. Then they carefully lowered their paralysed friend on his mat into the room where Jesus was speaking.

Jesus saw that they had faith in him and he said to the man, "My friend, your sins are forgiven."

Some religious leaders who heard this were shocked. Who did this man think he was, they wondered, angrily. Only God himself could forgive sins.

Jesus knew what they were thinking, and said, "So that you know that I have the authority to forgive sins, I will heal this man." And he turned back to the paralysed man, and said in a firm voice, "Get up, pick up your mat, and go home!"

The man twitched his legs to see if he could move, then jumped up and boldly walked out in front of everyone.

The crowd were amazed at this miracle, and went away praising God.

Jesus has the power to heal
One of the purposes of Jesus' miracles was to show that he was God. When the four friends boldly lowered the paralysed man down through the roof, Jesus realized that they had faith, and he healed the man. His power to heal was a visible sign of his power to forgive sins.

Flat-roofed houses
In Jesus' time, most houses had a flat roof which was reached by an outside staircase. The roof was built by daubing a thick coating of mud onto a layer of reeds or brushwood laid over supporting wooden beams. The surface was then rolled flat. Roofs are still made in this way in some areas of the Middle East. These modern-day houses are in Jordan.

LORD OF THE SABBATH

✤ Luke 6 ✤

Plucking grain on the Sabbath
The Sabbath was supposed to be an enjoyable day of physical and mental rest and spiritual refreshment, but the religious leaders had made it a burden. They added many restrictions on activities which the Old Testament allowed; travellers could pick grain to eat on the Sabbath day.

Inside a synagogue
A synagogue is the place where Jews meet each Sabbath (Saturday) to pray and to hear the Bible read and taught. Even today in Orthodox synagogues, women sit separately in a gallery or behind a screen and are not allowed to speak. A box or "ark" containing the scrolls of the Torah is in the middle of the building.

REMEMBER THE SABBATH DAY
The Sabbath is meant to be a day of rest for everyone. Muslims celebrate it on Friday, Jews on Saturday and Christians on Sunday. The command to keep it holy (that is, set aside for God) is one of the Ten Commandments given to Moses in the Old Testament. One day's rest in seven reflects God's pattern of "work" in creation; he rested on the seventh "day". In Jesus' time the Pharisees had strict rules about what did or did not consist of work.

One Sabbath Jesus and his disciples were strolling through some cornfields. As they did so the disciples casually plucked some ears of corn, rubbed them between their hands and picked out the grain to eat.

Noticing what they were doing some Pharisees asked, "Why are you breaking the Sabbath laws?"

Jesus replied on behalf of his disciples, "Have you forgotten what you have read about the time when King David and his followers were hungry? He entered the temple, took the consecrated bread, and ate it, even though by rights only the priests were allowed to do so. What is more, he allowed his followers to do the same thing." Jesus paused and then concluded by saying, "The Son of Man is Lord of the Sabbath."

On another Sabbath, Jesus was teaching in a synagogue. In the congregation was a man whose right hand was crippled. It was all withered and useless. The

Pharisees and teachers of the law watched carefully to see if Jesus would heal the man on the Sabbath, because they were looking for an excuse to denounce him and take him to their religious court. Jesus knew exactly what they were thinking and so he deliberately told the man to stand up in a place where everyone could clearly see him.

Jesus then addressed the congregation, "I have a question for all of you. What is the correct way to behave on the Sabbath? Is it right to do good, or evil? To save a life or take it away?"

He looked around to see if anyone was courageous enough to give him an answer, but when no one said anything, he faced the man and said, "Stretch your hand right out."

In an instant the hand became powerful once again.

Jesus' opponents were outraged and they began to debate among themselves what ought to be done with him.

THE WATER OF ETERNAL LIFE

✢ John 4 ✢

Village well
Because most of the Holy Land is very dry, wells are an important source of water for people, animals and crops.

As Jesus was passing through Samaria he stopped on the outskirts of a town called Sychar, near the field that Jacob gave to his son Joseph. He was very tired and in need of a rest, so he sat down by Jacob's well while his disciples went to the town to buy some food.

Jesus was thirsty, so when he saw a Samaritan woman approach the well to draw water, he asked her, "Will you give me a drink, please?"

The woman was surprised by his request and answered, "How is it that you, a Jew, are asking me, a Samaritan, for a drink? Normally our peoples have nothing to do with each other."

Jesus replied, "If you realized who it is who is making this request, you would have asked him and he would have given you living water."

The woman was intrigued, "But sir, this well is very deep and you have no means of reaching the level of the water. Where do you hope to find this living water? Perhaps you are more resourceful than Jacob who discovered this well and used it to serve his flocks and family!"

Jesus replied, "Anyone who drinks from this water will become thirsty again, but whoever drinks from the water that I am able to give will never again be thirsty. In fact, my water will form a spring inside that will rise up to eternal life."

"Give me some of that water so that I won't have to keep coming back here to satisfy my thirst," the woman asked him.

"Fetch your husband and come back here," Jesus told her.

This embarrassed the woman. "I haven't got a husband," she mumbled.

"I know," said Jesus gently. "You have been married five times and the man you now live with is not your husband." The woman tried to change the topic of conversation. "You are obviously a prophet, sir. We have always worshipped here but you Jews say we must worship in Jerusalem. Who is right?"

"Soon it will not be important where a person worships. God is Spirit. He is bigger than any earthly location. Those who genuinely worship him will do so in spirit and in truth," responded Jesus.

"When the Messiah comes, he will explain these things to us," said the woman.

"I am the Messiah," Jesus declared.

The woman left him and raced back to the town. "I've met a man who knew my life history despite never having met me before. Perhaps he is the Messiah!" she told the people.

Samaria
The most direct route from Jerusalem to Galilee lay through Samaria. But because the Jews hated the Samaritans as "unclean" heretics they usually made a detour by travelling up the east side of the river Jordan.

THE SERMON ON THE MOUNT

✤ Matthew 5-7 ✤

The birds in the air
The house sparrow was common in Israel in Jesus' day. According to Jewish law, sparrows were ritually clean, so they could be eaten, but they were considered to be of little worth. Live sparrows are still sold in market places in the Middle East today, but fetch low prices. In his sermon, Jesus says that God looks after small birds, like the sparrow, but he cares even more for each of us.

The Mount of Beatitudes
This hillside near Capernaum is thought to be the place where Jesus gave his most famous teaching, the Sermon on the Mount. This church, which stands on the Mount of Beatitudes, was built to commemorate the event. The word "beatitude" means a blessing. It comes from the start of the Sermon on the Mount, where Jesus makes a number of statements, starting "Blessed (or happy) are people who..."

Salt
Salt was used to season food and also to preserve it. Salting fish was the main industry at Magdala on the Sea of Galilee. Much of the salt used in Israel came from the Dead Sea. In the Bible, covenants were often sealed with salt, and so it also came to symbolize faithfulness.

Jesus climbed up a hill near Capernaum and sat down. Many people followed him, and he began to teach them:

"How happy are the poor, the downcast, the humble and those who long to please God. They will receive heavenly riches, comfort, position, and deep satisfaction. How happy are people who long to be good, people who show mercy, people who are pure, people who work for peace and people who are victimized. Their desires will be fulfilled, they shall receive mercy, they will see God, and they will certainly enjoy heaven.

"You are the salt of the earth and the light of the world. Let everyone taste your flavour and see your good actions, for then they will praise God in heaven.

"I have not come to do away with the laws that Moses and the prophets taught you; indeed I am here to fulfill their laws and teaching. Every part of the law must be obeyed.

"You have heard it said, 'Do not murder'. But I tell you that even if you are angry with your brother, you will be judged. You must forgive the person who has made you angry, before you offer a sacrifice to God.

"You have heard it said, 'Do not commit adultery'. But I tell you that even looking at a woman with improper thoughts is an act of wickedness. Whatever makes you sin must be removed. It is far better to lose a part of you than to lose your life in hell.

"You have heard it said, 'An eye for an eye and a tooth for a tooth'. But I tell you that if someone hits you on the right cheek, then you should offer him your left cheek too.

"Love and pray for your worst enem and remember that God your Father mak the sun shine and the rain fall on good people and bad people alike, without discriminating. Everyone loves the people who love them. You must do more, imitating your perfect heavenly Father.

"When you give money, or when yo pray or fast, do not do it so that everyone can see and compliment you on your good behaviour. Instead do it secretly. Your heavenly Father will see what you do and reward you.

"Do not store up wealth on earth, where you can never stop it being stolen o destroyed. Instead store up wealth in heaven, where it will be completely safe.

"As you obey these commands, do not worry about what you will wear or what you will eat and drink. Life is too important to worry about these things. God cares for the flowers in the fields and the birds in the air, so he is well able to look after you, who are much

ore precious to him than they are. Search
st for God's kingdom and his goodness,
en everything else will be given to you.
o not worry about tomorrow, but
ncentrate on one day at a time.

"As you judge other people, so you
urself will be judged. It is pointless
ghlighting someone else's faults when
ur own are even bigger. Deal
th your own failings, and
en you can think about
her people's.

"Your heavenly Father is
rfect and will give you only
od things. What father
uld give his child a
ake if he asked for
ead, or a stone if he
ked for a fish? Ask God,
d he will give you good
ings. Seek and you will
nd. Knock and the door
ill be opened.

"In everything you do, remember to
treat others in exactly the same way that
you would like to be treated.

"Enter through the narrow gate.
Many people choose the wide gate that
leads to destruction. Only a few find the
life that lies through the
narrow gate."

The flowers in the fields
In spring, the hillsides of Galilee
are covered with wild flowers,
including poppies, crocuses,
daisies, anemones and these crown
marguerites. In some translations
of the Bible, Jesus speaks of the
"lilies of the field", but he may
well have been thinking of wild
flowers in general, rather
than any one plant.

BUILDING ON THE ROCK

♣ Matthew 7 ♣

Jesus was coming to the end of his long sermon on the hillside near Capernaum, but he had one more story to tell.

"Everyone who not only listens to what I say, but actually obeys me, is like the wise man who built his house on the rock," he explained. "He was sensible and realistic. He knew that the dry season would not go on for ever. Storms would come and his house would be battered by the winds. So he dug down deep till he came to rock. He then laid strong foundations and built the house on them. When the rain came, filling the streams until they flooded, and the winds blew in violent gusts, the house did not collapse. That's because its foundation was built on the rock, which was solid and firm.

"On the other hand, anyone who listens to what I say but does not obey me, is like the foolish man who built his house on sand. He saw no need to take time to lay any foundations – he simply built his house on the loose sand and shingle. When the storms came, the rainwater undermined the walls and the gale-force winds blew the precarious structure over with an enormous crash. The house was totally destroyed. Your life will only be secure if you put into practice everything I have told you."

As the crowds began drifting home, they took with them many challenging new ideas to think about. Jesus had spoken so much truth, and yet he was very different from some of their religious teachers. Their strict religious rules that made God appear harsh and unreasonable no longer seemed to make sense.

Built to stand
All buildings need deep foundations in order to withstand bad weather. These remains of a synagogue in Capernaum date back around 2,000 years. Jesus would have taught in or near here.

THE HOUSE THAT WAS BUILT ON SAND
Jesus used the example of building on sand to illustrate the foolishness of hearing his words and not putting them into practice. Sand conveyed instability, and it would have been stating the obvious to ordinary people to say that a house had to have firm foundations if it was to stand. To build on shifting sand was asking for trouble.

JESUS CALMS THE STORM

✤ Matthew 8; Mark 4; Luke 8 ✤

Jesus and his disciples had spent a tiring day teaching the crowds by the Sea of Galilee. When evening came and it was time to leave, Jesus said, "Let's go over to the other side of the lake," and so they all got into a small fishing boat.

Jesus was tired, so he lay down on a cushion at the end of the boat and, as the disciples set sail on the calm water, he fell fast asleep. Soon, a violent wind blew up across the lake, making the waves toss the boat furiously. Water crashed into the boat and lapped around the disciples' ankles, threatening to sink them.

Although they often fished on the lake, the disciples were terrified and woke Jesus up. "Teacher, look at the storm! Don't you care that we're all about to drown?"

But Jesus was not afraid. Slowly he stood up, and then spoke to the wind and the waves. "Be quiet and still!" he ordered. Immediately the wind died down and the lake became calm once more.

He turned to his companions and asked, "Why were you so frightened? After everything you've heard me say, do you still have no faith that God will look after you?"

The disciples looked at each other in complete astonishment. "What kind of man is this, who commands even the wind and the waves and they obey him?"

Jesus is Lord
Incidents such as the calming of the storm helped the disciples discover that Jesus was God in human form. He is often shown in stained glass windows as the true ruler of the world.

Sea of Galilee
The Sea of Galilee is nearly 250 metres below sea level in the rift valley of the river Jordan and surrounded by hills. This makes it liable to sudden violent storms. In the semi-tropical climate, draughts of colder air rush down from the hills and whip up the waves.

Fishing on the Sea of Galilee
Fishing was the main occupation in the towns and villages bordering the Sea of Galilee, especially around the northern shores where shoals fed on the vegetable matter swept down by the Jordan. Small boats, not unlike dhows in appearance, were propelled by sails and oars. When the wind was contrary, the crew had to row into the wind.

RAISING THE DEAD

✦ Matthew 9; Mark 5; Luke 8 ✦

Jesus realized that some of his power had left him. He looked around and asked, "Who touched my clothes?"

His disciples were amused. "With all this mob pushing and shoving, everyone is touching you!"

Jesus continued to look for who had touched him. The woman felt she could no longer hide herself in the crowd, so she nervously confessed to what she had done.

Smiling, Jesus said to her, "Daughter, your faith has made you well. Go in peace."

Even as he was talking to her, messengers arrived from Jairus' home with tragic news. "Your daughter has just died. Don't worry the teacher any more."

But Jesus paid no attention and said, "Don't worry, Jairus, trust me."

He then told everyone to wait there and he continued with only Peter, James, and John. At the entrance to the house there was a terrible noise with people wailing at the tops of their voices.

"What is all this uproar for?" asked Jesus. "The girl is not dead, merely asleep."

But everybody sneered at him, so he sent them all out of the house. With his disciples and the child's parents, he went into her room.

He took her hand and whispered, "Wake up, little girl!" In that instant she opened her eyes and stood up. Everyone was amazed, but Jesus warned them not to tell anyone what they had seen.

Jesus was with a large crowd of people near the Sea of Galilee when Jairus, one of the synagogue leaders, came up to him and fell on his knees.

"My young daughter is dying. Please come and place your hands on her so that she will recover and live," he begged.

So Jesus went with him. A large crowd milled around them as they walked. There was a woman there who, for twelve long years, had suffered from unpleasant bleeding. She had wasted all her money on doctors who were unable to help her. In fact, her condition grew steadily worse.

When she heard of all that Jesus had done, she crept up behind him thinking, "If I can just touch his clothes I will be healed." As soon as she touched him, her bleeding stopped.

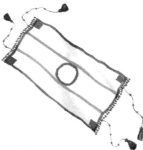

Tallith
In accordance with the law of Moses, every Jewish male was required to wear a fringe or tassel at each of the four corners of his outer garment. The tallith, as it was called, was a rectangular outer garment worn over the upper part of the body on top of a full-length tunic.

ANGER IN THE TEMPLE

✤ Matthew 21; Mark 11; Luke 19; John 2 ✤

Just before the Passover was due to begin, Jesus went up to Jerusalem. As he wandered around the temple's outer courtyards he came upon merchants buying and selling all manner of things. They were trading cattle, sheep and doves, while others were seated around tables haggling over the price of money that they wished to exchange. Jesus was horrified and he made a rough whip out of cords of rope and forced them all out of the temple area. He drove out the animals too and he overturned the tables of the money dealers, scattering their coins everywhere. Then he turned upon the dove sellers, shouting, "Take those birds and get them out of here! What right have you to turn my Father's house into a common market-place?"

Jesus' disciples had never seen him act in this way before, and they remembered the passage from the Psalms that said, "I will be overcome with zeal for your house, O God."

The Jews were indignant at Jesus' behaviour. They came to Jesus and challenged him, "Perform a miracle in order to prove that you have the right to do these things."

But all Jesus said in reply was, "If you destroy this temple then I will rebuild it within three days."

They sneered back at him, "Do you realize how long it took to build this magnificent temple? Forty-six years! And yet you come along and say that you can rebuild it in three days!" They did not realize that the temple he was referring to was his own body.

Indeed it was only when Jesus had come back to life, three days after his death, that his disciples remembered this conversation and finally understood that he had been talking about himself and not about the temple in Jerusalem.

Coins in the temple
These Jewish coins from the time of Jesus were the only currency accepted in the temple area. When Jews from other countries came to Jerusalem, they had to change their money in order to buy animals to sacrifice in the temple. Money-changers had set up tables in the Court of the Gentiles to exchange foreign currency, for which they charged more than was fair.

YOU MUST BE BORN AGAIN

✣ John 3 ✣

Torah cupboard

Every modern-day synagogue has a cupboard or chest in which the scrolls of the law, or Torah, are kept. Readings from the Torah are still given in Hebrew, and the large scrolls are handled with great respect. Pharisees like Nicodemus studied and interpreted the Torah law.

Baptism

When Jesus talked to Nicodemus about being "born with water and the Spirit", he may have been referring to baptism. Baptism symbolizes the start of new spiritual life.

Nicodemus

Nicodemus was a Pharisee and a member of the Jewish ruling council. He came to visit Jesus at night. He may have been afraid to come in the day because of his position, or he may just have wanted to talk to Jesus for a long time. This would have been difficult during the day, when Jesus was surrounded by crowds.

One of Jesus' admirers was a man who belonged to the ruling council of the Jews. His name was Nicodemus. One night, under the cover of darkness, he visited Jesus.

"Rabbi," Nicodemus addressed him, "everyone knows that you have been sent by God. Otherwise you would not be able to perform all the miracles that you are doing."

Unwilling to rise to such flattery, Jesus replied, "I tell you that it is only when someone has been born again that they can see God's kingdom."

Nicodemus was surprised by this answer, so he tried to understand what Jesus meant. "A man cannot be born again," he answered. "It would be impossible for him to go back inside his mother's womb and emerge a second time!"

Then Jesus said, "Unless a person is born with water and the Spirit they will never enter God's kingdom. Physical life gives birth to physical life, but spiritual things are born of the Spirit.

"You shouldn't be surprised that I said, 'You must be born again'. The wind blows wherever it wants to. Even though you can feel the wind and hear it, you do not know where it has come from or where it is going to. It is the same for anyone who is born of the Spirit."

Nicodemus was confused. "What do you mean?" he asked Jesus.

"How is it possible that you, a teacher of Israel, cannot understand these things, even though I have used everyday illustrations? What chance would you have if I were to speak about things in heaven? The Son of Man will be raised to give eternal life to all who trust him.

"God loves the world so much that he has sent his only Son, and everyone who trusts in him will not die, but live for ever. But anyone who does not trust in him is already lost. God did not send his Son into the world to condemn people, he sent him to offer them life and hope."

JESUS SENDS OUT HIS DISCIPLES

✤ Matthew 10; Mark 6; Luke 9 ✤

Traveller's bag
A scrip was a small bag made from woven strips of leather or other fibre. Farmers, shepherds and travellers used a scrip as a money-bag and for carrying other small personal possessions. Jesus told his disciples not to carry any possessions with them, because God would provide for their needs. They were to rely on the hospitality of the people they met.

Jesus called his twelve apostles to him and gave them authority to cast out demons and heal people. Then he sent them in pairs on a special assignment to the neighbouring towns. As they set out, he gave them these instructions:

"Teach everyone that the kingdom of heaven is near. Cure every disease, raise the dead and free people who are possessed by demons.

"Take nothing extra for the task other than the clothes you are wearing. If anyone refuses to welcome you and entertain you, leave them. Do not try to force yourselves upon them.

"The situations you are going to will not be easy. You will need to be as cunning as snakes and as trusting as doves. People will look for opportunities to trap you and punish you. But even if they bring you before the highest courts in the land, do not worry. When they challenge you, the Father himself will tell you what to say.

"Your presence will split families and you will be hated because of your relationship with me. But do not worry. Be brave and speak out what I have taught you. You have nothing to fear from someone who can only kill the body. The only person you should fear is God – and you have my word that he loves you more than anything else on earth.

"My appearance in this world has not brought peace but war. Mothers, fathers and children are divided in their opinion about me. Yet anyone who loves his family more than he loves me is worth nothing to me.

"All of my followers must be prepared even for death. Anyone who loses his life for me will find it, but anyone who thinks he is alive apart from me will lose his life.

"Remember that when someone welcomes you, they are really welcoming me. If someone gives you even a drink of water because you are one of my disciples, that person will be rewarded."

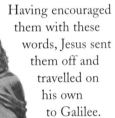

Having encouraged them with these words, Jesus sent them off and travelled on his own to Galilee.

Staff
In Jesus' day almost everyone, from the richest man down to the blind beggar, carried a staff. Travellers particularly benefited from having one, because journeys often meant walking long distances over rough ground. A walking-stick not only acted like a third leg, but was also a useful support when resting, and could even be used to fight off wild animals or snakes.

THE SOWER AND THE SOILS

❖ Matthew 13; Mark 4; Luke 8 ❖

Thistle

Thistles spring up in uncultivated or neglected ground, but are also troublesome weeds in grain fields. Jesus says that his message can be abandoned because of difficulties or temptations in life, but people with receptive minds and hearts allow the message to take root in their lives and bear fruit.

Almonds

Almonds are the first fruit trees to blossom in Palestine and the nuts were a popular food in Bible times. The chief fruits were dates, figs, grapes, olives, and perhaps apricots. But most people's diet consisted of bread and vegetables, which is why Jesus often spoke about grains and harvest.

Sowing seed

This wall painting from an Egyptian tomb shows the farmer scattering the seed by hand from a bag. The seed was ploughed into the ground by oxen. Inevitably some fell on the pathways that went through many fields, and was eaten up by birds because the surface was too compacted for it to take root.

Often Jesus told simple stories, called parables, with powerful messages lying beneath the surface. Once when he was teaching a large crowd from a boat anchored by the shore, he told them:

"A farmer set off to sow some seed on his land. He threw it in huge sweeps, and as he did so, some fell onto the well-trodden path on which he was walking. Almost as soon as the seed bounced on the hard ground, hungry birds swooped down and ate it.

"Other seed fell on rocky patches with just a thin covering of soil. The plants grew quickly at first, but soon shrivelled up, because their short roots could not find enough water to protect them from the scorching sun.

"Some seeds landed among thorns that choked the young plants.

"Others, however, fell on rich soil and gave rise to thirty, sixty or a hundred times the crop."

Jesus concluded, "Whoever hears my words, let them hear with understanding."

"Master," his disciples then asked him, "what does this parable mean?"

Jesus replied, "The seed that was sown along the path is like a person who listens to the message of the kingdom of God, but does not understand it. The devil comes and plucks away what has been sown in that person's heart.

"The seed that landed on the rocky soil is like someone who gladly listens to the message and is full of joy. But without any roots it is impossible to last. As soon as any form of difficulty or trouble comes, all enthusiasm is lost and the person falls away.

"The seed that fell among the thorns is like the person who hears the word, but is suffocated by the worries and concerns of this life and is unable to produce any fruit.

"Lastly, the seed that fell on productive soil is like the person who hears and understands the message. That person then produces a crop thirty, sixty or a hundred times what was originally sown."

JESUS TEACHES US TO PRAY

✤ **Matthew 6; Luke 11 & 18** ✤

A s the disciples watched Jesus praying, they said, "Lord, you pray all the time, so we know how important it is. Please teach us how to pray."

"What matters most is that you love God," Jesus explained. "Pray in secret and don't try to impress anyone else. Your prayers won't be more powerful if you use lots of clever words, so keep your words simple. And remember that God knows what you need, even before you open your mouth, so trust him to answer you."

Prayer
Jesus taught that prayer is a way of talking and listening to God. He gave his disciples the Lord's Prayer as an example of how to pray to God. Instead of just asking for things, it includes worship and confession.

GOD THE FATHER
One of the main teachings of Jesus was to show us that God is like a father who loves and cares for us.

Then Jesus said what they should pray.
"Our Father in heaven,
May your holy name be honoured,
may your kingdom come,
may your will be done on earth as it is in heaven.
Give us food today.
Forgive the things that we have done wrong
as we forgive the people who have wronged us.
Lead us not into temptation.
But protect us from evil.
For yours is the kingdom,
the power and the glory,
for ever and ever.
Amen."

GIVE ME HIS HEAD!

✤ Matthew 11 & 14; Mark 6; Luke 7 ✤

John the Baptist
John the Baptist had been thrown into prison because he spoke out against the marriage of Herod Antipas with Herodias, the wife of his brother Philip. The law of Moses forbade anyone to marry their brother's wife while that brother was still alive. Herod was afraid of John, but Herodias hated him, so she had him executed and his head brought to her on a meat plate.

public that she wished he was dead.

In prison John had his doubts. Even though he was in prison, he was allowed visitors. He became more and more puzzled and disappointed as Jesus went about teaching and healing people. Why hadn't Jesus set up the kingdom that John and others had expected? Word came to Jesus that John was uncertain whether Jesus really was the Messiah. So Jesus told John's disciples to report back to him about all the healings that they had seen.

At King Herod's grand birthday feast, his wife's daughter Salome got up and danced so gracefully for him that King Herod rashly promised to give her whatever she wanted as a present, even up to half his kingdom. Salome went to Herodias and said, "What shall I ask for?"

Herodias saw this as her chance to get rid of John, so she wickedly replied, "Ask Herod to give you the head of John the Baptist on a plate."

When King Herod heard what Salome wanted, he felt very afraid about killing such a good man.

John the Baptist was a bold person. He wasn't afraid to speak up for what he knew was right. On one occasion he told the Jewish leaders and the ordinary people face to face that God's kingdom was coming so they needed to turn back to God. He was very blunt as he criticized the religious leaders. He told them that it was no good relying on their religious background – a new beginning was necessary. Everyone had to get ready for the Messiah who was coming. But John didn't draw attention to himself – he was happy when people followed Jesus.

Later, when John found out that King Herod had taken Herodias, his brother's wife, and married her, he told the crowds that this was clearly wrong. King Herod ordered John to be chained up in prison, but because he respected John's holiness and was afraid to anger the people by killing their prophet, he allowed him to live. However Herodias, Herod's wife, hated John so much for shaming her in

He knew that it would be wrong to order the execution of John, but because he had made the promise in front of all his important guests, he could not change his mind without a great deal of embarrassment.

So King Herod gave the order to have John's head cut off.

A servant brought John's head to Salome, and she proudly presented the plate to her mother, who smiled with satisfaction. Meanwhile, John's disciples took his headless body away to bury it, and then told Jesus the sad news.

Bronze dancer
In Jesus' day rich people often hired beautiful women to entertain them with suggestive dancing at their banquets. Herodias's daughter Salome danced at her step-father's birthday party, and so enticed him and his guests that he foolishly vowed to give her anything she wanted.

Herod Antipas
The Herods ruled in Palestine from 48BC to AD100. Herod Antipas was the son of Herod the Great and ruled Perea and Galilee. It was he who imprisoned and beheaded John the Baptist and judged Jesus before he was crucified. He became friends with Pilate as a result of Jesus' trial.

Tiberias
Today Tiberias is a sizeable spa-town on the west shore of the Sea of Galilee. It was founded by Herod Antipas, who named it after the emperor Tiberius. Herod made it his capital because it occupied a good defensive position. Roads from all parts of his territory converged here.

JESUS FEEDS THE HUNGRY CROWD

✤ Matthew 14; Mark 6; Luke 9; John 6 ✤

Loaves and fishes
This 5th-century mosaic of the basket of five barley loaves and two Galilean mullet is set within a stone altar in the Byzantine Church of the Multiplication at Tabgha. The original food was given to Jesus by a young boy.

Tabgha, Galilee
Tabgha on the Sea of Galilee is the traditional site where Jesus took, blessed, and broke the bread and the fish and gave them to the disciples to be distributed to the 5,000. Jesus often taught crowds of people on these hillsides.

Jesus multiplies the loaves and fishes
When Jesus fed many people by a miracle, he was showing them that God is concerned for people's physical well-being as well as about their spiritual relationship with him. Christians are told in the Bible to care for people in any kind of need. They are also taught to trust God to provide for their needs and not to worry too much.

On their return from telling the good news to villages and towns, the disciples were eager to report to Jesus all that they had seen and done. It was difficult to do so, because so many people were milling around Jesus that there was not even time for them to rest, eat and regain their strength.

So Jesus said to them, "Let's go to some secluded spot away from these crowds, so that we can be alone together and you can rest."

But even as they left, many raced on ahead of them and so when Jesus arrived with the disciples, the secluded place was brimming with people. When Jesus saw them, he was filled with pity because they were wandering around like sheep without a shepherd. So he began to teach them.

As dusk began to settle, his disciples came to him and said, "It is already late and we are a long way from the nearest town. Order the people away so they can find something to eat in the villages."

"Why don't you give them something to eat?" replied Jesus.

"It would cost the same as a person earns in eight months to buy food for all these people," they said crossly.

Andrew, Peter's brother, spoke up. "There's a young boy here with five barley loaves and two small fish – but that's like a drop in the ocean to feed everyone here!"

Jesus then told the disciples to make the people sit down on the grass. There were at least 5,000 men.

Jesus then took the loaves and the fish. He prayed, and in front of everyone he broke the loaves into pieces. When he had done this, he gave them to the disciples to distribute to the expectant crowd. Next he divided the fish up as well.

In this way every single person present was able to eat as much as they wanted. In fact, when everyone had finished eating and the disciples had collected up all the remains, they were amazed to discover that there were twelve whole baskets full of leftover pieces of bread and fish.

COME TO ME, PETER

✤ Matthew 14 ✤

As soon as Jesus had fed the large crowd, he told his disciples to get back into their boat and set sail for the other side of the lake. He then dispersed the crowd before climbing up the mountainside in order to pray by himself.

Meanwhile, the disciples' boat had run into difficulty way out in the lake. Strong winds were stirring up huge waves that were crashing against the sides of the boat.

When Jesus saw this, he went to meet them, walking on the water as if it were dry land.

When the disciples noticed a figure walking to them across the tossing waves, they were petrified. "It's a ghost," they screamed in terror.

As soon as he heard their cries, Jesus reassured them, "It's me. Don't worry!"

Peter was the first to open his mouth. "Lord, if it really is you," he stuttered, "tell me to join you on the lake."

"Come towards me," Jesus ordered gently.

So, without thinking, Peter swung his legs over the side of the boat, stepped out onto the water, and began to walk towards Jesus.

When he realized what he was doing and heard the wind whistling around his head, Peter was overcome with fear. He began to sink and yelled out, "Lord, save me!"

Jesus thrust out his hand and held onto him.

He stared at Peter and said, "You have such little trust! Why did you begin to doubt me?"

Together they continued towards the boat and as soon as they were inside, the wind calmed down.

Seeing this, those who were inside the boat fell down on their knees and worshipped Jesus.

"Without doubt you are the Son of God," they exclaimed.

Sea of Galilee
This is not a sea at all but a big pear-shaped lake about 21 kilometres long and 11 kilometres wide. It lies below sea level and is surrounded by high hills and narrow ravines. The cold air on the hills sometimes rushes down and causes sudden storms on the lake; they can blow up almost without warning.

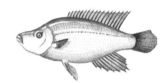

St Peter's fish
Of the twenty or so species of fish in the Sea of Galilee, the most famous is St Peter's fish, so named from the fish Peter caught with the coin in its mouth to pay his and Jesus' annual temple tax. The male is able to carry the spawn in a tiny sac under the mouth. It is known to be attracted to bright objects.

Location of the miracles
This map shows the places in Galilee where many of Jesus' miracles were performed. The Sea of Galilee was the centre of a thriving fishing industry in New Testament times and the towns around the lakeshore were busy and prosperous. Today only Tiberias remains as a town, and the precise location of many places in the Gospel narratives is uncertain.

A WOMAN'S FAITH

✦ Matthew 15; Mark 7 ✦

Dogs

These pictures of dogs are taken from Egyptian carvings and wall paintings. Although dogs were highly regarded in Egypt, they were viewed very differently in Palestine. Here, they were rarely kept as pets and usually roamed wild in the streets, living off refuse and dead animals. Jewish people regarded dogs as unclean and a source of disease. Calling someone a "dog" was not a compliment!

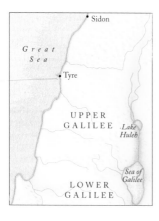

Tyre and Sidon

The wealthy and magnificent cities of Tyre and Sidon lay about 50 kilometres northeast of Galilee. In New Testament times, these cities were heavily influenced by Greek culture, but they were also proud of their historic heritage as centres of Canaanite religion and worship.

THE GENTILES

The Greek woman in this story was a Gentile – someone who was not Jewish. The Jews considered the Gentiles unlikely to receive God's blessing, and often described them as "dogs". Jesus says that he had come to minister first to the Jews, "the lost sheep of Israel." But the Gentile woman, instead of being offended, was willing to settle for the "crumbs" that even the pet dogs ate from their master's table. Jesus rewarded her faith and healed her daughter.

Jesus and complained, "Send that woman away. She is bothering us with all her begging. She does nothing but rant and rave!"

In reply Jesus said, "I was sent to save only the lost sheep of Israel."

But the woman flung herself on her knees in front of him and begged again, "Lord, please help me! Save my daughter from this evil spirit."

"It would not be right to take bread from the children and throw it to the dogs to eat," Jesus said to her.

"What you have said is true," the woman admitted. But then she added, "However, when crumbs and scraps fall from the table, then even the dogs are allowed to eat them up."

Jesus smiled and spoke one more time to the woman. "Your reply shows how great your faith is! Go home – your request has been granted."

So the woman got up and rushed straight home. When she got there, she found that her little girl was lying quietly on her bed and that the demon had left her, just as Jesus had said.

Shortly afterwards, Jesus left that area and travelled back to the shores of Lake Galilee.

He went up on a mountainside and huge crowds of people came to him, bringing with them the lame, the blind, the crippled, people who could not speak, and many others.

They came to Jesus and he healed them all. The lame could walk, the blind could see, people who had never been able to speak suddenly found that they could talk, and the crippled were made strong!

Then all the people gave thanks to God and praised him for what he had done for them.

Jesus and his disciples travelled to the area of Tyre and Sidon. They stayed in a house, hoping that no one would hear of their presence.

But a Greek woman from the area found out that Jesus was staying there and came to see him.

She was in great distress and wailed at the top of her voice, "Son of David! Be merciful to me, my Lord! I have a daughter who is possessed by a demon and is suffering terribly."

But Jesus did not reply to her. After a while his disciples went to

JESUS IS GLORIFIED

✤ **Matthew 16-17** ✤

One day, while they were in Caesarea Philippi, Jesus asked his disciples, "Who do people say that I am?"

They replied, "Some people say that you are John the Baptist, other people think that you are one of the prophets – Elijah or Jeremiah."

"But what about you?" Jesus asked. "Who do you say that I am?"

Peter answered, "You are the Messiah, the Son of the living God."

"Peter, you are blessed, because God himself has shown you this," Jesus replied. "You, Peter, are a rock, and on this rock I will build my church."

Jesus then explained to his disciples that he was destined to die in Jerusalem.

About a week later, Jesus took three of them, Peter, James and John, up onto a high mountain. While they were there, his appearance changed before their eyes. His face shone brightly like the midday sun and his clothes turned a dazzling white. At that moment, Moses and Elijah appeared and began talking with Jesus.

Peter was overawed by what he saw and said to Jesus, "Lord, how good it is that we are all here together. Would you like me to make three shelters for you?"

But just as Peter was speaking, a dazzling cloud descended and covered them all. From somewhere inside the cloud, they heard a voice say, "This is my beloved Son. Listen to everything that he says, for I am very pleased with him."

This alarmed the three disciples, who fell flat on the ground, too terrified to look up. They lay there until a hand touched each of them softly on the shoulder. It was Jesus. "Get up," he said. "Do not be afraid." When they plucked up courage to look round, they saw that only Jesus was left.

As they walked back down the mountain, Jesus warned them, "Do not tell anyone what you have seen. You can only mention it when the Son of Man has been brought back to life from the dead."

Jesus transfigured
This story is often called the "transfiguration", which means a change in form or appearance. When Jesus was transfigured on the mountain, God's glory shone through him. This is often shown as a halo of light around his head, enabling his disciples to recognize that he was indeed the Son of God.

Church of the Transfiguration
This modern church stands on Mount Tabor in Galilee – the traditional site of the transfiguration. In the sixth century, three churches were built here in memory of the shelters that Peter wanted to make for Jesus, Moses and Elijah. But many experts now believe that Mount Hermon, near Caesarea Philippi, was the site of the transfiguration.

THE GOOD SAMARITAN

♣ Luke 10 ♣

Dry wadi
This dry wadi near Jericho illustrates the barren landscape on the road from Jerusalem to Jericho, a journey of 30 kilometres. The quiet road descends steeply from 850 metres above sea level to about 250 metres below sea level, and the rocky terrain affords many hiding places for robbers.

Once, a teacher of the law challenged Jesus. "Teacher," he said, "tell me what I have to do to inherit eternal life."

"What does the law say?" Jesus replied.

"'Love the Lord with all your heart, soul, strength and mind' and 'Love your neighbour as much as you love yourself,'" came the answer.

"That is right," said Jesus. "If you do that, you will live."

"But who exactly is my neighbour?" the man asked. Jesus answered him with a story:

"A man was journeying from Jerusalem down the remote road that leads to the city of Jericho. He was attacked by thieves who overwhelmed him and took everything that he had, before leaving him for dead. Later, a priest came by, but all he did was cross over and continue walking as if he hadn't seen anything out of the ordinary. A Levite came along and did exactly the same. Eventually a Samaritan saw the battered body lying in the dust, was filled with compassion and immediately went to help the injured man. He bandaged him up as best he could. Then he gently eased him onto his donkey and took him to an inn.

"The next morning he had to leave, but left some money with the innkeeper saying, 'Take care of this man for me. When I return I will pay you for any extra expenses necessary for his care.'"

Jesus finished the story and then asked the teacher of the law, "Which of these three men acted as a neighbour to the man who had been so ruthlessly attacked?"

"The one who showed kindness towards him," he replied.

"Then go and do the same," Jesus concluded.

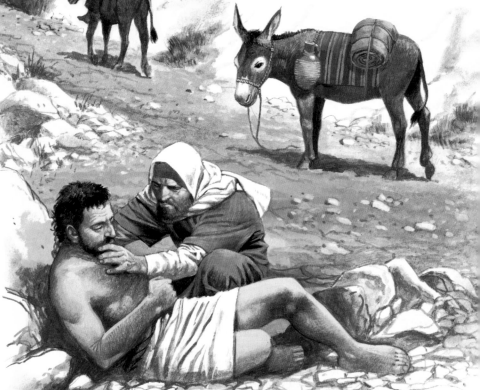

Olive press
Olives are rich in oil which was squeezed out of them by rolling a heavy stone over them. The oil, which is recognized today as one of the healthiest sources of fat, was used for cooking and also burned in lamps. The "good Samaritan" used it as an antiseptic, but it would not have been very effective.

THE GREAT WEDDING FEAST

✤ Matthew 22; Luke 14 ✤

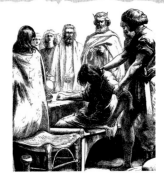

hoped would come were unsuitable. So I want you to go out into the highways and byways, inviting anyone you should meet to come and share in my joy.'

"The servants set off and invited everyone they came across as they went out into the streets of the city. So many people came that the banqueting hall was full of people from every corner of society.

"Later, as the king was mingling with his guests, he came upon a man who was not dressed in the appropriate wedding clothes. 'My friend,' the king said, 'why is it that you are not wearing wedding clothes?'

"The man was at a loss for words so the king called his servants and ordered them, 'Tie this man up and expel him from my party into the night.'"

Jesus then concluded the parable by saying, "Many people are given invitations but only a few are chosen."

The wedding hall
Weddings were occasions of great rejoicing, with sumptuous foods and unlimited wine. Guests were expected to wear special clothes. To refuse an invitation was an insult. Jesus' parable shows that God invites undeserving people to participate in the blessings of his kingdom.

Servants cooking
The wall painting shows servants preparing geese and other meats for a banquet. A special steward was responsible for sampling all the food and drink before it was set before the guests.

Jesus told the people another parable: "If you want to know what the heavenly kingdom is like, I will tell you.

"There was once a king who made extravagant preparations for the wedding feast of his son. When everything was ready he told his servants to invite the guests, but they all refused to attend.

"Undeterred, he commissioned more servants to go and fetch the guests saying, 'Inform everyone that the banquet is ready. Tell them that I have killed my finest oxen, and that the cows which have been fattened specially for the occasion are roasting on the spit. Everything is in place. All that I now lack is people to share my joy with. Come at once to my feast.'

"But the guests were not interested in going and they carried on their affairs as if nothing had happened. Some even grabbed hold of the messengers, beat them and killed them. When he heard about this, the king was livid. Consumed with anger, he called out his army and gave them orders to kill the murderers and destroy their city.

"Once more the king turned to his servants and said, 'My banquet is still waiting to be enjoyed. The guests I had

LOOKING FOR THE LOST

♣ Luke 15 ♣

When the Pharisees saw Jesus talking with tax collectors and sinners, they were very disapproving. If Jesus was truly holy, then surely he would not mix with such dubious people, they thought. But Jesus wanted to show them how much God wants everyone to know him, whether they are good or bad.

"Imagine that you owned a flock of a hundred sheep, but then discovered that one of them had gone missing," Jesus began telling the crowd.

"Wouldn't you leave the other ninety-nine safely grazing in their field, then search high and low for your lost sheep? What joy and relief you would feel when you found it! You would want to hurry home with it on your shoulders to share your happiness with your friends and neighbours."

Jesus looked kindly at the people in the crowd, so many of whom were treated as outcasts. "Take courage, my friends, because the angels in heaven rejoice whenever just one sinner says sorry and turns to God. In fact, they are more delighted with the one sinner than with ninety-nine people who are already living a good life."

"I will give you another example," Jesus continued. "Imagine that a woman owned ten very precious silver coins, but then lost one. Wouldn't she carefully sweep every nook and cranny of her home, and search with her lamp until she found it? And when she found it, wouldn't she rush out to celebrate with her friends and neighbours? God, too, searches carefully for everyone who is lost. He is so happy when even one sinner turns to him."

The lost piece of silver
In this story, the woman sweeps the floor with her straw broom as she searches her house for the silver coin. In New Testament times, houses were very dark because they had only small windows, set high up in the walls. The woman would have found it difficult to spot the missing coin on the beaten earth floor. The coin may have been part of her head-dress. It was very precious and would have been worth a whole day's wages.

WELCOME HOME!

✤ Luke 15 ✤

Jesus told the crowd another story about God's great love and forgiveness.

"A man had two sons. The younger son asked his father to give him his share of the inheritance, so that he could leave home," Jesus began. "But the son was foolish, and wasted his money on wild living in a foreign country until he had nothing left. When famine struck, he had to take a job looking after the pigs there. He was so desperately hungry that he longed to eat their food.

"At last he could bear no more. Perhaps if he said sorry to his father, he could get a job on the family farm, he thought.

"So he set off for home, but before he arrived, his father spotted him and rushed out to meet him. The father's heart was bursting with love and forgiveness for his son, and he hugged him warmly.

Carob pods
The carob is an evergreen tree. It produces pods which are about 15–25 centimetres long. When they are ripe, the pods contain a sweet syrup which can be used for food and to make cloth and cosmetics. In New Testament times, carob pods were fed to pigs and cattle, and were also eaten by poor people because they were very cheap. Carob pods may well have been the food that the son in this story fed to the pigs.

Illuminated Bible
Stories like this parable were first passed on orally and later written down to form the New Testament of the Bible. Before printing was invented, all Bibles had to be copied out by hand. This work was often done by monks, who decorated the books with beautiful lettering and illustrations.

"'Father, you have every right to disown me as your son,' said the son, ashamed of his past behaviour.

"But his father simply replaced his son's rags with expensive clothes and declared, 'Let's have a feast to celebrate your return!'

"When the older son heard the music and dancing, he felt jealous. 'This is not fair!' he protested to his father. 'I have worked hard for years without causing you any trouble, but you have never thrown a party for me!'

"His father calmly explained, 'My son, everything I have has always been yours. But please share my happiness, because your brother has come back from the dead.'

"In the same way," Jesus ended, "God also welcomes every sinner who comes home to him."

Wild boar
The domestic pig of the Middle East is descended from wild boar, like the one pictured here. Wild pigs lived in Palestine in Jesus' day and sometimes destroyed an entire vineyard or field of crops as they foraged for food. Pigs were forbidden food to the Jews, who considered them filthy and ugly animals. The son in Jesus' story must have been truly desperate to take a job looking after pigs and consider eating their food.

THE GOOD SHEPHERD

✣ John 10 ✣

to them. I am the gate, and whoever come in through me will be saved. Such a perso can come and go as they please and they will find good land on which to graze. When a thief comes he steals and destroy but I have come in order that my people may enjoy life to the full.

"I am the good shepherd. I lay dow my life for my sheep. When a casual worker sees the wolf approaching the sheep, he will run away because the fate o the sheep is of little interest to him. As soon as he has deserted the flock, the wol gets in among the sheep and creates havo as he pleases. But my sheep are protected and secure in my love.

"I am the good shepherd. As my Father knows me, and I know him, so I ar known by my sheep. I am going to give m life for the sheep. I care for my sheep. An when I have given my life for the sheep, I will take it up again.

"As well as the sheep of this pen I have others, too. When I have brought them, there will be one flock and one shepherd for all my sheep.

"My Father loves me because I am about to lay down my life for the sheep. I lay down my life of my own free will – no one can force me to do it, it is my own decision."

The good shepherd
Every shepherd carried a rod, or staff, so that he could catch hold of and rescue any sheep that fell down a ravine or got caught in a bush. At night the shepherd held his rod across the entrance to the sheepfold and the sheep passed under it as they were counted into the fold. The shepherd was also armed with a wooden club with which to beat off any wild animals that sought to attack the flock. Jesus is often described as the Good Shepherd and his people as the sheep, whom he protects and keeps secure from danger.

Jesus told his followers, "The truth is that anyone who does not enter the sheep pen by the gate, but seeks to gain entry by another entrance, is a thief. The shepherd enters by the gate, and when he does, the watchman gladly opens it for him. The shepherd knows the name of each of his sheep and they recognize his voice so that when he calls them they follow him. They will never go after someone they do not know; instead they will run away, because they do not recognize his voice.

"I am the sheep's gate. Everyone who ever came before me was a thief or a robber, but no matter what they said the sheep paid no attention

COMING TO JESUS

✤ Matthew 19 ✤

Many people brought their children to Jesus so that he could pray for them and bless them by laying his hands upon them. His disciples objected to this and became angry with the parents.

When Jesus heard about their attitude, he said, "Do not stop small children from coming to me. The kingdom of heaven belongs to them and all those like them." He then placed his hands upon them and left.

Once a young man approached Jesus and asked him, "Teacher, tell me what good things I must do to receive eternal life."

"Why are you asking me about what is good?" Jesus replied. "God is the only one who is good. If you want eternal life, then you must obey the commandments."

"Which commandments?" the man asked.

"Do not murder, do not commit adultery, do not steal or tell lies about other people. Honour your parents and love your neighbour as you love yourself," Jesus answered.

"I have obeyed them all," said the young man. "Is there anything else that I must do?"

"Yes," said Jesus, looking at the man directly yet lovingly. "If you are seeking perfection, then go and sell all that you have and give the proceeds to the poor and then follow me. Then you will have treasure in heaven."

The young man left Jesus deeply upset, because he was very rich.

Jesus turned to his disciples and said, "See how hard it is for rich people to enter heaven's kingdom! The truth is that it is easier for a large camel to go through the eye of a tiny needle than for a rich man to enter God's kingdom."

"If that is so, then who can be saved?" the disciples asked themselves.

"What is impossible for human beings is possible for God," said Jesus.

Peter then exclaimed, "We have given up everything to follow you. What will our reward be?"

"When the new age begins and the Son of Man is upon his throne, his followers will judge the twelve tribes of Israel. And every person who has left family or possessions for my sake will receive a hundred times as much in return as well as eternal life. But," concluded Jesus, "many who are first in line will become last and many who are last in line will become first."

Camels
The camel can travel great distances carrying heavy loads. The camel's hump is a store of fat, which allows the animal to go for days with little food or water.

The needle's eye
A needle's eye was a smaller door within a large city gate that allowed people access to the city at night when the main gates were shut. A camel would be too big to squeeze through this small door.

185 ✤

LAZARUS BROUGHT BACK TO LIFE

✤ John 11 ✤

Death and burial
In the hot climate of Palestine, a dead body would begin to smell very quickly, so when people died, they were buried on the same day. The body was washed and then wrapped in strips of linen with aromatic spices. A linen napkin was placed over the face.

Flax spinner
The manufacture of linen from flax fibres was a domestic industry of Jewish women in biblical times. It is the oldest of the textile fibres, and was used by the Egyptians.

Women working
Women did much of the hard work in New Testament times, but they had a low position in society. Jesus' attitude towards them, however, contrasted markedly with the prevailing views of the day. By honouring women, he put them on an equal footing with men. Various women gave Jesus hospitality and provided for him as he travelled.

Mary and Martha, sisters of Lazarus, sent a message to Jesus explaining that their brother was very ill. Although he was a great friend of the family, Jesus did not go and visit them straightaway.

A few days later Jesus said to his disciples, "Lazarus is asleep, but I will go and wake him up."

"If he is merely asleep, then he will get better," they replied.

"You misunderstand me," continued Jesus. "He is dead, and in a way I am glad, because now you will believe. Come, let us go."

When they arrived, they discovered that Lazarus had been buried for four days.

"If you had been here," Martha said, "Lazarus would still be alive. But even now God will grant whatever you wish."

"He will rise once more," declared Jesus.

"Of course he will rise on the great day of the resurrection," replied Martha.

"I am the resurrection and the life. If anyone trusts in me they will never die."

Martha then rushed to Mary and told her that Jesus had arrived. When she went out to Jesus Mary repeated what Martha had said. "If you had come, then Lazarus would never have died!" she wept.

Jesus was overcome with emotion and cried. They took him to the tomb – a cave closed by means of a stone.

"Remove the stone," Jesus ordered. Immediately Martha protested, "But he has been dead for four days. It will smell terribly."

"Just believe me," Jesus replied.

They edged the stone back and Jesus prayed, "Thank you, Father, for hearing my prayer. Thank you that you have also given these people here the chance to see your glory." Having said that, he called into the tomb, "Come out, Lazarus!"

The crowd fell silent as the figure of a man emerged from the tomb, covered in the linen that had wrapped his body.

"Remove the grave clothes and let him go," ordered Jesus.

WHO DESERVES FORGIVENESS?

✤ Luke 18 ✤

Poll tax receipt
This is a fragment of a receipt for poll tax paid, written in Greek. Under the Roman occupation regular taxes were collected for the emperor. The Pharisees hated tax collectors because they took money from Jews to support the Gentiles, worked on the Sabbath, and used generally extortionate practices.

Rue
Rue is a perennial herb which grows in rocky places in Palestine. It grow up to 80 centimetres high and has aromatic grey-green leaves. It was valued for seasoning food, but it also had disinfectant and antiseptic properties. Jesus criticized the Pharisees for their scrupulous tithing of it, while they neglected more important matters.

Many people were full of self-confidence and their own importance. They looked down on others, believing themselves to be far better people than the commoners. So Jesus told them a parable:

"One day two men entered the temple in order to pray. One of them was a Pharisee and the other was a tax collector.

"The Pharisee stood up in front of everyone and, making sure that he was the centre of attention, he offered up a prayer in honour of himself. 'God, I give you thanks that you have not made me like other people, such as thieves, criminals, or those who commit adultery, not to mention this miserable tax collector beside me. I go without food two times a week and give a tenth of all my income.'

"The tax collector did not even dare go into the heart of the temple, but stayed on the fringes. Without so much as a glance towards heaven, he thumped his chest in sorrow and muttered, 'Please have mercy upon me, O God, for I am nothing

but a wicked sinner.'

"The truth is that this second man, not the Pharisee, was the one who returned to his home, accepted and forgiven by God. Every person who is full of their own self-importance will be humbled but everyone who is humble will become important."

SHOWING OFF

The Pharisee in the story is more interested in the outward show of his religion rather than responding humbly to God. God is not impressed when we boast, but cares about how much love we have in our hearts.

Prayer shawl and phylactery
The tallith or prayer shawl is still worn by orthodox Jewish men at synagogue services. Very strict Jews wear it all day. The phylactery is a little box containing a summary of God's commandments. It is strapped to the forehead as a reminder to keep God's words "in front of you".

COME DOWN ZACCHAEUS

❧ Luke 19 ❧

One day Jesus had to pass through the town of Jericho. It was the home of Zacchaeus, an extremely wealthy man who was the chief tax collector of the city. He had heard a great deal about Jesus and wanted to see what sort of person he was. As he arrived the place where Jesus was walking, he tried in vain to see him, but he was a short man and the crowd was so large that it was impossible to catch even a glimpse of him. So he raced ahead and climbed a spreading sycamore tree that was along the route.

Zacchaeus lay there waiting for Jesus and the crowd to come by. As Jesus reached the tree, he stopped and looked up into the branches.

Jesus called out to Zacchaeus who could scarcely believe his ears when he heard his name: "Zacchaeus, come out of the tree straightaway. I want to stay with you at your house today."

Immediately Zacchaeus clambered down, greeted Jesus warmly and led the way back to his house.

Not all of the people who saw this were as pleased as Zacchaeus was. They began to grumble about what Jesus was doing. "Doesn't he realize that he has gone to stay with a well-known cheat and sinner?" they whispered among themselves.

But Zacchaeus said to Jesus, "Lord, this very day I have decided to give away half of what I own to the poor. What's more, if I have taken anything from anybody by dishonest means, then I will repay them four times what I took."

Jesus was pleased and said to Zacchaeus, "Today God's salvation has entered into this house. This man is a true son of Abraham. The Son of Man has come to find and rescue those who are lost like Zacchaeus."

Jericho

Jericho is one of the oldest cities in the world. Some archaeologists claim that its history goes back 11,000 years. The flourishing agriculture of this oasis city is dependent on a perennial spring known as Elisha's spring. Palm trees line the streets and the city is strategically placed to guard the crossing of the Jordan. Jericho was the first Canaanite city to be captured by the Israelites when they entered the Promised Land.

ALL TREATED THE SAME

✤ **Matthew 20** ✤

eaven's kingdom," said Jesus, "is like the owner of a vineyard who went out early one morning to hire men to harvest the grapes. As the owner spoke to each man, he agreed the day's wage of a denarius and told them what to do.

"Three hours later he went and did the same thing. As he entered the market place he saw men idly standing around chatting in small groups.

"He approached them and said, 'If you go and work in my vineyard I guarantee that you will earn a fair sum of money.' So the men followed him and set about working on his land.

"Another three hours went by and once more he employed some men. Even then he still needed more workers and so, when he was in the square, three hours afterwards he hired yet more men.

"Just before darkness was due to fall, he went back into the market place and came across more men doing nothing.

"'Why have you been standing around here in the market place all day when you could have been working?' he asked them.

"'No one has hired us,' they replied.

"'I will,' he said, and so they too went with him to begin working in his vineyard.

"As night fell the owner said to his foreman, 'Give all the workers their pay. Start with the men that I hired last.'

"So the foreman began as his master had instructed him. He gave the last group of workers one denarius each. When those who had been working the longest came to receive their wages they were expecting to get more, but the foreman handed them exactly the same amount, one denarius. They complained, 'Those men who have only worked a short time have received the same amount that you've given us. They've only done a little, while those of us who have been sweating all day under the hot sun have done most of the work,' they grumbled.

"But the owner said, 'My friends, I am not treating you unfairly at all. Remember that you agreed to work for one denarius. Collect your wages and go. It is my wish to give to those I took on at the end of the day exactly the same as I have given you. Are you annoyed because I am a generous employer?'"

Jesus ended by saying, "In this way those who are first will become last and those who are last will become first."

Treading the grapes
Growing grapes is labour-intensive, and workers were often hired to gather the crop into baskets, and to tread those being made into wine in a winepress hewn out of solid rock. Grapes were trodden with bare feet while the men held onto ropes above them. The grape juice ran out into containers placed round the bottom of the winepress.

Denarius
Three different systems of coinage – Roman, Greek and Jewish – were in circulation in Palestine in New Testament times. The denarius was a Roman coin minted in silver. The one pictured here bears the image of Caesar Augustus, the Roman emperor who ruled at the time Jesus was born. The denarius was the standard pay for a full day's work.

River Jordan
There were no bridges over the river in Jesus' time (the Romans built some later) but there were a number of places where the river was shallow enough to be forded, especially in summer. Jesus told this story on the east side of the Jordan, so he must have crossed the river several times.

SHE GAVE ALL SHE HAD

♣ Mark 12 ♣

One day, when Jesus and his disciples were teaching in the temple courts, Jesus sat down opposite the money collecting boxes to watch the crowd putting in their offerings. Some boxes were for collecting tax from the Jewish men, while others were for extra gifts that people wanted to make to God.

Many rich people threw in large numbers of coins, some of them gold, which made a loud crashing noise as they fell on top of other coins. Some were so proud of their contributions that they made sure that the others saw how generous they were.

Then along came a poor widow, dressed in shabby clothes. She had no husband to look after her, and so didn't have much money even for food. She reached over and quietly put in two very small copper coins, which together were worth less than a penny.

Gathering his disciples around him, Jesus said, "It may surprise you to hear the truth that this widow has put more into the temple treasury than anyone else today."

The disciples looked at each other in astonishment. How could two small copper coins be worth more than all those gold coins they had seen thrown into the boxes?

"You see, the others were wealthy," Jesus explained, "and had plenty of money left in their pockets to buy whatever they wanted. This widow lives in poverty, yet she gladly put in everything she had. She held nothing back from God, showing the true devotion of her heart."

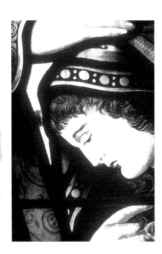

Woman blessed
Life was difficult for widows in biblical times. Without a husband they were often left in very poor circumstances, and unless they remarried they had no status. Without anyone to support and protect them, they all too easily became the victims of injustice and oppression. Bearing children was considered a great honour, so for a woman of child-bearing age to be widowed was considered shameful. Widows were often neglected and exploited by society, but Jesus showed that God had a special concern for their welfare.

THE WISE AND FOOLISH GIRLS

✤ Matthew 25 ✤

One day, the disciples asked Jesus how they might know when the end of the world was coming.

"No one knows when," Jesus replied, "but if you are wise, you will make sure that you are ready for my return, so that I can take you with me to heaven."

Then Jesus told them a story about ten girls waiting to join a wedding feast. "Five were foolish, and took no extra oil to light their lamps, but the other five were wise, and took jars of extra oil so their lamps wouldn't go out," he said.

The bridegroom took a long time to come, so all ten girls fell fast asleep. Then someone woke them up at midnight, saying, "Look, he's on his way! Come and meet the bridegroom!"

Excitedly, they lit their lamps, but the foolish girls' lamps began to flicker weakly.

"Our lamps are going out," they complained to the wise girls. "Please give us some of your oil."

But the wise girls refused. "There may not be enough oil for all of us, so quickly go and buy your own."

But while they were gone, the bridegroom arrived. The wise girls followed him into the wedding feast, and the door closed firmly behind them.

Later, the foolish girls rushed back with their lamps now full of oil. They knocked on the door, crying, "Let us in!"

But the bridegroom simply said, "I don't know who you are. You've come far too late."

Jesus told his disciples, "Always make sure you are ready, because you don't know on which day or at which hour I will return."

Jesus, the light of the world
In the New Testament Jesus is often portrayed as a bridegroom, and the church as his bride. As weddings were always held in the evening, the bridesmaids carried lamps and escorted the bridegroom to the wedding feast in a torchlit procession. In the same kind of way Jesus promises to guide his people through their lives.

The five foolish virgins
For outdoor processions, the lamps consisted of a wick – an oil-drenched rag or a strip of flax – and a container of oil, held high on a wooden pole. Because the supply of oil would last for only a few minutes, it was important to have spare oil available. Jesus' future return to earth is compared to the sudden arrival of the bridegroom. The parable teaches us to be ready, whenever that time may come.

THE TALENTS

✤ Matthew 25 ✤

"When the kingdom of heaven finally comes," Jesus told his disciples, "it will be like the man who decided to go on a long journey.

"Before he left, he summoned his servants, put them in charge of his property, and gave each of them a sum of money.

"He gave the first servant five talents, the second servant two talents, and the third servant one talent. Then the master set out on his journey.

"The first servant put his five talents to work straightaway and soon made another five talents. The second servant also used his two talents to make two extra talents. But the servant who had received only one talent went and dug a hole in the ground, hid the money, and left it there.

"Eventually, the master returned and called his servants, so that he could put his affairs in order.

"The first servant came in and said to his master, 'Sir, you entrusted me with five talents. Look, I have earned you five more.'

"'Well done!' his delighted master exclaimed. 'You have been a good and faithful servant, and proved yourself capable of looking after small things. As a reward, I have decided to trust you with greater things. Come and share with me in my happiness.'

"Then the second servant came in and said the same thing, 'Sir, you entrusted me with two talents. Look, I have earned you two more.'

"Again the delighted master praised the servant, and promised to give him greater responsibilities as a reward.

"Finally, the servant who had received just one talent came in. 'Sir,' he began, 'I know that you are a ruthless ma[n] expecting to find a harvest where you hav[e] not sown. I was afraid, so I hid the mone[y] you gave me in a hole. Here it is again.'

"His master was angry. 'What a wicked servant you have been. If you kne[w] what a hard master I was, why didn't you [at] least put my money in a bank to earn som[e] interest to give me when I returned home[?]

"Then he called his other servants and commanded them, 'Take away that man's talent and give it to the servant wh[o] now has ten talents.

"'Whoever has will be given more, [so] that he has more than he ever could have hoped for. Whoever does not have, will have what little he possesses taken from him. Now throw that useless servant out into the night.'"

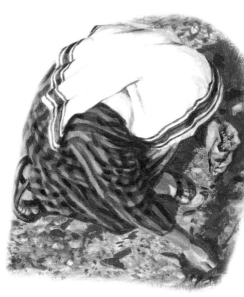

The talents
A talent was originally a weight, equivalent to about 34 kilograms. By Jesus' time, the talent had come to be used as a unit of money. A talent was a valuable coin, worth 3,000 shekels. Our modern use of the word "talent" for a gift or an aptitude comes from this Bible story, which is often called "The Parable of the Talents".

MAKING THE MOST OF OUR GIFTS
God gives each of us unique talents. Whoever we are and whatever family o[r] job we find ourselves in, we all have a responsibility to make the most of these gifts. Being careless with our opportunit[ies] is a sad waste when life is comparative[ly] short. God wants us to have the most fulfilling life possible, and one day he w[ill] ask us how we have spent our time and how we have used our talents.

THE SHEEP AND THE GOATS

✤ Matthew 25 ✤

"The time will come," Jesus told his disciples, "when the Son of Man will appear in glory, surrounded by angels, to take his rightful place upon his throne. On that day, all people will be gathered in front of him. Just as a shepherd separates the sheep from the goats, he will divide up the people, placing the sheep on his right and the goats on his left.

"Then the king will say to the people on his right, 'Come and inherit the kingdom that belongs to you. It is yours, because when I was hungry, you fed me. When I was thirsty, you offered me a drink; when I was a stranger, you welcomed me to your home; when my clothes were in rags, you gave me new ones; when I was ill, you cared for me; and when I was in prison, you visited me.'

"And the good people will reply, 'But Lord, we have never seen you hungry and fed you, or thirsty and given you a drink. When did we invite you into our homes? When did we give you new clothes? We have never seen you sick or a prisoner and come to visit you.'

"But the king will reply, 'The truth is that whenever you did something for the least of these brothers of mine, you did it for me.'

"Then he will turn to the people on his left and say, 'You are cursed. When I was hungry or thirsty, you offered me nothing; when I was a stranger, you shut the door in my face; when my clothes were in rags, you ignored me; when I was ill and in prison, you left me to my fate.'

"'But Lord,' they will reply, 'we never saw you hungry, thirsty, a stranger, in need of clothes, sick, or in prison. How could we help you?'

"And he will answer, 'The truth is that every time you chose to ignore one of the least significant of these people, you ignored me.'

"Then they will be sent away to eternal punishment, but the people who have done what is right will enjoy eternal life."

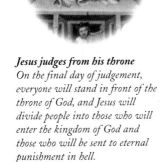

Jesus judges from his throne
On the final day of judgement, everyone will stand in front of the throne of God, and Jesus will divide people into those who will enter the kingdom of God and those who will be sent to eternal punishment in hell.

Feeding the hungry
Disasters like famine, floods, earthquakes and war can happen at any time. We can demonstrate Jesus' teaching in a practical way by feeding and clothing people who are in desperate need.

JESUS ARRIVES IN JERUSALEM

✤ Matthew 21; Mark 11; Luke 19; John 12 ✤

As Jesus rode into Jerusalem, his followers began to throw their cloaks onto the road in front of him. Others cut branches off palm trees and laid them down in his path.

Everyone began to sing and shout and praise God, thanking him for all the wonderful miracles they had seen Jesus perform. "Hosanna!" they shouted. "Blessed is the king who comes in God's name! Hosanna!"

Very soon, there was such a commotion that it seemed as though everyone in Jerusalem had come out to welcome Jesus. But some Pharisees in the crowd were not impressed. They said to Jesus, "Tell your disciples not to shout in this way."

But Jesus replied, "If they were to keep quiet, the stones themselves would cry out for joy."

Lulab
When Jesus rode into Jerusalem, the people cut leafy branches from the nearby fields and placed them in the path of the donkey. They also waved lulabs, like the one pictured here. Lulabs were made of palm or willow branches. They were symbols of triumph and victory and were used on occasions of great rejoicing.

Riding on a donkey
In the Bible, horses were associated with war, so in peacetime kings rode donkeys instead. The donkey was a symbol of humility and peace. A donkey that had not been used before was regarded as especially suitable for religious purposes.

Jesus was on his way to Jerusalem. Before he reached the village of Bethphage by the hill called the Mount of Olives, he told two of his disciples to go ahead.

"As you enter the village, you will see a young donkey tied to the entrance of a house. Untie it and bring it here. If anyone tries to stop you, tell them that the Master needs the donkey."

So the two disciples did as Jesus had instructed. They found the donkey, and just as they were untying it, some of the villagers asked what they were doing. "The Master needs the donkey," they replied, and with this answer they were left in peace.

Then they led the donkey back to Jesus, put some cloaks on its back as a saddle, and Jesus mounted it.

THE SIGNS OF CHRIST'S RETURN

✤ Matthew 24 ✤

Jesus' last week
Jesus rode his donkey about three kilometres from Bethphage across the Kidron Valley to enter Jerusalem by the Eastern Gate. The places associated with the last week of Jesus' earthly life are shown on this map.

"You will see people becoming more and more wicked, and my followers will be punished and put to death," Jesus continued, as the disciples listened carefully to every word.

"Many people will turn away from me. But have courage, because I will save those who stand firm. Once the whole world has heard the truth about me, then I will be ready to return.

"I will come in the clouds for everyone to see clearly, like the lightning that flashes across the sky from east to west. And then the angels will gather my people safely together and I will take them up to heaven.

"Remember that I will come at an hour when no one expects me, so keep watch and lead good and faithful lives," Jesus encouraged them. "Make the most of all your opportunities to serve God."

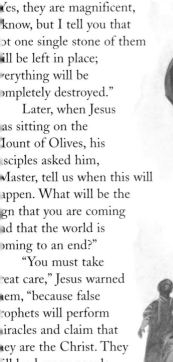

Two days later, as Jesus was leaving the temple, his disciples came to him and said, "Just look at these buildings!"

Jesus answered them, "Yes, they are magnificent, I know, but I tell you that not one single stone of them will be left in place; everything will be completely destroyed."

Later, when Jesus was sitting on the Mount of Olives, his disciples asked him, "Master, tell us when this will happen. What will be the sign that you are coming and that the world is coming to an end?"

"You must take great care," Jesus warned them, "because false prophets will perform miracles and claim that they are the Christ. They will lead many people away from the truth.

"There will be wars and famines and earthquakes, and even the planets will shake in the sky, but try not to be afraid.

Mosaic map of Jerusalem
This section of a mosaic map of Jerusalem dates from the 6th century AD. It was discovered by archaeologists in 1896 during excavations on the floor of St George's church at Medeba in modern-day Jordan.

THE LAST SUPPER

✤ Matthew 26; Mark 14; Luke 22; John 13 ✤

Jesus washes his disciples' feet
People's feet got very dirty and dusty in the open sandals they wore as they walked through the streets, and it was the custom for servants to bathe a guest's feet with water. When Jesus washed the disciples' feet, he was performing a menial task. He set an example for his followers, showing them how they should humbly serve one another.

Communion chalice
In the Holy Communion (also known as the Mass, Eucharist, or Lord's Supper), Christians take bread and drink wine from a chalice or cup, as a thanksgiving for Jesus' sacrificial death, just as Jesus told them to at the Last Supper.

Fresco of the Last Supper
Fresco, or "fresh" in Italian, is a painting made on fresh lime plaster using pigments mixed with water. This 15th-century example was painted during the Italian Renaissance. The Last Supper is portrayed here as a Roman banquet scene. In the early church, the "communion" was often part of a proper meal.

It was time to celebrate the Passover, so Jesus told Peter and John to go into Jerusalem and follow a man carrying a water jar. "Then ask the owner of the house which he enters to show you to a large, upstairs room, where you can prepare the Passover meal," he told them.

When they arrived at the house that evening, Jesus poured water into a bowl, took off his outer garment and wrapped a towel around his waist. He then poured some water into a bowl. Kneeling down, he began to wash his disciples' feet which were dusty from the road outside.

Peter was shocked to see his master behaving like a servant. "You will never wash my feet!" he protested.

"If I don't wash you," Jesus told Peter, "then you don't really belong to me."

Peter said, "Lord, don't wash just my feet. Wash my hands and my head as well!"

Jesus replied, "If you've just had a bath, you need only wash your feet. The rest of your body is clean. And you are clean – that is, all except one of you." He said that not all of them were "clean", because he knew one of them would betray him to his enemies.

When Jesus finished washing his disciples' feet, he put his outer garment back on and sat down. He explained that he was setting them all an example. "Although I am your Lord, I have shown you how to be humble and kind. Now you must learn to serve each other the same way."

They began eating and, knowing it was time for him to return to his

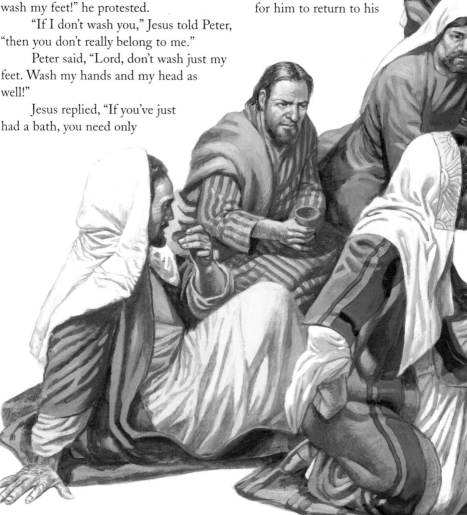

...ather in heaven, Jesus suddenly felt sad ...d announced, "One of you sitting here ...ill betray me."

The disciples were very distressed. ...urely it won't be me, Lord?" they ...xiously asked him, one by one.

In answer, Jesus dipped a piece of ...read into a bowl and gave it to Judas, ...ying, "God alone has decided what will ...ppen to me, but this is the man who will

betray me." But they didn't understand what he meant.

Later, Jesus took some bread, gave thanks to God and broke it in pieces. "Eat this," he told his disciples, "for it is my body."

Then he handed them the wine cup. "And drink this, for it is my blood which I will shed so that many may be forgiven. Do this to remember me when I am gone."

The Upper Room
The Coenaculum on Mount Zion is the traditional site of the Upper Room in Jerusalem. How it looked in Jesus' day is unknown. Some think it was built onto the roof of a house, but others believe that it was the most important room in a house and used only on special occasions.

Judas Iscariot
Judas was the treasurer of the twelve disciples: he looked after the money for the group. However, he was greedy and sometimes used to take some of the money for his own use. He chose to betray Jesus for thirty pieces of silver, but in the end he committed suicide in grief over Jesus' death.

Bread and wine
During a traditional Jewish Passover meal Jesus gave a new meaning to the shared bread and cup. The Passover commemorated Israel's deliverance from slavery in Egypt. Christians think of Jesus as their "Passover lamb" who forgives their sin, and they celebrate his forgiveness of them with the bread and wine.

197 ✤

DO NOT BE AFRAID

✤ John 14-17 ✤

Fruit and branches
A gardener prunes away dead branches to make a fruit tree more healthy. In this story, Jesus says that God is sometimes like a gardener – he has to prune away dead or useless parts of our lives.

Gordon's
Calvary and
garden tomb

Traditional
Calvary
and tomb
Antonia
Fortress

Temple

Bethphage

Bethany

Herod's
Palace

Garden of
Gethsemane

Caiaphas' House

Mount
of
Olives

Upper
Room

Kidron
Valley

To the house of Caiaphas
This map of central Jerusalem shows the main sites associated with Jesus' arrest, trial and crucifixion. After he was arrested in the Garden of Gethsemane, Jesus was taken as a prisoner to the house of Caiaphas, the high priest. We do not know the route that was taken – he may even have passed through the temple.

The Dominus Flevit Chapel
Half-way up the Mount of Olives is the church of Dominus Flevit. It is often called the "teardrops chapel", because it marks the site where the Bible tells us that Jesus wept for Jerusalem. He was upset because he knew that people in the city would reject him, and years later the city would be destroyed.

Jesus knew that the time for him to die was drawing near, and tried to prepare his disciples for the tragedy that was about to unfold.

"Do not be afraid," he comforted them. "Trust in me and trust in God. I am going to my Father's house to prepare a place for you. Then I will come back and collect you.

"I am the way, the truth, and the life. No one comes to my Father without going through me. If you really knew me, you would know my Father too. Indeed, anyone who has seen me has seen the Father. I am in the Father and he is in me. All that I have said and done has been inspired by my Father.

"If you love me, you will obey my teaching. And when the Father sees your obedience, he will love you and come and live with you.

"I am the true vine and you are the branches. My Father is the gardener. If you do not bear fruit, he will cut you off, but if you do, then he will prune you to make you even more fruitful. Then you will go on to produce eternal fruit.

"When the world sees your fruit, then it will hate and despise you, just as it has hated and despised me. But do not worry – when I am gone, I will send the Holy Spirit, who will teach you and remind you of everything that I have said.

"Soon you will be filled with sorrow, because you will not see me any longer. While you are overwhelmed with sadness, the world will be glad. But, just as a woman forgets the pain and struggle of labour when her child is born, so your tears will turn into joy.

"I have told you these things so that you will be prepared when they happen."

Then Jesus prayed, "Father, glorify your Son, so that he may glorify you. Protect my disciples. May all the people who believe in me because of their message be united in everything they say and do."

BEING FRUITFUL
Jesus described himself as the vine and us as the branches. Just as grapes cannot ripen without being fed by the vine on which they grow, neither can we be truly good and fruitful without God's life flowing freely through us. Using only our own strength we often fail, but Jesus tells us to depend on him for real power.

ARRESTED IN THE GARDEN

✤ Matthew 26; Mark 14; Luke 22; John 18 ✤

Later that evening, Jesus and his disciples went to a garden, called Gethsemane, outside the walls of Jerusalem. Jesus was very sad, and asked his disciples to stay awake and pray with him. But they were tired, and kept falling asleep.

Suddenly, Judas appeared out of the gloom with a band of soldiers and religious officials. They were armed with swords and clubs and carried lanterns so that they could see their way.

To be sure that they arrested the right man, Judas had told them that he would kiss Jesus. When Judas saw Jesus, he went up to him and said, "Greetings, Teacher!" and then he kissed him.

"Judas, is this the way that you have chosen to betray the Son of Man?" asked Jesus.

No sooner had he spoken than the soldiers pounced on Jesus and arrested him. When Simon Peter realized what was happening, he grabbed hold of his sword and sliced off the ear of one of the high priest's servants.

"Put your sword away!" Jesus ordered him. "Everyone who uses a sword in anger will die in the same way. Don't you realize that I could appeal to my Father and he would immediately send his angels to protect me? But if I did that, it would be impossible to fulfill the words of the prophecy that says things must happen in this way."

Then Jesus touched the servant's ear and healed it.

Peering through the darkness, Jesus turned to his captors and asked them, "Why have you come armed with all these weapons? Do you think that I am in charge of a rebellion? Every day you have seen me teaching in the temple, yet you never lifted a finger against me there.

"You deliberately chose a fitting time and place for your deed – the hour when darkness is supreme. Yet what you are doing now is all happening in order to fulfill the prophecies."

Then the soldiers seized Jesus and led him away to the high priests house to face his fate alone. Simon Peter followed at a distance.

Judas
Judas Iscariot was one of Jesus' twelve disciples. He betrayed Jesus for thirty silver coins, which was not a lot of money. The Bible does not tell us why Judas turned against Jesus, although in his Gospel Luke explains it by saying that the devil entered Judas.

The Garden of Gethsemane
The name Gethsemane comes from an Aramaic word meaning "oil press". The garden was an olive grove on the lower slopes of the Mount of Olives. The Romans later chopped down the original trees, but there are still eight ancient olive trees growing in the garden which may be shoots from the trees that stood there in Jesus' day.

Judas betrays Jesus with a kiss
Judas brought a crowd armed with swords and clubs to arrest Jesus in the Garden of Gethsemane. He had already arranged with the Jewish authorities that he would identify Jesus with the signal of a kiss. This was a sign of respect which disciples customarily gave to their rabbi as a greeting.

THE PRIESTS ACCUSE JESUS

✣ **Matthew 26-27; Mark 14-15; Luke 22-23** ✣

The king's game

The picture shows part of a game played by Roman soldiers, called "the king's game". It is carved on the stones in a place called the Lithostratus, or "pavement", in Jerusalem. This is said to be the courtyard of the Antonia Fortress, where Jesus was tried and condemned to death.

THE SANHEDRIN

The Sanhedrin was the Jewish high court, which met in Jerusalem. Its name came from the Greek word for "council". The seventy members of the Sanhedrin were chief priests and teachers of the law. They could pass judgement in all sorts of cases, but they did not have the power to put a prisoner to death. For this they needed the confirmation of the Roman governor. At the time of Jesus' trial, the governor was Pontius Pilate.

The steps to Caiaphas' house

After Jesus was arrested in the Garden of Gethsemane, he would have been brought up these stone steps to Caiaphas's house, where the members of the Sanhedrin were assembled to try him. Caiaphas was the Jewish high priest and therefore the head of the Sanhedrin. The council may have met in his house to ensure that the trial was kept secret.

of the one and only God, tell us the truth! Are you the Christ, the Son of God?"

"I am indeed," replied Jesus. "But I want to add this: there will come a time when you will see the Son of Man seated next to God, coming on the clouds of heaven."

At this the high priest began tearing his robes in disgust. "We don't need to hear any more witnesses. We have heard this man speak against God with our own ears. What is your verdict?" he shouted to his colleagues.

"He must die!" they responded. Some of them then spat at Jesus and others hit him with their clenched fists. Then they blindfolded him and slapped him. "Which one of us was it that hit you, Christ?" they taunted him.

Then they led Jesus away to Pilate, the Roman governor, to be sentenced.

Jesus was ushered into the presence of Caiaphas, the high priest, who had assembled all the teachers of the law and the elders of the Sanhedrin.

They were hoping to find someone who would give false evidence against Jesus, so that they could put him to death. They called many witnesses, but none of them could produce any convincing evidence.

Eventually, two disreputable men came forward and said, "We heard this man say that he could destroy the temple of the Lord and then rebuild it in three days." Jesus remained silent.

When the high priest heard this charge, he looked at Jesus and said, "You have heard the evidence against you. What do you have to say in your defence?" But Jesus said nothing.

Caiaphas was running out of patience, so he said to Jesus, "In the name

PETER DISOWNS JESUS

✤ **Matthew 26; Mark 14; Luke 22; John 13 & 18** ✤

Peter began to curse himself. Then he rounded on them all swearing, "I have already said that I don't even know the man!"

No sooner had these words left his mouth, than a cock crowed.

Then Peter remembered what Jesus had said to him earlier that evening: "Before the cock crows, three times you will pretend that you never knew me."

Heartbroken, Peter left the courtyard and went out into the cold, forsaken night, crying bitter tears of grief and shame.

Saint Peter
When Jesus called Peter to become his disciple, he was a fisherman called Simon. Jesus renamed him Peter which means "rock" in Greek. Traditionally, Roman Catholics believe that he was chosen by Jesus to be the first head of the Christian church.

Peter's denial
Peter's denial was prophesied by Jesus. When Peter heard the cock crow for the third time, he was bitterly disappointed at his own weakness and failure in disowning his Lord and Master.

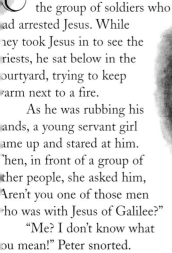

nobserved, Peter had followed the group of soldiers who had arrested Jesus. While they took Jesus in to see the priests, he sat below in the courtyard, trying to keep warm next to a fire.

As he was rubbing his hands, a young servant girl came up and stared at him. Then, in front of a group of other people, she asked him, "Aren't you one of those men who was with Jesus of Galilee?"

"Me? I don't know what you mean!" Peter snorted.

He decided to move away from her and went and stood at the gate. But as he was standing there, another girl spotted him and said to the people around her, "This fellow was with Jesus of Nazareth."

But Peter denied it. "As heaven is my witness, I have never met the man!" he exclaimed.

He huddled closer to the wall, hoping to avoid any more attention, but soon someone else approached him.

"How can you say that you were not with Jesus?" the man asked Peter. "Your accent is from Galilee – you must be one of his disciples!"

PILATE JUDGES JESUS

—— ✤ **Matthew 27; Mark 15; Luke 23; John 18-19** ✤ ——

When the religious council decided to kill Jesus, they brought him before Pontius Pilate, the Roman governor of Judea, who was the only person who could pass a death sentence. They accused Jesus of trying to encourage the people to rebel.

"Are you really the king of the Jews?" asked Pilate, surprised that Jesus would say nothing to defend himself.

"Yes, that is true, but my kingdom is not of this world," Jesus replied.

Pilate wanted to free Jesus because he could plainly see that he was no threat to the Roman government, and had probably only been arrested because the chief priests were jealous of him. He asked the crowd to choose one prisoner to be set free during the Passover celebrations: Jesus or a murderer called Barabbas, who had joined a rebellion against the Romans.

"We want Barabbas!" shouted the crowd.

"But why?" Pilate asked them. "I see no evidence that Jesus has committed any crime. I will punish him and then let him go."

But the crowd grew restless, and Pilate began to fear that they could riot and lose him his job. So to avoid trouble, he publicly washed his hands, to show that he took no responsibility for an innocent man's death.

Pilate let Barabbas go, and had Jesus savagely whipped before handing him over to the soldiers to be crucified.

The crucifixion
Crucifixion was a cruel way of executing people. As well as the terrible pain they suffered, it was a struggle to breathe because their bodies were stretched out. The cross became the symbol of Christianity because Christians believe Jesus died in their place, taking on himself God's punishment for their sins.

NAILED TO A CROSS

✣ Matthew 27; Mark 15; Luke 23; John 19 ✣

When Pilate ordered his soldiers to take Jesus away to be crucified, they dressed him like a king, with a royal purple robe and a pretend crown made of twisted thorn branches. "Let's all worship the king of the Jews!" they mocked, before beating him.

They wanted Jesus to carry a heavy wooden cross to Golgotha where he was to be executed, but as he was injured, they forced a passer-by to take it instead. They hammered long nails through his outstretched hands and feet, and lifted Jesus upright on the cross, before sharing out his clothes between them by casting lots.

"Father, forgive them, for they don't understand what they are doing," Jesus said.

"Forgive me, too!" cried out one of the two robbers being crucified on either side of him, though the other simply hurled insults.

Several women followers stood watching nearby, including Mary, his mother. Their hearts were filled with grief at the pain Jesus was suffering. But others did not care. "If he really is God's son, then why doesn't God rescue him?" jeered some religious leaders in the crowd. Jesus was thirsty so a sponge soaked in wine vinegar was lifted to his lips.

At midday, an unusual darkness fell across the sky, until three hours later Jesus cried out, "My work is finished! I give my spirit to you, Father," and he breathed his last breath and died.

At that very moment, an earthquake shook the ground and the temple curtain tore from top to bottom, showing that the barrier between God and people had now been removed.

As evening came on, Joseph of Arimathea – who was a rich man and a member of the Jewish religious council, and who had become a follower of Jesus – went to Pilate and asked for Jesus' body. Pilate allowed him to have it, and after Joseph had taken down the body, he wrapped it in linen. Joseph then put Jesus' body into a tomb, one that had not been used and that he had had cut out of the rock for himself. Then a big stone was rolled in front of the tomb's entrance.

Via Dolorosa

The route taken by Jesus from his trial to his crucifixion is known as the Via Dolorosa, or the Way of Sorrows. Traditionally fourteen "stations of the cross" mark various incidents along the way, and pilgrims to Jerusalem retrace this 15th-century Franciscan route every Easter. The street today is much higher than it was in Jesus' day.

Bronze coin

Pontius Pilate was the Roman governor in Judea in AD26-37. He was cruel and unpopular and had little regard for Jewish feelings. One way in which he offended Jews was by issuing this bronze coin. It shows a lituus, or fortune-teller's staff, which was used in pagan religious ceremonies and bears the name of the emperor Tiberius Caesar.

Spiny burnet

We cannot be certain from which plant Jesus' crown of thorns was made. There are many different varieties of plants with sharp prickles which grow in Palestine, including the spiny burnet shown above. The Roman soldiers made the crown and placed it on Jesus' head before the crucifixion. They did this to mock and humiliate him because Jesus said he was the king of the Jews.

JESUS IS ALIVE!

❖ Matthew 28; Mark 16; Luke 24; John 20 ❖

and crept inside, only to discover that the body was missing. Terror gripped them – even more so when they saw a young man sitting on the right side of the tomb, near where the corpse should have been. He was dressed in clothes as white as snow and his body shone like lightning. The women bowed down with their faces to the ground.

"Don't be frightened," he reassured them. "I know that you are looking for Jesus, the prophet from Nazareth. But why do you look for the living among the dead? He is not here. He is alive! He has risen from the dead just as he said he would. Look, this is the exact spot where his body was laid. He is going on ahead of you to Galilee, where he had arranged to meet you. If you go there, you will see him, as he promised. But first, go and tell Peter and the other disciples what has happened: that he has risen from the dead."

The women left the tomb dazed and shocked, yet at the same time filled with joy at everything they had seen and heard. They stumbled back to the disciples and, scarcely believing what they were saying, related everything that had happened that morning.

Most of the men thought they were mad, but Peter and one other disciple sprinted to the tomb. The other one was faster than Peter and so reached it first but was too afraid to go in.

When Peter finally appeared he went straight inside and saw the eerie scene: strips of linen lying there along with the burial cloth, neatly folded by itself. Finally his friend plucked up enough courage to go in and the two of them stared in wonder and surprise. What the women had said was true. Jesus was no longer there! He really was alive!

The Garden Tomb
This is a well-preserved example of a Jewish tomb from the first century AD. It is set in a garden where there is an older winepress and cistern. The tomb matches the Bible's description of the one in which Jesus' body was laid.

Very early on the first day of the week, Mary Magdalene, Mary (James's mother) and Salome made their way through the still, early morning gloom to the tomb where Jesus' body lay.

"Who will roll back the stone so that we can anoint Jesus' body with oil?" they asked, as they stepped silently through the empty streets carrying bundles of spices for the purpose.

As they approached the tomb, however, there was a violent earthquake. The ground shook and cracked apart. Afraid, the women were appalled to see that the heavy stone had been pushed to one side. Nervously, they crouched down

Jesus Appears to the Disciples

✤ Luke 24; John 20 ✤

Mary stood alone outside the empty tomb. As she turned to look inside just one more time, she began to weep once again. Two angels were inside and they asked her, "Why are you crying?"

"Because they have taken his body away and laid him in some unknown place," she sobbed.

As she said this, she heard the tread of footsteps behind her.

A man asked, "Why are you weeping? Are you looking for someone?"

Assuming it was the gardener she replied, "Kind sir, if it was you who took his body away, please tell me where it is."

"Mary!" came a familiar voice.

She lifted up her head and turned towards the speaker.

"Teacher!" she gasped and reached out for Jesus.

But he said to her, "Do not hold me, for I must still return to my Father. Go and tell the others."

Immediately she sped off with her joyful news.

Later that day Cleopas and a friend were walking with a heavy step to a small village outside Jerusalem called Emmaus. The curious events of the day dominated their sad conversation.

"What are you talking about?" a stranger inquired.

Taken aback, Cleopas replied, "Surely you must be aware what has happened here in Jerusalem in these last few days?"

"What things?"

So they explained all about Jesus and all that he had done before being crucified by the Roman authorities.

"But the strangest thing of all is that his body is no longer in the tomb. It has disappeared off the face of the earth."

"If only you had believed the holy prophets!" the man said, and he began to explain all that the Scriptures had said about these things.

Later that evening they invited him to share a meal with them. As they were eating, he broke the bread and gave thanks. At that moment they realized that it was

Jesus, but he vanished before them.

"That explains our excitement as he was talking to us along the road," they said.

Without delay, the two friends hurried back to Jerusalem. Bursting in on the disciples, they told them all that happened on their journey. "It's true, the Lord is alive again!" they said.

The supper at Emmaus
Emmaus was a village which, according to Luke, was 60 furlongs or 11 km away from Jerusalem. Although the site cannot be definitely identified, some people believe it may be modern-day El-Qubeibeh.

The Turin Shroud
The Turin Shroud is a 4-metre length of ivory-coloured linen bearing the shadowy imprint of a crucified man. During the Middle Ages there was a flourishing trade in religious relics and the shroud appeared at this time. People claimed it was the burial cloth in which Jesus' body was wrapped. Controversy has raged over its genuineness ever since.

THOMAS IS NOT SURE

✤ John 20 ✤

Doubting Thomas

A "doubting Thomas" is a name given to any sceptical person. Thomas was one of Jesus' disciples, but he was not with the others when Jesus appeared to them on that first Easter Day. Thomas said he would not believe that Jesus was alive unless he could actually see and touch the scars on his body. A week later his doubts and scepticism vanished when he saw Jesus for himself.

כלב יהודים

REX IVDAEORVM

OBACIΛΕΥCΤWΝΙΟΥΔΑΙWΝ

Superscription

A superscription was a board that was hung around a criminal's neck on the way to his execution and then fixed to the cross over his head. It bore his name and the offence for which he was being executed. The superscription that Pilate had written for Jesus read, "Jesus of Nazareth, King of the Jews". Part of it is reproduced here, written, from top to bottom, in Hebrew, Latin and Greek.

O n the evening of that day, the disciples were huddled together in a locked room, hiding from the Jewish authorities. Suddenly Jesus appeared before them. When they realized who it was, they were amazed and delighted.

"Peace to you all!" he said. Then he showed them the scar marks on his hands where the nails had been banged in, and the wound in his side.

"Just as I have been sent by the Father, so you will be sent by me," he told them. Then he breathed on them saying, "Receive the Holy Spirit. If you forgive a person's sins, they will be forgiven. If you do not forgive them, they will not be forgiven."

One of the disciples, Thomas, was absent when all this happened. When the others told him that they had seen Jesus, he refused to believe them. Thomas said, "I will only believe if I am able to see the scars on his hands and side and touch his wounds with my own hands."

A week later, they met once again, and this time Thomas was with them. Even though the doors were locked as before, Jesus appeared in the room again. "Peace to you all!" he said.

Then Jesus said to Thomas, "Touch the holes in my hands. Put your hand into my side. Stop doubting and believe!"

Thomas fell on his knees. "My Lord and my God!" he exclaimed.

"You have believed only because you have seen me," said Jesus. "How blessed will be those people who believe even though they have never seen me."

SEEING IS BELIEVING?
Sometimes we can be like doubting Thomas. We think that if only we could see and touch God, we would find it easier to believe in him. In this story, Jesus promises a special blessing for people who believe, even though they have never seen him, and he promises to send the Holy Spirit to help us overcome our doubts.

BREAKFAST WITH JESUS

✠ John 21 ✠

After their return to Galilee, some of the disciples went fishing with Simon Peter one night. But despite all their efforts, when they returned to the shore in the early hours of the morning they had not caught a single fish.

A man on the bank called out to them. "Have you caught anything?" he asked.

"Nothing," they replied.

"Cast your nets on the right-hand side of your boat and you will catch something," the man said.

Scarcely knowing why, they did as he said, and when they came to pull in their nets they found they were so full that it was impossible to get them on board.

"It is Jesus!" exclaimed John. At this, Peter quickly jumped into the water and waded towards him. The others followed, trailing their bulging nets behind them.

When they arrived, they found that Jesus was already cooking a meal of fish and bread for them on some hot coals.

"Add some of the fresh fish to the fire," he said, "and join me for breakfast." He then handed over the food he had prepared, and they ate together.

After they had eaten, Jesus took Peter to one side. "Simon, do you love me?" he asked.

"Of course, Lord, you know that I love you," Peter replied.

"Feed my lambs," said Jesus.

"Simon, do you really love me?" Jesus asked again, as he stared deep into Peter's eyes. Peter replied that he did. "Look after my sheep," said Jesus.

One more time Jesus said to him, "Simon, do you love me?"

Peter was upset because Jesus had repeated his question. In frustration he said, "Lord, you know everything, you know that I love you."

"Feed my sheep," Jesus said. He then added, "When you were a young man, you did as you pleased, but when you are old other people will stretch out your hands and force you to go where you do not want to go."

Jesus said this in order to show Peter how he would die. After this solemn warning he then said, "Follow me!"

Fishing at night
In this story, the disciples had been out all night fishing on the Sea of Galilee. Fishermen often went out at night, because they could catch more fish than during the day. In the day, many fish lurk at the bottom of the lake, where they are safe from birds and other predators. But at night they swim nearer the surface of the water and are easier to catch.

THE SEA OF GALILEE
Despite its name, the Sea of Galilee is not a sea at all, but a large freshwater lake. It is about 20 kilometres long and 11 kilometres wide. The lake has had many names. Today it is often called the Sea of Tiberias, but its earliest name was the Sea of Chinnereth. This comes from the Hebrew word for a harp, because the lake is roughly harp-shaped.

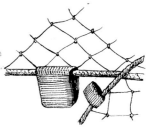

Fishing nets
In Bible times, three types of fishing nets were used. The casting net was bell-shaped, about three metres wide, and weighted at the edges with lead to make it sink. This type of net could be thrown from the shore and was used for small-scale fishing. The drag net was a long net that was lowered from a boat in a semi-circle. The ends were pulled together at the shore, to trap all the fish. The third type was the gill net. This was a long net fitted with floats. It would float in the water all night and be pulled in by the boat the next morning. The disciples were probably using a gill net in this story.

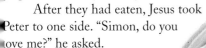

207 ✠

JESUS ENTERS HEAVEN

✤ Luke 24; Acts 1 ✤

Apostles at the ascension
After his resurrection from the dead, Jesus remained on earth for a further forty days before he returned to heaven to resume his place of authority at God's right hand. His return to heaven, or ascension, was in the presence of his disciples on the Mount of Olives. He was taken up into the sky until he was hidden from their sight in a cloud.

After Jesus rose from the dead, he appeared to his disciples many times, bringing them comfort and instruction, and telling them a little about what to expect in the future.

One day, when Jesus met them on the Mount of Olives in Jerusalem, the excited disciples were still bursting with questions for him. Jesus was their Messiah, the Saviour of Israel whom the Old Testament prophets had spoken about. He was their king, and they longed to see the Romans thrown out of their country at last.

"Lord, you've taught us so much about the kingdom of God, but when will you give the kingdom back to Israel?" they asked.

Jesus understood their impatience, but answered firmly, "You don't need to concern yourselves about the times or the dates when the Father has decided that I will return. Just wait here in Jerusalem, because soon I will send you the Holy Spirit, who will give you the power to tell everyone in the world about me. I am building my spiritual kingdom here on earth, and you have an important part to play in that."

When Jesus finished speaking, a cloud hid him from their sight. They strained their eyes, searching for him in the sky, but he was gone.

Suddenly, two men dressed in white – two angels – appeared beside them. "Why are you looking for Jesus in the sky?" they asked the puzzled disciples. "He's been taken up to heaven, and one day he will come back to earth in the same way."

THE HOLY SPIRIT COMES

✤ **Acts 2** ✤

Ten days after the apostles saw Jesus taken up to heaven, they began to celebrate the Jewish feast of Pentecost, along with Jews of many nations who had come to Jerusalem.

On Sunday morning, the Christians met together as usual when, suddenly, the sound of a mighty wind blowing from heaven filled the whole house. Amazed, they watched what looked like tongues of fire rest on each of them, filling them with the power of the Holy Spirit.

A tremendous joy bubbled up from inside them all and, loudly, they began praising God. A crowd gathered to see the commotion, and to their astonishment the apostles began speaking to the visitors in their own languages.

"Aren't these men from Galilee?" someone in the crowd asked his companion. "Then how are they able to talk about the wonderful things God has done in our own language?" Others thought the apostles were drunk.

"We're certainly not drunk," Peter told the crowd. "Why, it's only nine o'clock in the morning! No, God has poured out his Holy Spirit on us, and, just as the prophet Joel foretold, we will now prophesy, see amazing visions and dreams, and perform wonderful miracles. Jesus, whom you crucified, is alive, and God has made him Lord over everyone!"

When the crowd heard this, they were deeply ashamed, and asked the apostles what they should do.

"Don't be afraid," Peter told them. "Tell God that you are sorry for your sin, and be baptized. God will forgive you and give you the Holy Spirit, too."

And that day, about three thousand people became believers.

The Spirit as a dove
The Holy Spirit is God as he is experienced personally by Christians. The symbol of fire reminded Christians of his holiness, and the wind spoke of his powerful presence. At Jesus' baptism he came as a dove, showing God's love and peace.

THE FIRST CHRISTIANS

On the day of Pentecost, the Holy Spirit came upon the disciples. Peter preached boldly to those in Jerusalem and 3,000 people responded and joined them that day: this marked the beginning of the Christian church.

Apostles

An apostle is one who is "sent" by Jesus Christ. The word refers especially to Jesus' twelve disciples, but also specifically to Paul who was commissioned by the risen Jesus as the apostle to the Gentiles. Apostles in the early church had the following in common: they were witnesses to the resurrection of Jesus; they were servants of Christ and figures of authority in the church; they preached and taught; and they began many new churches.

Jews and Gentiles

The Gentiles were those nations and people who were not physical descendants of Abraham, and were therefore seen as excluded from the promises God made to Abraham and his descendants. Initially Jesus told his disciples to preach to the Jews, but after his resurrection they were commissioned to preach the gospel to all nations. From the very beginning the church made no distinction on the grounds of race or colour and accepted both Jews and Gentiles.

Paul

Saul, later called by his Roman name Paul, was a Jew and a Roman citizen. He was born in Tarsus, an important city in Asia Minor, of wealthy parents, and was brought up in the orthodox Jewish tradition. He was educated as a Pharisee under Gamaliel in Jerusalem, and zealously persecuted the church from its very beginning – he was one of those present at the stoning of Stephen, the first Christian martyr. Although his persecution threatened to destroy the church, it actually had the effect of spreading Christianity beyond Jerusalem as believers fled to other cities to escape the persecution.

Apostles

On the road to Damascus

Paul's conversion

Saul was undertaking a six-day journey to Damascus to arrest believers, when he was blinded by a dazzling light. He fell to the ground and heard Jesus saying, "Saul, Saul, why do you persecute me?" He was led into Damascus, and for three days neither ate nor drank until a disciple came and restored his sight. He was then baptized, and astonished everyone by preaching in the synagogues that Jesus was the Messiah. The Jews began to plot his death, but the believers lowered him down from the city walls in a basket and he escaped back to Jerusalem. The church realized his faith was genuine and they sent him to Tarsus for safety.

Paul's journeys

Paul was the first apostle to travel extensively in order to share the Christian message. He made several missionary journeys. On his first journey he sailed to Cyprus and then to the southern coast of Asia Minor. On his second trip he travelled to places in northwest Asia Minor. He then went to Macedonia and brought Christianity to Europe. He also visited Greece and Malta and was later imprisoned in Rome.

Evangelists

The first evangelists travelled by ships like this.

Evangelists are those called by God to proclaim the good news of the gospel, to bear witness to its truth, and to urge people to respond by believing. The task was first given to the apostles, and then to other believers whom the Holy Spirit had specially gifted for the work. The role of evangelist is seen as vital in the context of missionary journeys like those undertaken by Barnabas and Philip, and within the local church, where its leaders (like Timothy) are instructed to do the work of an evangelist. The first evangelists made many journeys across the Mediterranean Sea.

The spread of the church

Apostles like Paul deliberately went to key cities to start churches, but some Christians had to leave Judea because of persecution and they started new churches wherever they settled.

Paul's teaching

Paul considered the importance of the death and resurrection of Jesus Christ as central to God's salvation. He emphasized that people are put in a right relationship with God only when they trust Jesus. Those who become Christians are "in Christ": the Holy Spirit comes to live in them. Paul also taught the second coming of Jesus when the dead will be raised, all evil and opposition to God will be destroyed, and the kingdom of God will arrive. He urged Christians to lead lives of faith, holiness and obedience as they await Jesus' return.

The Holy Spirit

The Holy Spirit is the mysterious unseen force of God's power, sometimes likened to the wind. Usually, people were aware of the Spirit's power when others believed in Jesus or were healed. At Pentecost, the wind and fire were signs from God that the gift of the Spirit had come. After being blessed like this a person was truly a Christian.

Antioch

Antioch was the capital of Syria and the third largest city in the Roman empire. It had a large Jewish community. After the death of Stephen, many persecuted believers fled from Jerusalem to Antioch, and one of the largest and most active of the early Christian churches began. This was where converts were first called "Christians". Paul and Barnabas taught here, and it was the church at Antioch that sent them out on their missionary journeys to Cyprus and beyond. The city was destroyed by an earthquake in AD526.

Reading the good news

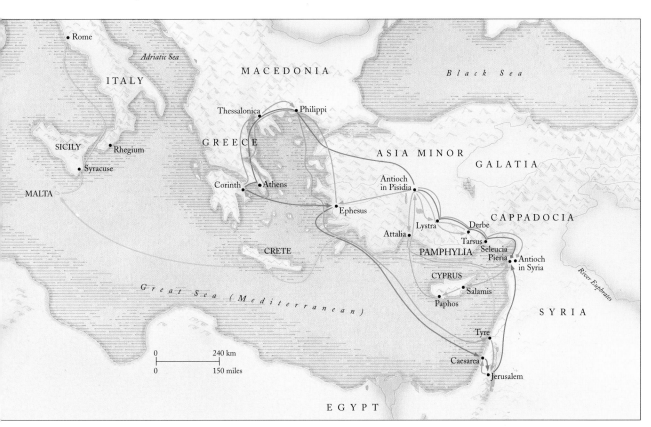

THE FIRST CHRISTIAN BELIEVERS

✤ Acts 2, 4, 5, & 9 ✤

Benedictine monks at prayer
Benedictines are Christian monks and nuns who live a simple life following rules set by St Benedict. The early Christians had a similar lifestyle. They sold their possessions to help the poor, shared meals, and met together every day to pray and hear the apostles teaching about Jesus.

Joppa
The town of Joppa, where Peter brought Tabitha back to life, is a port on the Mediterranean Sea, northwest of Jerusalem. Joppa was founded in the 17th century BC, so by New Testament times it was already an ancient city. For many years, it was occupied by the Philistines. Today, Joppa is known as Jaffa, and forms part of the city of Tel-Aviv.

The four Gospel writers
The life and teaching of Jesus are recorded in the four Gospels. The writers – Matthew, Mark, Luke and John – were all disciples or early followers of Jesus. St Luke also wrote the book of Acts, which tells us about the first Christians.

The number of Jesus' followers continued to grow. Every day they met in the temple courtyards, where the apostles spoke with great authority, talking boldly about the resurrection of Jesus. The believers shared meals in each other's homes, praising God with thankful hearts.

All the believers were united in their desire to help one another, and they made sure that no one was ever in need. One man, called Joseph, sold a field and handed the money to the apostles. His unselfish, caring attitude earned him the nickname Barnabas, which means "son of encouragement". He was just one of many people who sold their land or houses and gave the proceeds to the apostles to distribute to the needy.

Peter also journeyed around the country. One day, when he was visiting some of the believers in Lydda, he met a man called Aeneas, who had been paralysed for eight years.

"Jesus Christ heals you, Aeneas," Peter declared. No sooner had he said this, than Aeneas got up off his mat. When the inhabitants of Lydda saw Aeneas standing on his own two feet they were amazed and believed in Jesus.

While Peter was in Lydda, a woman called Tabitha died in nearby Joppa. Tabitha was loved a great deal, because she was extremely kind to the poor, making clothes for people who were in need of them. Her friends sent a message to Peter, asking him to come at once.

When Peter arrived, he was taken to the upstairs room where Tabitha's body had been placed. Peter told everyone to leave, then he knelt down and prayed. Turning to the dead woman, he said, "Get up, Tabitha!"

Her eyes opened and she sat up. Peter helped her to stand, then called the believers to join him. Everyone who witnessed this miracle spread the news all over the city and many people came to believe in Jesus as a result.

In Jerusalem, the other apostles continued to heal many people. Soon a stream of people suffering from all kinds of illnesses, and even people possessed by demons, came to see them in the hope that they would be made better. Not one of them went away disappointed – everyone was healed.

PETER HEALS THE BEGGAR

✤ Acts 3 ✤

As Peter and John were walking to the temple one afternoon, a man was being carried to one of the temple gates, known as the Beautiful Gate. This man had never been able to walk and was being taken to his usual begging position inside the temple courtyards. When he saw the two apostles, he called out to them, asking for money.

Peter stared at him and said, "Take a good look at us!" The man did so, because he was hopeful that they might give him something.

"I have neither gold nor silver," Peter told him, "but I do have something for you. In the name of Jesus of Nazareth, I tell you to get up and walk."

Then Peter took the man by the hand and pulled him to his feet. As he was doing so, the man sensed that his feet and ankles were being strengthened. He leapt to his feet and went with them into the temple courtyards. He jumped and skipped along like a child, praising God.

Everyone recognized him as the poor cripple who used to beg at the gate, and they were astounded to see what had happened to him. The man's behaviour caused quite a stir and soon a crowd had gathered round Peter and John.

Peter said to them, "Fellow Israelites, why are you so shocked? Why are you looking at us as if we had made this man walk by our own power?

"This is the work of God's servant Jesus, the man you handed over to Pilate for execution. You preferred to release a killer than have anything to do with this good and holy man. You thought you had put an end to his life, but God brought him back to life and it is by his power that this man is now able to walk.

"What you did to Jesus, you did in ignorance. But God used his death in order to fulfil all that the prophets had written.

"I urge you to turn away from your sins and trust in God. Remember the promise that God first made to Abraham? God told him that all the nations of the world would be blessed through him. Now that God has brought Jesus back to life, he is sending him to you first. And as you turn away from your sins, God will bless you."

The Wailing Wall
The Western Wall, known as the Wailing Wall, is all that is left of the temple that stood in Jesus' time. The rest of the temple was destroyed by the Romans in AD70. Jewish people still go to the Wailing Wall to pray and lament for the loss of the temple. Some people write their prayers on pieces of paper, which they slip between the stones of the wall.

213 ✤

ANANIAS AND SAPPHIRA TELL LIES

❖ Acts 5 ❖

The dove
The dove is often used as a symbol of the Holy Spirit. The bird has a loving nature which is seen in its loyalty to its mate and devotion to its young. This, together with its gentleness, purity and innocence, made it natural for the early Christians to associate the dove with the Holy Spirit. This mosaic of a dove was excavated in a bath in the town of Tiberias.

The crucifixion of Peter
According to tradition, Peter is said to have died in Rome during the reign of the emperor Nero by being crucified upside down. Nero blamed the Christians for the huge fire which destroyed much of Rome in AD64. He had them persecuted and put to death.

Hiding the money
Ananias and his wife Sapphira wanted the apostles to think that they were generous givers. They gave them part of the money which they had raised by selling some land, but pretended that they were giving all of it. They paid for their dishonesty with their lives.

One of the believers was a man named Ananias. He sold some of his possessions to raise money for the poor, but he and his wife Sapphira decided to keep part of the profit for themselves. Ananias took the rest of the money and handed it over to the apostles, claiming that it was the full amount of all the proceeds.

But Peter said sternly to Ananias, "Why have you let Satan fill your heart? You have kept some of the earnings from the sale of your land for yourself. Why have you lied to the Holy Spirit?

"Before you sold the land, it belonged to you. After you had sold it the money was yours to do with as you pleased. What possessed you to do what you did? You thought you were lying to us, but really you were lying to God."

Overcome with fear and shame, Ananias collapsed and died where he stood. Peter

called for some strong young men, who wrapped up Ananias's body, carried it out and buried it.

About three hours later, Sapphira came in, unaware of what had happened to her husband. Peter showed her the money that Ananias had given him.

"Can you confirm that this is the full amount that you and Ananias received for the land you sold?" he asked her.

"Yes," she replied, rather curious at the nature of his question.

"Why did you agree with your husband to test God? The men who have just buried Ananias are back from the graveyard and now they will leave to bury you as well," pronounced Peter.

Just as Ananias had done, she crumpled to the ground, dead. Once more the men picked up the body and repeated the grim task that they had so recently performed for her husband.

When the news of these dramatic events became common knowledge, everyone in the church and all the others who heard about it were gripped with fear.

PHILIP AND THE ETHIOPIAN

✤ Acts 8 ✤

An angel told the apostle Philip to travel southwards on the desert road Gaza. So, obediently, Philip set out, ondering what God wanted him to do.

On the same road was an important thiopian official, whose job was to look ter the Ethiopian queen's wealth. He had one to Jerusalem to worship God, and was ow travelling home. As he sat in his hariot, the Ethiopian was reading the riptures of the prophet Isaiah.

The Holy Spirit told Philip to catch o with him, so Philip quickly ran ongside the chariot, and asked the thiopian, "Do you understand what you e reading?"

"I have been longing for someone to xplain it to me," the Ethiopian replied. Please come and join me." So Philip ambered into the chariot.

"Isaiah talks about someone being led his death like a sheep going to be aughtered," the Ethiopian said, with a uzzled expression. "He was treated badly, says, and was killed by people who would not give him a fair trial. Was Isaiah talking about himself or about someone else?"

"He spoke of the Messiah who would die to save all of us from our sins," Philip explained. Then he told the Ethiopian that Jesus was the Messiah and that he had risen from the dead. At last, the Ethiopian had his answer.

They travelled on until they arrived at some water. "Now that I understand and believe in this Jesus, why shouldn't I be baptized?" the Ethiopian asked.

Gladly, Philip baptized him. As soon as they came out of the water, the Holy Spirit took Philip away, and the Ethiopian did not see him again. But he continued his journey joyfully.

Ethiopia
This city is Addis Ababa, the capital of modern-day Ethiopia. The country is situated in northeast Africa, an area which is mainly Muslim. However, Ethiopia has always been home to large numbers of Christians. Today more than a third of all Ethiopians are Christians. They belong to the Ethiopian Orthodox Church, which was founded in the 4th century AD.

JESUS CHALLENGES SAUL

✦ Acts 9 ✦

Damascus
Damascus was the capital of the Roman province of Syria, which lay to the north of Palestine. The city stood at the centre of a network of important trade routes. Saul's journey along the road from Jerusalem to Damascus would have taken him four to six days. This house is built into the ancient city wall, which still stands today.

One of the early church's most dangerous enemies was a young man from Tarsus, called Saul. He was a Jew, who mistakenly thought that he would please God by persecuting Christians.

Saul was there when Stephen, one of the first Christian believers, was stoned to death. He supported those who killed him.

After that event, Saul tried to destroy the church in Jerusalem. He went from house to house searching for Christians; any that he found were thrown into jail, and even executed. Many believers had to leave the city to escape Saul's persecution.

Then Saul went to the high priest and asked for authority to go to the city of Damascus. He intended to arrest any followers of Jesus that he found there and bring them back to Jerusalem. The high priest gave his permission, so Saul set out on his grim journey to Damascus.

But, as he was travelling along the road, a bright, heavenly light suddenly flashed all around him. He covered his eyes and fell to the ground.

Then he heard a voice call out, "Why are you persecuting me, Saul?"

Fearfully, Saul asked, "Who are you, Lord?"

"I am Jesus," the voice replied. "Now get up and go into the city, and you will be told what to do."

So Saul got up and opened his eyes, but he found that he had been struck completely blind. The men he was travelling with had to lead him into Damascus. Saul remained blind for three long days and, feeling humbled by his meeting with Jesus, he could not eat or drink anything.

In Damascus there was a disciple called Ananias. One day, God spoke to him and told him to go to a house on Straight Street and ask for a man from Tarsus, called Saul.

St Paul
After he became a Christian, Saul was known by the Roman version of his name – Paul. He became one of the greatest of all the apostles. Paul founded many new churches and was responsible for spreading Christianity into Europe. The letters that he wrote to some of the early churches form a large part of the New Testament of the Bible.

But Ananias felt afraid. "Lord, I have heard all about this man and the trouble he has caused for your people in Jerusalem," he said, nervously. "And now he has come here to arrest us."

God repeated his command, and explained, "I have specially chosen Saul to spread the good news about me. I will show him how much he must suffer for my sake."

So Ananias went to the house, found Saul, and placed his hands on him. "Brother Saul," Ananias said, "I have been sent by the Lord Jesus, who appeared to you on the road." Immediately, something like fish scales fell from Saul's eyes. He could see again and he was filled with the Holy Spirit.

Saul was baptized straightaway. Then he joined the other disciples in Damascus, who were amazed at the change in him. Soon he began to preach the good news about Jesus in the synagogues.

GOD'S LOVE IS FOR EVERYONE

✧ Acts 10 ✧

Leopard mosaic
This leopard mosaic was discovered when the synagogue at Maon was excavated. It dates from the 4th-6th century AD. Maon lies 14 kilometres south of modern-day Hebron in Israel. It is surrounded by pastureland – probably the "wilderness of Maon" where the Bible says that David hid from Saul.

In the town of Caesarea there lived a God-fearing centurion, called Cornelius. One afternoon, an angel appeared to Cornelius in a vision. "God has heard your prayers," the angel said to him. "Send your men to Joppa to collect Peter. He is staying at the home of Simon, the tanner."

Straightaway Cornelius summoned some of his servants and instructed them to do as the angel had told him. They set off and arrived in Joppa the next day.

When they arrived, Peter was on the roof of the house. He had gone there to pray, but as he prayed he fell into a trance. He saw what appeared to be a large sheet coming down from heaven. Inside the sheet were all sorts of animals, reptiles and birds.

"Arise, Peter. Kill and eat," said a voice.

"No!" he replied. "Never in my life have I eaten anything that is unclean."

The voice spoke again, "What God has cleaned you must not call unclean."

This happened three times and then the sheet disappeared as mysteriously as it had come.

While Peter was trying to understand the meaning of this vision, the Holy Spirit spoke to him, saying, "Some men have come to find you. Leave with them."

The next day Cornelius's men and Peter returned to Caesarea. After they had greeted each other, Cornelius told Peter about the angel's visit.

Peter then realized what his vision meant. "God has shown me that he has no special favourites," he said. "He accepts anyone, whatever their nationality, as long as they fear and obey him. I am a witness to the message of Jesus Christ. Although my people executed him, God has brought Jesus back to life and chosen him to judge the living and the dead, as the ancient writings prophesied."

As he was speaking, the Holy Spirit came, just as he had done on the day of Pentecost. The Jewish men who were with Peter were astonished that even people who weren't Jews were praising God and speaking in different languages.

"I see no reason why these people should not be baptized, for the Holy Spirit has come to them in the same way that he came to us," announced Peter.

So Cornelius and those with him were baptized in the name of Jesus Christ.

AN ANGEL FREES PETER

✦ Acts 12 ✦

King Herod arrested some of the believers and executed James, John's brother. Then he had Peter arrested and flung into prison, where he was guarded by sixteen soldiers. Herod intended to bring Peter to trial at the Passover. During the intervening period, Peter was kept under lock and key. But the people of the church kept praying for him.

The night before the trial was to take place, Peter was fast asleep. He was chained securely between two soldiers, and more soldiers were guarding the entrance to the jail.

Suddenly, an angel appeared in the cell, filling it with light. The angel shook Peter and said, "Get up!" As Peter did so, the chains around his wrists tumbled off and crashed to the floor.

"Get dressed and follow me," the angel continued. Peter thought he was dreaming, but he followed the angel.

They passed the first guard, then the second guard and finally they arrived at the heavy iron gate of the prison. The door creaked open by itself and Peter stepped out into the city. The angel went with him along the street, then vanished into thin air.

Peter finally realized that he was not dreaming. "The Lord really has rescued me," he said to himself. Then he sped to the house of Mark's mother, Mary.

Inside, some of the believers were at prayer. A girl named Rhoda answered his knocking. When she realized who it was, she forgot to open the door and rushed to tell the others. "Peter is here!" she shouted.

"Don't be so ridiculous!" they told her. But the sound of Peter's knocking could still be heard, so they went to see what was happening. To their surprise, there was Peter, just as Rhoda had said!

They could scarcely believe their ears as Peter told them what had happened. Finally, he told them to pass on to the others the exciting news of how God had rescued him.

Angels
Angels appear on several occasions in the book of Acts. They rescue people from prison and sometimes give people guidance and instructions, either directly or through dreams and visions.

Prison keys
Prisoners were chained or placed in stocks and were closely watched at all times. Their guards would face certain death if they allowed a prisoner to escape. Peter's prison was probably the Antonia Fortress in Jerusalem.

SHARING THE GOOD NEWS WITH OTHERS

✦ Acts 13-14 ✦

where Paul talked about the resurrection of Jesus. They were invited to return on the next Sabbath. This time, when they entered the synagogue virtually everyone in the city had assembled to hear their message.

"We came first to the Jews, but as they have rejected our teaching we will also speak to the Gentiles," said Paul, "for the Lord himself speaks of bringing his light to the whole world."

The Gentiles were delighted, but the Jews stirred up many of the chief people of the city against them and so they were forced to leave.

Next, Paul and Barnabas preached in Iconium, but the Jews there plotted to kill them so once more they had to leave.

In Lystra they healed a cripple and were acclaimed as gods by the crowds. Paul was horrified, and tried to convince the crowds that he and Barnabas were just ordinary humans. Even so, the people tried to offer sacrifices to them.

Soon after this, some Jews arrived from Iconium and turned the people of Lystra against Paul. They attacked him, stoned him and left him outside the city, thinking he was dead. But some of the disciples came and revived him and the next day he left.

Then Paul and Barnabas made their way back to Antioch to report on everything that had happened.

Zeus
Zeus was the Greek god of the heavens and the patron god of the city of Lystra. According to an ancient legend, the gods Zeus and Hermes had once visited the area and had only been recognized by an old couple. The people of Lystra did not want to make the same mistake twice, so when Paul and Barnabas healed a cripple, they were convinced that they must be Zeus and Hermes and tried to offer sacrifices to them.

The leaders of the church in Antioch were fasting and praying together when the Holy Spirit spoke to them. He told them that Paul and Barnabas must leave Antioch because they had important work to do elsewhere.

So Paul and Barnabas sailed to Cyprus, where a false prophet named Bar-Jesus spoke against them. Paul said to him, "Why don't you stop opposing the Lord? Now he will strike you, and you will be blind for a while."

At once Bar-Jesus was unable to see a thing and had to be led away. Sergius, the governor of the island, was so amazed by this that he became a follower of Jesus.

From Cyprus, Paul and Barnabas travelled to Pisidian Antioch. On the Sabbath, they went to the synagogue,

TELLING OTHERS THE GOOD NEWS
God encourages every Christian to talk to other people about their faith. After all, the message of Jesus is good news, and the best news that anyone can hear is that God loves them. We needn't be shy to tell people about God, because we can trust him to show us when to speak, and to tell us what to say.

AN EARTHQUAKE SHAKES THE PRISON

✤ Acts 16-17 ✤

Soon Paul set out on a second journey, taking with him a friend called Silas. They travelled to Philippi, in Macedonia.

There was a slave girl in the city who was possessed by a demon. She earned a lot of money for her owners by telling fortunes. For days, the girl followed Paul and his companions everywhere, shouting, "These men are telling you the way to be saved." Finally, Paul had had enough, so he commanded the demon to leave her.

When the girl's owners realized that the demon had gone, they were upset because they had lost their source of income. They took Paul and Silas to the magistrates and made false accusations against them. Their lies were accepted and Paul and Silas were flogged and thrown into prison.

In the middle of the night, a huge earthquake struck the prison. The doors opened and the prisoners' chains fell off. When the jailer woke, he was stunned to see the doors wide open. Convinced that all the prisoners had escaped, the jailer drew out his sword and was about to kill himself. But Paul shouted, "Don't – we are all here!"

The jailer called for torches, and was able to see that what Paul had said was true. He was amazed and asked Paul, "What must I do to be saved?"

"Trust in the Lord Jesus and you and your family will be saved," replied Paul. Then he told the man and his household all about Jesus. They were filled with great joy and asked to be baptized.

The next morning, the magistrates sent word that Paul and Silas should be released, but they refused to leave. "We have been beaten and thrown into prison without a hearing, even though we are Roman citizens," Paul protested. "If the magistrates want us to go, they must come here themselves and release us."

When the magistrates discovered that Paul and Silas were Roman citizens they were very worried. So they came to escort them from the prison and urged them to leave Philippi.

After paying a brief visit to encourage some of the believers in the town, Paul and Silas left for Thessalonica.

Greek amphora
The people of Philippi would have used pots like this one, called an amphora, for storing wine or oil. Philippi was situated in the Roman province of Macedonia, in the northern part of modern-day Greece. It was originally a Greek city, but was conquered by the Romans in 168BC.

Christ's blessing
A "blessing" is a statement that God will do good things for us. Jesus "blessed" his followers before he returned to heaven. Paul experienced God's goodness in the miraculous release from prison. He told the jailer that in order to be "saved" (to know God personally and receive his blessing), he must trust in Jesus.

ARGUING WITH HIS ENEMIES

❖ Acts 21-26 ❖

In many places he visited, Paul faced danger as people tried to stop him preaching about Jesus. When his friends heard the prophet Agabus warn that he would be imprisoned in Jerusalem, they pleaded with Paul not to go.

"In every city God warns me that I face prison and hardships," Paul said, refusing to be discouraged. "But my whole life is dedicated to preaching the wonderful gospel of God's grace. Why are you crying? I am more than willing to die for my beloved Jesus."

At the temple in Jerusalem, certain Jews stirred up the crowd into a violent frenzy until they viciously beat Paul, wanting him dead. The Roman commander ordered his arrest, but when he heard that Paul was a Roman citizen,

he did not punish him because he had not been found guilty. Instead, wanting the truth, the commander brought Paul before the Jewish council to answer their charges, but they simply quarrelled among themselves.

When Paul's nephew discovered a plot to ambush and kill Paul, the commander ordered his soldiers to escort Paul to Caesarea. There, he spent two years in prison. But Paul cleverly used the opportunity to tell the Roman leaders about Jesus. "I am only repeating what the prophets said would happen, that Jesus would suffer, then rise from the dead," he protested. "I have committed no crime against the religious law or Caesar."

And the authorities agreed with him.

Ruins of Caesarea
Caesarea was a deep-water port, built by Herod the Great and named in honour of Caesar Augustus. The city became the capital of the Roman province of Judea and the residence of the Roman governors. Recent excavations revealed a stone with Pontius Pilate's name inscribed on it. Paul visited the city at least three times before being brought to be tried before Governor Felix. He spent two years in prison at Caesarea, but then he appealed to have his case heard by Caesar in Rome. Under Roman law, Paul was entitled to have a fair trial in Rome.

SHIPWRECKED ON THE WAY TO ROME

✤ Acts 27-28 ✤

Paul remained a prisoner for several years until he decided that he would ask the emperor of Rome to hear his case. So with other prisoners and some friends, he boarded a ship bound for Italy.

The season of Mediterranean storms began, and strong winds kept blowing their ship off course. Finally, Paul warned the Roman centurion, Julius, "It's too dangerous to go on. Our lives are at risk."

The ship's captain didn't agree so they continued. As they neared Crete, a hurricane blew up and tossed the boat about so violently that everyone on board gave up hope of staying alive.

"You should have listened to me," Paul told them, "but don't be afraid. God has told me that, although we will be shipwrecked, none of us will die."

After two weeks of storms, the sailors realized that they'd reached shallow water and tried to escape in the lifeboat to avoid hitting rocks. "They must stay with the ship!" Paul insisted to Julius, "otherwise they will all drown." Paul knew that God would protect them. He began eating, and encouraged everyone else to join him.

When at last they spied land, the ship hit a sandbank and was smashed to pieces. The soldiers wanted to kill all the prisoners in case they escaped, but Julius stopped them because he wanted to save Paul. All 276 people reached the shore and were saved, just as God had promised.

The island on which they had landed was Malta. They stayed the winter there before going on to Rome. When he reached Rome, Paul was kept under house arrest for two years as he awaited his trial. But all the time he continued to preach boldly the good news of Jesus.

Julius Caesar
With the rise of the Roman empire in the first century BC, ambitious men began to struggle for power. Julius Caesar is probably the best known. He defeated Pompey and took the title 'dictator', assuming special emergency powers. He was a brilliant ruler, but he was assassinated by Brutus and Cassius in 44BC.

Crete
Crete, where the storm began, is the largest Greek island. The climate is mild and dry and a chain of mountains covers the centre of the island. The Romans made it a province in 66BC. Today many Cretans belong to the Greek Orthodox Church.

Roman chair of state
The Romans brought law, order, and stability to the countries they governed, enforcing peace by maintaining garrisons of soldiers throughout the empire. The city of Rome became the seat of civil government. This Roman chair of state would have been used in the conduct of official business.

IN A RIGHT RELATIONSHIP

✤ Romans 1-16 ✤

Romans is the first of twenty-one letters, or "epistles", in the New Testament. Thirteen of them are believed to have been written by the apostle Paul. These letters were sent either to churches or to individuals and many of them were written to follow up visits that Paul had made on his missionary journeys. He wrote to encourage the new believers in their faith, and to try to warn them of the dangers and difficulties they faced. This is part of a letter that Paul wrote to the Christians in Rome:

Roman costume
Citizens of ancient Rome wore an outer garment called a toga. This was a semi-circular piece of cloth, which was draped around the body and fell to the feet in folds. At first, both Roman men and women wore togas, but in time, women began to wear a cloak, called a "palla", instead.

The Roman forum
The forum was a public square in the centre of ancient Rome. All the city's most important government buildings, temples and monuments were around the forum. It was also the central meeting place, where Romans went to discuss important questions of the day.

Abraham
In this letter, Paul says Abraham did not become the father of the Hebrew nation because of anything special that he did, but because he trusted God. Paul says that in the same way, we are to trust God in order to receive the gift of new spiritual life.

Ever since the world was created, God has clearly shown us his power and character, yet we have chosen to ignore him. There is not one person on earth who obeys God with the full honour that he deserves. All of us have failed to keep the holy commands of God's law. We are all sinners. But God has now shown us a way to be in a right relationship with him, that is not dependent upon keeping the law. God sent his Son, Jesus Christ, to suffer and die in our place.

Our ancestor Abraham was accepted not because of what he did, but because of his simple act of trust when he took God at his word. God blessed Abraham. He gave him a son, and life through his descendants. Abraham became the father of many nations. In the same way, God has given us his own Son. Like Abraham, we were unable to do anything for ourselves, but we too have received life through the gift of God's Son to the world.

We no longer have to try to please God by obeying the law. The old system of the law died with Jesus. The more we studied and tried to obey the law, the more we were tempted to disobey it. Now that it is dead and buried, we are free to live in a way that pleases God. Just as he made Jesus alive again, so he makes us alive to serve him. We used to be slaves to our sinful ways, but now we are slaves to good and right behaviour.

We still have to battle to overcome our old way of life and the daily temptations that try to destroy us. But God has sent his Holy Spirit to guide us and to fill us with the strength and determination to live for him. The power of the Spirit gave Jesus back his life. If the Spirit lives in us, his limitless power and energy will help us to serve God. So all the good things that we do come from God, and not from our own efforts. To God alone be the glory! Amen.

GOD'S ARMOUR PROTECTS US

✤ Ephesians 6 ✤

Ephesus was the most important city in the western part of Asia Minor (modern-day Turkey). It was situated on the caravan route between Europe and Asia, and was a great commercial, political and religious centre. During his third missionary journey, the apostle Paul stayed in Ephesus for two years. He later wrote to the Christians there about the great spiritual blessings that were theirs because of Jesus Christ, and about God's plans for his people, and of how these work out day to day. Here is an extract from the end of his letter:

Ruins at Ephesus
Ephesus was the capital of the Roman province of Asia. Saint Paul and Saint John helped to establish a flourishing church there, which became the leading Christian community of Asia. Archaeologists uncovered the ruins of Ephesus in the late 1800s.

Finally, be brave. Trust in the Lord and in his immense power. Put on the full armour of God, so that you can resist the devil and all his wicked plans. Remember, living as a believer in the world is not easy. We are in a battle. We are not fighting against things that we can see, but against all the rulers and kingdoms of this sinful world and against the forces of evil in the heavens.

For this reason, you must dress yourselves with every piece of God's armour, and with all his weapons. Then when evil attacks, as it will, you will be able to stand your ground. Strap the belt of truth around your waist. Put the breastplate of righteousness on your chest. For shoes wear the alertness that is inspired by the gospel of peace. Protect yourself with the shield of faith, using it to deflect everything that the devil will throw at you. Place the helmet of salvation proudly on your head and hold the sword of the Spirit, which is the word of God, firmly in your hand. You cannot manage without any of these weapons.

And keep on praying, because prayer is indispensable. Whatever the circumstances, be sure to pray under the Spirit's inspiration, and always remember other believers in your prayers.

Finally, pray for me too, so that whenever I have the opportunity to speak for the Lord, I will preach his gospel boldly. Pray that I may declare the gospel without fear, as I ought to.

Artemis of Ephesus
The temple of Artemis at Ephesus was one of the seven wonders of the ancient world. Worship of the goddess Artemis was connected with a kind of fertility-cult. When Paul visited Ephesus, he preached at the temple of Artemis and caused a riot.

Joan of Arc
Christians know that they are fighting a spiritual battle, which requires putting on the spiritual armour of Ephesians 6. Some Christians, however, have had to fight real battles for their faith or their country, like Joan of Arc, pictured above.

USING OUR SPIRITUAL GIFTS

✤ 1 Corinthians 12-14 ✤

Rock gecko
Lizards are by far the most conspicuous reptiles in the Mediterranean, and they can often be seen basking on rocks in the early morning sunshine. This rock gecko's feet have suction pads on the toes, enabling it to cling to smooth walls. Sometimes it clings upside down to the ceiling in houses.

Byzantine Cross
The cross is the chief symbol of Christianity and is often depicted in Christian art. It shows that Jesus died to make God's forgiveness and new life possible. However, Jesus' resurrection from the dead is equally important. It shows that Jesus conquered death, so that his followers can live in God's presence for ever.

Aphrodite
The Corinthians were wealthy people and enjoyed a variety of leisure pursuits. But their culture and wealth led them into bad ways, centred on the cult of Aphrodite, the Greek goddess of love, whose worship involved immorality. The temple to Aphrodite had over 1,000 pagan priestesses.

Paul wrote a letter to the church in Corinth explaining how God gives every Christian spiritual gifts to use:

When you meet on a Sunday to worship, remember that you all have something valuable from God to encourage others with, perhaps a hymn or a message. The same God works through the same Spirit, but in different ways. One person might receive a message of wisdom from God to share, someone else a message of knowledge. One might be given a special gift of faith, another healing, or the power to work a miracle. Others can prophesy, or distinguish between spirits. Then there is the gift of speaking in tongues and interpreting what has been said. But don't be proud, because none of the gifts is better than any other.

Think of the church as being like a human body. Each part has a purpose, working together with the other parts. Don't think that any one part is more important than another. For instance, there would be no sense in the eye saying to the hand, "I don't need you!" People in the church who don't seem important have also been given a special role by God.

In the body of Christ on earth, God chose apostles, prophets, teachers and workers of miracles. Others have gifts of healing or administration, or speak in different tongues. Each person can discover the gifts God has given them.

WE WILL LIVE AGAIN

✤ 1 Corinthians 15 ✤

When Paul heard that some of the Christians at Corinth claimed that there was no life after death, he wrote firmly correcting them:

My friends, Jesus was punished on the cross for our sins, buried in the tomb, then on the third day raised from the dead. We know this, because once he appeared to more than five hundred believers, and also to Peter and the other apostles. In fact, I saw him with my own eyes on the road to Damascus!

So why do some of you say that there is no resurrection of the dead? Because if Jesus isn't alive, then our whole faith is worth nothing, and you'd still be unforgiven! If we didn't have an eternal home in heaven to look forward to, we might as well eat, drink and enjoy ourselves, instead of being careful how we live because one day God will judge us.

You ask, "What will our bodies look like when we are raised from the dead?"

Our natural bodies will rot away, but then we'll have beautiful new spiritual bodies, better than before, never suffering from any sickness.

Look forward to that day when the trumpet will announce the raising of the dead! As quickly as the twinkling of an eye we'll be changed to be like Jesus himself, although it's a mystery how it will happen. We can thank God because Jesus has won the final victory over death.

So don't let anything stop you from doing God's work, because even though life may be difficult, you will be rewarded in heaven.

THE SECOND COMING

✤ 2 Thessalonians 1-2 ✤

The Christians in Thessalonica became confused about Jesus Christ's second coming. Some claimed that he had already come back from heaven. Paul wrote to them, explaining the truth:

Brothers, remember that none of us knows exactly when Jesus will return to earth, so don't be fooled when you hear people saying that the day of the Lord's coming has already arrived. That day will come just as a thief comes in the night, when we least expect it.

And don't despair that some of your family and friends have already died, because when Jesus comes back, they will rise from the dead. Then we who are still alive will join them in the clouds and be with Jesus for ever.

Meanwhile, the most important thing is to please God by living a pure life. Although your enemies are making you suffer badly, this doesn't mean that the end of the world is in sight. Before then, evil will increase, but stand firm in the truth that we have taught you, and may God our Father strengthen you.

Some of you have become lazy, but you must always be ready to meet God without being ashamed of your behaviour. Be kind to each other, and work hard. Help the weak and be patient with everyone. Always be joyful and pray all the time, thanking God and avoiding every kind of evil.

Greek Orthodox church
Thessalonica was (and still is) an important Greek city. It was built at the junction of major trade routes. It was the first city where large numbers of people responded to Paul's message. Today, it has many churches like these.

Saints in heaven
No one knows quite what heaven will be like, except that people there will see and know God completely, and there will be no more suffering or evil. The haloes on this Greek painting suggest the purity of heaven, where everyone is called a "saint".

LETTERS TO CHURCH LEADERS

✤ 1–2 Timothy; Titus ✤

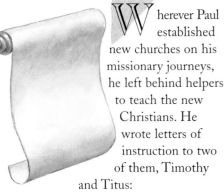

Wherever Paul established new churches on his missionary journeys, he left behind helpers to teach the new Christians. He wrote letters of instruction to two of them, Timothy and Titus:

To Timothy, my dear son. Make sure you appoint mature Christians as leaders, testing them to see that they are well behaved and able to teach. Point out to your brothers that everything God has made is good so that they will not be confused by false teachers.

Don't let anyone look down on you, Timothy, just because you are young, but set them a good example in what you say and do, and in showing love, faith and purity. Teach people that the love of money is a cause of all kinds of evil, and that God will make you content with the money you already have.

Remember that God's Spirit gives us power, love and self-control, so be brave about preaching the gospel. As a good soldier of Jesus, you will suffer – just as I have! But I have fought hard and finished the race, and look forward to God's reward.

Paul urged Titus to encourage the believers on Crete to turn away from their old ways of laziness and lying:

Choose godly leaders for each church, and always set a good example yourself. Make sure that everyone respects you when you encourage and correct them.

First-century anchors
In New Testament times, anchors were made completely of iron, or of wood with lead or stone arms. They could weigh more than 600 kg and had small marker-buoys attached to locate their position. Ships carried three or four anchors and when riding out a storm these were dropped from the stern of the ship.

The Minoan civilization
From about 3000 to 1150BC, Knossos on Crete was the main centre of the Minoan civilization, named after King Minos of Crete. When Paul visited Crete many examples of Minoan art and architecture would have been in evidence.

Merchant ship
In New Testament times many merchant ships sailed across the Mediterranean, and Paul used them for his missionary travels. Propelled by sails and oars, some were 90 metres long. Few ships sailed between November and March when the seas were rough and, as it was the rainy season, clouds often obscured the stars, making navigation impossible.

The faith of Moses
The letter to Hebrews ends with an appeal to Christians to show the same faith and trust in God that the heroes of the Old Testament had. Moses, for example, had faith that God would part the Red Sea.

Seal and inscription
In Bible times, letters were often marked with a seal to show who the letter came from. A seal was proof that a letter was authentic. The seal of an important person or official meant that the letter carried their authority.

St Paul
St Paul wrote many of the letters in the New Testament and was once believed to be the author of the letter to the Hebrews. Experts now think that this letter was written after St Paul's death, and its true author is still not known.

THE IMPORTANCE OF FAITH

✤ Hebrews 11 ✤

The letter to the Hebrews was sent to Jewish Christians to encourage them, but we don't know for certain who wrote it. In the letter, the author describes the relationship between Jesus Christ and the Old Testament, and sees Jesus as fulfilling the Old Testament law. The letter says the following:

True faith is being sure of what we hope for and certain of things that we cannot see. It is faith that allows us to know that God created the world. This is the faith that was seen in the men and women who served God in the past.

Abel showed faith when he offered a more appropriate sacrifice than his brother Cain did. Because he had faith, Noah built an ark even though he could not see the gathering rain clouds.

When God commanded, Abraham left his own country to live in an unknown land. He became a father when he was a very old man and eventually produced a nation as numerous as the stars in the sky. Yet Abraham did not receive anything for himself. His eyes were fixed on the future, as he strained to see what God had in store for him. Even when God told him to kill his own son, Abraham did not hesitate, because he had faith that God could bring Isaac back to life again.

By faith, Isaac and Jacob blessed their children. By faith, Moses' family protected him at his birth. When he grew up he repaid them by showing faith in the face of Pharaoh's stubbornness, preferring to suffer with his own people rather than enjoy the luxuries of Egypt. By faith, the Israelites passed through the Red Sea. By faith, the walls of Jericho crumbled to the ground and Rahab survived the slaughter of its citizens.

The list is endless. I could speak of Gideon, Samson, David, and all the prophets. Some people faced lions, survived burning, escaped death in battle, or were raised from the dead; some were tortured and whipped; others were imprisoned and executed. Many wandered around in rags without house or home.

Each and every one of these heroes lived by faith in God, so that one day they, like us, would be made perfect, according to God's holy plans.

LIVING FOR GOD

✤ 1 Peter 2 & 4; 2 Peter 1 ✤

Peter was one of Jesus' closest disciples. After Jesus ascended into heaven, he became a leader of the early Christians in Jerusalem. Peter was one of the first people to preach the good news about Jesus to Gentiles – people who were not Jews. Peter's first letter was written to persecuted Christians, both Jews and Gentiles, who were scattered throughout much of northern Asia Minor (present-day Turkey). Peter writes:

Jesus is the living foundation stone on which you are being built. You have been chosen by God himself, so that you can tell other people about Jesus, who called you from the dark shadows into his brilliant sunshine.

You are a company of royal priests, a holy nation joined together to form the people of God. You do not belong to this world any more, but are subjects of a heavenly kingdom. Therefore I plead with you not to make this world your home. Do not get bogged down in the wrong ways of the world. Instead conduct yourself in such a way that, even if people speak badly of you, they will see the good that you do and give glory to God.

Even if people abuse you because you have done what you know to be right, do not worry. In fact, you should not be surprised when people mock you because you follow Jesus. If you are suffering simply because you are a Christian, don't be downcast. Instead, you should be honoured and praise God. It is better to be victimized for doing what pleases God, than for disobeying him. Christ suffered, and you should expect to suffer too. But keep on going to the end!

Do everything that you can to build on what is already good in your lives – to possess goodness as well as the faith that you already enjoy. To goodness add understanding; to understanding add the ability to control yourself; to this, add persistence, and to persistence add godliness. With godliness you must show kindness to all those of the faith, and finally to this kindness, add love. If you keep growing in all these characteristics you will never be limited in what you can do for the Lord. But if you stop growing, it is a sign that you have forgotten all that he has done for you.

Therefore, live in a way that pleases God. If you do this, nothing will ever trip you up and you will be welcomed with joy when you enter the eternal kingdom of Jesus Christ. Amen.

Jesus Christ
In his letter, Peter concentrated on the theme of suffering, because the Christians he was writing to were facing terrible persecution. But Peter reminded them that Jesus suffered for us, and told them that they should be glad to share with Jesus in this way.

Suffering today
In some parts of the world, Christians are still persecuted for their faith today. Other Christians, like these refugees, suffer because of wars or natural disasters. Peter encourages Christians who are suffering to trust God and draw on his power.

Reed pen and ink pot
Peter would probably have written his letters with a reed pen and ink. One end of the reed was shaped to form a nib, which was dipped into the black ink. This was made from soot mixed with water, oil and gum, and was kept in an ink pot.

The vision of John
John's vision reveals the glory of the risen Jesus Christ. When John saw Jesus' power and majesty, he knew that, even in the face of death, believers were assured of eternity in his glorious presence, when evil will no longer come between God and his people.

Plain of Megiddo
Strategically situated in the valley of Jezreel, Megiddo has been the scene of countless battles, and has come to symbolize war. Some Christians believe that the last great battle described in the Book of Revelation will be fought there.

The seven churches of Asia
The Book of Revelation starts with letters to seven churches in the Roman province of Asia, in modern-day Turkey. The letters brought commendation, complaint, and correction.

JOHN'S VISION OF HEAVEN

✤ Revelation 1-3 ✤

Now an old man, John was imprisoned on the island of Patmos when Jesus gave him a magnificent vision of what he is like. John wrote:

I was praying one Sunday, when I heard a loud voice commanding me to encourage the seven churches in Asia.

Then a figure appeared, dressed in a long robe with the golden sash of a high priest around his chest. His head was snowy white, showing his wisdom, and his eyes blazed with the fire of judgement. His feet were like molten bronze, and his voice sounded like powerful rushing water. In his right hand he held seven stars - the angels of the seven churches - while the message he spoke was like a sharp two-edged sword coming out of his mouth. And his face shone as brilliantly as the sun.

When I saw his glorious splendour, I fell at his feet as though I was dead. But he told me not to be afraid.

"I am the First and the Last, alive for ever," he told me, "and I hold the keys to death and the world of the dead."

When John saw his Lord's majesty and power, he knew that whatever troubles faced the church, even death itself, God would always be stronger and keep them safe. They made mistakes, but God would forgive and change them. No evil power would ever separate them from his love.

A NEW HEAVEN AND EARTH

✤ Revelation 20-22 ✤

John's vision included a glimpse of the magnificent new heaven and earth that God will create in the future. He wrote:

I saw the holy city of Jerusalem made beautiful, like a bride dressing herself in fine clothes for her husband. Dazzling precious jewels decorated its walls and it shone brightly with the pure and holy glory of God. A high wall with twelve gates labelled with the twelve tribes of Israel surrounded the city, and on its foundation stones were the names of the twelve apostles.

Here God will make his home with his people, those who have been forgiven by Jesus, the Lamb of God, and whose names are written in the book of life. And, tenderly, God will wipe every tear from our eyes, and there will be no more death, or suffering, or crying or pain, because the past and every kind of evil will be gone for ever. Only peace and love will remain.

But, sadly, staying outside the city will be those who haven't been forgiven their sin. They won't share in this glorious new world. So let everybody who is thirsty for eternal life come and drink from the crystal clear river of the water of life that flows from the throne of God.

The one who has spoken these things to you says, "I am coming soon."

So, Lord Jesus, come soon!

The city of God
John's vision of the heavenly Jerusalem was of a city with walls of jasper, gates of pearl, and streets of gold, built on foundations encrusted with precious stones. The river of life runs through the city, and it is a place of perfection with no more death, pain or suffering. There is no need of the sun by day, nor the moon by night, because the glory of the Lord gives it light. The vision is full of symbols which describe beauty and peace. Heaven is unlike anything we know about on earth

BIBLE REFERENCE

Here we can find out about daily
life in bible times, the places people
lived in, and about the kinds of plants
and animals they would have seen.
We can find out about the spread of
Jesus' message to other lands
and the beginning of the
Christian church.

*The world and all that is in it belong to the
Lord; the world and all people who
live on it are his.*

(Psalm 24:1)

DAILY LIFE IN OLD TESTAMENT TIMES

The events described in the Old Testament took place over a vast period of time – probably more than 2,000 years. In this time, people's way of life changed dramatically. Characters in the early Bible stories, such as Abraham, Isaac and Jacob, were nomads who moved from place to place and lived in tents. But by the time of King David, the Israelites had become a settled people who lived in houses and made their living from farming the land.

The nomadic way of life

Abraham, Isaac and Jacob were nomads. They had no settled homes, but moved from place to place looking for grazing land and water for their herds of sheep and goats. They lived in tents, which they could pack up and carry on the back of their animals whenever they wanted to move on. Nomads usually travelled in family groups, led by the father of the family. According to the Bible, Abraham's family group included several wives, his sons with their wives and children, and slaves.

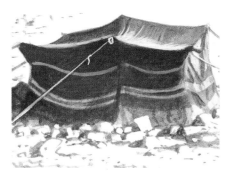

Nomad's today live in tents that have changed very little since the time of Abraham.

In a nomad's tent

Abraham and his family would have lived in tents made of woven goats' hair. They were held up with rows of poles and secured with guy ropes. This sort of tent was usually divided into two parts by a curtain. The women and children lived in the back part of the tent, while the front part was used by the men and for entertaining guests. The tent furnishings would have been very basic – just some straw mats for beds, and a goatskin spread on the floor as a table. Their only other possessions would have been cooking equipment and a few pottery lamps.

Keeping flocks

Nomadic families like Abraham's lived from their flocks of sheep and goats. They drank their milk and used the wool and skins for making tents and clothes. Their animals were very valuable to them, so they only killed them for their meat on special occasions. In later times when the Israelites had become settled farmers, flocks were still important. They were kept in the countryside outside the towns and looked after by a shepherd. His job was to lead his flock to grass and water, and protect them from the threat of wild animals.

In many parts of the world, a young goatherd or shepherd with his flock is still a familiar sight.

A typical house

Once the Israelites settled in Canaan, they abandoned their tents and started to live in houses. They were usually made from stone, timber and plaster and were often built into the city wall. Houses often had a courtyard and most had one main room which was used for cooking, eating and sleeping, and also as a stable for the family's sheep, goats and chickens.

On the roof

Outside the house was a staircase that led up to the flat roof. The roof was made of heavy wooden beams, covered with layers of reeds, mud, grass and clay. The family would have spent a

The word nomad comes from the Greek meaning "one who wanders for pasture". Most nomads travel in their family group or tribe.

lot of time on the roof of their house. Women often did their weaving and baking on the roof, and they also used it for drying figs, dates, flax and for washing. In the evenings, the family relaxed together on the roof and they even slept there in the summer.

Farming

As the Israelites settled in Canaan, they started to farm the land. Their main crops were cereals, olives and grapes. When the rains came in October, farmers ploughed the fields and then sowed the cereal crops. These crops were harvested in April and May. The grain was cut with a curved knife called a sickle and then tied into bunches called sheaves. During the summer months, farmers concentrated on their vines, which needed to be constantly pruned and hoed.

Grapes were picked in September, and the farmer would often have to hire extra workers to help with the harvest.

A typical Israelite house was built of mud bricks and had a flat roof. Inside there was just one room, lit by tiny windows and oil lamps.

Food

A typical family meal would have been a stew made from beans, lentils and peas, flavoured with onions and garlic, and served with bread. This would be followed by fruit, such as figs, melons, dates or pomegranates. Sheep or goat's milk was also an important part of the diet. It was churned to make butter and the curds could be used to make cheese or a kind of yoghurt called "leben". People only ate meat on special occasions, such as religious festivals, or when they were entertaining honoured guests.

Jewish food laws

In Bible times, all Israelites followed the laws about food that are written in the books of Leviticus and Deuteronomy. According to these laws, pigs, rabbits, camels, shellfish, and any animal that had died of natural causes could not be eaten. It was forbidden to eat meat and milk in the same meal, or to eat the blood of animals. When an animal was killed for food, its blood had to be drained out. Meat that has been treated this way is called "kosher". Many orthodox Jews still follow these food laws today.

Israelite women spent most of their time working around the home. They were in charge of the household.

According to Jewish food laws, crayfish and other shellfish are regarded as "unclean" and may not be eaten.

Clothes

Israelite men wore a tunic made from wool or linen, which came down to their knees or ankles. Over this they wore a sleeveless coat – a square piece of woollen cloth with holes for the arms. This coat was very adaptable – it could also be used as a rug to sit on or a blanket at night. Women wore very similar outfits to men, but their clothes were often made of more brightly coloured fabric. Israelite people often wore leather sandals, especially if they were travelling.

Women's work

One of a woman's most important and time-consuming chores was baking bread. She had to grind grain between two flat stones to make flour, then mix the dough and bake the loaves. Twice a day, the woman also had to fetch all the water that the family needed from the village well or cistern. She carried it home in a large pot balanced on her head. Another duty was spinning wool and weaving cloth for the family's clothes.

237 ❖

DAILY LIFE IN NEW TESTAMENT TIMES

Unlike the Old Testament, the New Testament spans a relatively short period of time. The events it describes start with the birth of Jesus (now believed to have taken place in 6 or 7BC) and ends about seventy years later with the death of St Paul. In New Testament times, most people in Palestine still made their living from farming, but more people were living in the towns and cities. One big difference from the Old Testament period was that Palestine now formed part of the Roman empire, and was occupied and governed by the Romans.

Life in a small town

Jesus was brought up in the town of Nazareth, in the region of Galilee. Like other towns it was very small by today's standards and had only a few hundred inhabitants. Many of them would have been farmers, but a few would have been craftsmen, such as carpenters, potters or weavers. Jesus' own father, Joseph, was a carpenter in Nazareth. The main meeting places in the town would have been the synagogue and the market place where the craftsmen had their shops.

During the time of Jesus, Nazareth was a small insignificant town. Today it is popular with pilgrim visitors and has many churches.

Going to the synagogue

By the time of Jesus, most towns would have had a synagogue – a

The Torah was written on long scrolls of paper, which were kept in a special niche or shrine in the synagogue like this one.

building where Jewish people went to worship God and study the law. Inside the synagogue was a prayer hall, which always faced towards Jerusalem. Men and women sat in separate areas. The most important part of a service was reading and studying the Torah, the first five books of the Old Testament, which contained the Jewish law. Visiting teachers were often invited to read the Torah out loud, and there are several stories in the Bible of Jesus reading and teaching in the synagogues of Galilee.

Going to school

There was often a school attached to the town's synagogue, where the rabbi (teacher) taught boys about the Jewish law. In the New Testament period, most Jewish people spoke Aramaic, so pupils first had to learn to read and

write Hebrew, the language in which the Torah was written. Then they had to learn the law by heart. Girls did not attend school. They were taught weaving, cooking and other household skills by their mothers at home.

Fishing

Many people in Galilee made their living from fishing. Every evening, the fishermen would set out on the Sea of Galilee in their small wooden sailing boats. They fished using nets which they pulled through the water and then hauled back into the boat. The main catch was a fish called tilapia, or St Peter's fish. At dawn they would return to the shore and sort the fish into baskets, ready to be sold fresh or salted and dried. They spent the day repairing their boats and mending their nets and sails.

Tilapia are a kind of fish found in the Sea of Galilee. They are also known as St Peter's fish .

Orthodox Jewish boys on their way to school in the Mea Shearin district of Jerusalem.

Many religions observe a Sabbath, or day of rest. For Muslims this is a Friday, for Jews a Saturday, and for Christians, a Sunday.

The Sabbath

In the story of creation, God worked for six days and then rested on the seventh day. Each Saturday, Jewish people have a day of rest, or Sabbath, to remember this. In New Testament times, the Sabbath started at sunset on Friday evening and ended at sunset on Saturday. Families would gather together on Friday evening to eat a meal together. After the meal, a special prayer of blessing called the Kiddush was said. On the Sabbath itself, Jews were not allowed to do any form of work. Even cooking and fetching water were forbidden.

Travel

If ordinary people wanted to go somewhere, they either had to walk there or ride on a donkey, so journeys were not quick or easy. For example, in the story of Jesus teaching in the temple, he and his family walked from Nazareth to Jerusalem for the Passover, a journey that would have taken them about six days. Gangs of thieves often lurked in lonely spots waiting to rob travellers, so people tried to travel in groups for protection. The road from Jerusalem to Jericho, where the man was attacked in Jesus' story of the Good Samaritan, was known to be particularly dangerous.

In many parts of the world, donkeys are still used as a means of transport.

Roman coin
Every five years the Romans put the job as tax-collector up for auction. It went to the highest bidder as the collector could charge people as much tax as he liked and keep any profit for himself.

The Romans

During the New Testament period, Palestine was not an independent country. It formed part of the Roman empire, a huge territory covering much of western Europe, western Asia and north Africa, and was known as the province of Judea. Although the country was technically ruled by a local king, real power lay with the Roman authorities. There were Roman soldiers everywhere, and Jewish people had to pay taxes to Rome. All this made the Romans very unpopular.

The seven-branched candlestick, or menorah, is one of the main symbols of the Jewish faith.

Jewish feasts and festivals

Rosh Hashanah
(September-October)
Jewish New Year.

Yom Kippur
(September-October)
The Day of Atonement, when Jewish people fast and pray.

Succoth
(September-October)
Celebration of the grape and olive harvest and the end of the farming year. People camped in huts or booths for Succoth, which means the "Feast of Booths".

Hanukkah
(December)
The Feast of Lights celebrates the

rededication of the temple in Jerusalem by Judas Maccabeus in 164BC. Candles are lit on each of the eight days of the festival.

Purim
(February-March)
Celebration of how Queen Esther saved the Jews from their enemies.

The Passover
(March-April)
Commemoration of the Exodus from Egypt. The angel of death killed every first-born Egyptian, but "passed over" the Israelites.

Shavuot
(May-June)
Remembers the day that Moses received the Ten Commandments. It is also known as the Feast of Weeks.

PLANTS AND ANIMALS

The creation, Noah's ark, Jonah and the whale, and Jesus' parables about shepherds and their sheep are just some of the many Bible stories involving plants and animals. In Bible times, most people were dependent on growing crops or keeping domestic animals to make their living, so it is not surprising that they are mentioned so frequently in the Bible. There are more than 400 references to sheep alone. Unfortunately some of the animals that appear in the Bible, such as lions, bears and crocodiles, no longer live in Israel today because they have been hunted to extinction.

TREES
Cedars
Cedar trees grew in Lebanon, a country to the north of Israel. The wood was very strong and long-lasting, so it was often used for important buildings. King Solomon imported cedars from Lebanon to build the temple in Jerusalem.

Fig trees
When Zacchaeus the tax collector wanted to see Jesus, he climbed up a fig tree so that he could see over the crowd. Fig trees were grown all over Israel for their fruit. The figs were either eaten fresh, or dried and pressed into cakes.

Palm trees
Date palms were grown particularly in the area around Jericho. Palm trees are also mentioned in the story of Jesus' entry into Jerusalem, when people cut palm branches and laid them on the ground in front of him.

Olive trees
Olive trees live for a very long time and can produce fruit for hundreds of years. The olives were pressed between two large millstones to make olive oil. This was a vital product, used for cooking and as fuel for lamps.

CROPS
Vines
Vines were grown in rows on hillsides and were harvested in September. Some of the grapes were eaten fresh and some were dried to make raisins, but most were crushed and fermented to make wine.

Wheat and barley
Barley was the most widely grown cereal crop because it could grow in areas with poor soil. Both wheat and barley were

ground to make flour for bread, and barley could also be used to brew beer.

Fruit
The Israelites grew figs, grapes, dates, apples, pomegranates and other fruits. The pomegranate became a symbol of fruitfulness and was used as decoration on the high priest's robes.

DOMESTIC ANIMALS
Sheep
Sheep were the most important domestic animals. They were kept for their milk, meat, wool and skins. The fattest and most perfect lambs would also be offered to God as sacrificial animals.

Cattle
The Israelites kept some cattle for their milk, but they were much less common than sheep or goats. We know from the parable of the prodigal son that a specially fattened calf was sometimes killed and eaten on very important occasions.

Goats
Goats were often kept in flocks with sheep. It was not always easy to see which was which, hence Jesus' story about separating the sheep from the goats. Goats could survive on very rough land and were kept for their milk, meat and skins.

Donkeys
Donkeys were used to carry people or heavy loads. Jesus rode into Jerusalem on Palm Sunday on a donkey.

Camels
Camels can survive for long periods without water, so they are ideal for use in desert conditions. In Bible times, camels were highly prized. Abraham's large herd of camels was a sign of his family's wealth.

Pigs
The Israelites did not keep pigs because their food laws forbade eating pork. There were pigs in Israel, but they were usually kept by gentiles (people who were not Jewish).

WILD ANIMALS
Lions
Lions were quite common in Israel in Old Testament times, and they often attacked people or their flocks. Samson was attacked by a lion, which he killed with his bare hands.

Wolves
Wolves often attacked flocks of sheep and goats. The shepherd had to be ready to defend his flock and was armed with a club called a rod to beat off wolves and other wild animals.

Ibex
The ibex is a type of wild goat that still lives in some rocky areas of Israel today. In Bible times it was hunted for its meat.

Snakes
Several species of adder and viper lived in Israel. People were very scared of them, because a bite could prove fatal. In the Bible, the snake is often used as a symbol of evil – the most famous example is the serpent in the Garden of Eden.

Locusts
Locusts are the most frequently mentioned insect in the Bible. Sometimes a huge swarm of them arrives in an area and eats every single plant. In the Bible, one of the ten plagues of Egypt was a swarm of locusts.

BIRDS
Ravens
The raven was the first bird that Noah released from the ark. According to the Jewish food laws, the raven was an "unclean" bird and could not be eaten or sacrificed.

Doves
In the Bible, the dove is a symbol of the Holy Spirit, who appeared in the form of a dove when Jesus was baptized in the river Jordan. It also represents peace. Perhaps this comes from the story of Noah, when it was a dove that returned to the ark carrying an olive branch.

Quail
The quail is a small, brown, speckled bird, related to the pheasant. When the Israelites were wandering in the desert, God sent a flock of quail for them to eat.

THE HOLY LAND

The country that we now call Israel, or the Holy Land, lies at the eastern end of the Mediterranean Sea, and is the setting for many of the stories in the Bible. In the Old Testament, this area was known as Canaan. It was inhabited from the earliest times, because it is a very fertile area where it is easy to grow crops. Canaan also benefited from its position at the meeting point of Africa and Asia, and many important trading routes ran through it. By the time of Jesus, the country formed part of the Roman empire and was known as Palestine.

The Promised Land

When God brought Moses and the Israelites out of slavery in Egypt, he said that he would lead them to a land that they could make their own. After forty years of wandering in the wilderness, the Israelites arrived in Canaan, God's Promised Land. They described it as "a land flowing with milk and honey", because it was so rich and fertile.

Jerusalem, the city of David

When the Israelites first settled in Canaan, Jerusalem was a small town called Jebus, that belonged to the Jebusites. It was built on a hill called Mount Zion, and surrounded by stone walls. King David conquered the city in about 1000BC and made it the capital of his kingdom and the centre of worship of Jehovah, the God of Israel. David brought the Ark of the Covenant to Jerusalem and his son, Solomon, built the first temple to house it. Although Jerusalem is described in the Old Testament as a mighty city, it was probably no bigger than a modern-day village.

Jesus and Jerusalem

By the time of Jesus' birth, Jerusalem had grown dramatically and probably had about 25,000 inhabitants. There was a new temple, built by King Herod, and the city was home to the Roman governor. Many of the most important events of Jesus' life took place in Jerusalem. When he was a baby, his parents took him to the temple to be dedicated, and later he taught his followers in the temple courtyards. Jerusalem was also the place of Jesus' death – he was tried and crucified there. Many sites connected with Jesus are still there today – the Garden of Gethsemane where he prayed on the night of his arrest, the route that he walked carrying the cross, and Golgotha, the place where he was crucified.

The Via Dolorosa is the route that Jesus walked, carrying the cross, to the site of his crucifixion. The name means the "way of sorrows".

Bethlehem

In Bible times, Bethlehem was just a small village, situated about eight kilometres south of Jerusalem. It is famous for being the birthplace of two very famous people. Israel's best-loved king, David, came from Bethlehem, and a thousand years later, Jesus was born there. The site traditionally thought to have been the place of Jesus' birth was a cave, used as a stable, on the outskirts of Bethlehem. This cave is now covered by the Church of the Nativity.

Jerusalem is a holy city for Jews, Christians and Muslims. The Dome of the Rock is an Islamic temple built over the rock where God asked Abraham to sacrifice Isaac.

Bethlehem has many historic places of worship. In Hebrew "bethlehem" means "house of bread".

Nazareth

Jesus' mother Mary and her husband Joseph lived in the small town of Nazareth, in the region of Galilee, and this is where Jesus was brought up. According to Luke's Gospel, Jesus started his ministry in Nazareth. He preached in the synagogue, but because the people recognized Jesus as a local man and the son of a lowly carpenter, they refused to accept him and drove him out of the town.

The miracle of Jesus calming the storm took place on the Sea of Galilee.

The Sea of Galilee

Despite its name, the Sea of Galilee is not a sea at all. It is a large freshwater lake, about twenty kilometres long and eleven kilometres wide. In Jesus' time, fishing was the main occupation in the area around the lake, and Jesus' first disciples were all fishermen. Many of the important events of Jesus' ministry took place in the cities and countryside around the Sea of Galilee. There he healed many sick people, performed miracles such as calming the storm and feeding the five thousand, and gave the Sermon on the Mount. After his resurrection, Jesus appeared to his disciples as they were fishing on the lake.

The river Jordan

The river Jordan is the biggest and longest river in Israel. It rises in the north of the country and flows southwards, through the Sea of Galilee, to the Dead Sea. The river Jordan is mentioned many times in the Bible. The Israelites had to cross the Jordan to enter the Promised Land, John the Baptist washed people in the Jordan to cleanse them from their sins, and Jesus himself was baptized there. Today people from all over the world travel to Israel to be baptized in the Jordan, like Jesus.

The desert

The Judean wilderness is a rocky desert area that lies west of the river Jordan. People couldn't grow crops or live there, so in biblical times it was a lonely and desolate place. But several Bible characters spent time in the desert. The prophet Elijah lived in the desert and was fed by ravens. Later, John the Baptist lived in the desert and survived by eating locusts and wild honey. Jesus spent forty days and nights in the desert, where he was tempted by the devil.

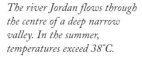

The river Jordan flows through the centre of a deep narrow valley. In the summer, temperatures exceed 38°C.

The Dead Sea was formed millions of years ago. It contains many minerals which are thought to have healing properties for the skin.

The Dead Sea

The Dead Sea is a salt lake that lies about 400m below sea level, making it the lowest place on earth. The water is so salty that no fish can live there, which is how the lake got its name. Experts now think that the Bible story of Sodom and Gomorrah took place in the Dead Sea area, and that the ruins of the two cities may lie submerged somewhere in the southern part of the lake. In places, deposits of salt stick out of the water, which remind us of the fate of Lot's wife, who was turned into a pillar of salt.

Elijah was fed by ravens when he was alone in the wilderness.

OTHER BIBLE LANDS

Although many of the events in the Bible take place in the area we call the Holy Land, some of the stories are set in other areas. For example, in the Old Testament, the Israelite people spent a long period in Egypt, then, many years later, they were forced into exile in Babylon. Jesus' ministry took place in the Holy Land, but Christianity spread rapidly to other countries. The New Testament tells us in detail of the journeys of St Paul and the other apostles, as they started to travel to Syria, Turkey and Europe, spreading the news about Jesus.

Ur

Before God commanded Abraham to leave his home and travel to Canaan, he lived in the city of Ur. It was the capital of the ancient kingdom of Sumer, and was situated on the Euphrates river in modern-day Iraq. In Abraham's time, the city was ruled by the Chaldeans, and it later became part of Babylonia. In the 1920s, archaeologists discovered the site of the ancient city of Ur. They found the remains of a pyramid-shaped temple, called a ziggurat, and a number of royal graves which contained gold jewellery, armour and other treasures.

This bull's head decorated a musical instrument called a lyre. It was one of the treasures discovered in the royal burial pits at Ur.

The Egyptians built huge pyramids which were burial monuments for their dead.

Egypt

Egypt was a very rich and prosperous country. Most of the country was desert, but there was a thin strip of fertile land along the river Nile, where most of the people lived. Egypt was ruled by kings called pharaohs, who built magnificent palaces, temples and tombs. The Israelites' link with Egypt began when Joseph was sold into slavery there and rose to become one of the pharaoh's ministers. He later brought his family to live in Egypt. Their descendants lived there for many years, but the Egyptians eventually treated them as slaves. The prophet Moses finally led the Israelites out of Egypt to the Promised Land in an event known as "the exodus".

Sinai

Sinai is a desert region that lies between the two forks of the Red Sea in eastern Egypt. According to the Bible, the Israelites spent forty years wandering in this wilderness as they travelled from Egypt to the Promised Land. Somewhere on the way, Moses climbed Mount Sinai and received the Ten Commandments from God. The exact route that they took and the location of Mount Sinai have never been definitely identified. However, many experts think that Jebel Musa ("the Mountain of Moses") in the southern part of Sinai was probably the mountain that the Bible calls Mount Sinai.

Sinai is a dry, barren region, where people cannot normally live.

Babylon

Babylon was the capital of the area known as Babylonia, which lay in the southern part of modern-day Iraq. It was a beautiful city, and contained the famous Hanging Gardens, one of the seven wonders of the ancient world. In the 6th century BC the Babylonians started to conquer neighbouring lands, including the kingdoms of Israel and Judah. In 586BC they seized Jerusalem, destroyed the temple, and took large numbers of Israelites back to Babylon as captives. Many of them worked as craftsmen, rebuilding the city during the reign of the Babylonian king, Nebuchadnezzar.

The Ishtar Gate was the ceremonial entrance to the city of Babylon. Its walls were decorated with figures of bulls, dragons and lions made of coloured glazed brick.

Damascus

Damascus, the capital city of Syria, is one of the world's oldest cities. It was already a well-established town in 2000BC. Damascus is mentioned several times in the Bible, but it is most famous as the place where St Paul was converted to Christianity. As Paul was travelling on the road to Damascus he had a vision of Jesus and was blinded. Paul's sight was restored a few days later in a house on Straight Street in Damascus – the street is still there today.

Rome

In New Testament times, Rome was the capital city of a huge empire which covered most of Europe and the area around the Mediterranean Sea. Rome was a magnificent city, and probably the largest in the world at that time. In the centre of the city was a square called the Forum, which was home to several important temples, triumphant arches, and the building where the senate (parliament) met to discuss and pass the laws. According to Christian tradition, both St Peter and St Paul were put to death in Rome. Today, it is the centre of the Roman Catholic church.

This is an example of a typical Greek Christian Orthodox church.

Corinth, Thessalonica and Philippi

St Paul travelled to Greece on two of his missionary journeys. He founded important early churches in the cities of Corinth, Thessalonica and Philippi, which was the first place that he visited in Europe. St Paul later wrote to the churches in these cities, and his letters appear in the New Testament.

Athens

Athens was once the most important of the Greek city states. Many magnificent temples and other buildings from this period still stand there today, especially on the hill called the Acropolis. By New Testament times, Athens had been conquered by the Romans and was part of their empire. St Paul visited Athens on his second journey. He disputed with the local philosophers in the market place and on the hill called the Areopagus, where the city council met.

Ephesus declined after the 4th century AD and has been uninhabited for centuries, but many ruins still stand there. The picture shows the ruins of the library at Ephesus.

Ephesus

The city of Ephesus was situated at the mouth of the River Cayster, on the coast of modern-day Turkey. The city was founded in the 10th century BC, and was the centre of worship for the goddess Artemis, known as Diana to the Romans. St Paul visited Ephesus on two of his missionary journeys and helped to establish a church there. His preaching upset the followers of Diana, and eventually caused a riot!

Athens was named after Athena, the Greek goddess of wisdom. Her most important temples were on the Acropolis.

WHO'S WHO IN THE BIBLE?

Aaron
Elder brother of Moses and high priest, Aaron assisted Moses.

Abraham
He obeyed God's call to leave Ur and journey to Canaan. He's known as the father of God's people.

Adam
The first man, created by God in the Garden of Eden.

Daniel
He interpreted the dreams of King Nebuchadnezzar and demonstrated his faith when thrown to the lions.

David
Israel's second and greatest king. and ancestor of Jesus. He was a shepherd boy when he was anointed king in place of Saul. He is famous for his victory over the giant Goliath.

Deborah
A prophet and (the only female) judge over Israel.

Elijah
A prophet who is most famous for his victory in the contest with the prophets of Baal at Mount Carmel.

Elisha
Successor to Elijah as the leading prophet of the northern kingdom of Israel in the 9th century BC.

Esau
Son of Isaac and elder brother of Jacob. He sold his birthright to Jacob for a bowl of stew.

Esther
A Jewish queen of Persia who risked her life to foil a plot to destroy the Jews. This is commemorated in the festival of Purim.

Eve
The first woman, whose name means "living". With Adam she disobeyed God and brought sin into the world. She was the mother of Cain and Abel.

Ezekiel
He prophesied to the Babylonian exiles and warned of God's judgement, but also brought a message of hope for the future.

Ezra
Priest and teacher of Moses' law, commissioned by the Persian king Artaxerxes to lead a return of exiles to Jerusalem.

Gideon
One of the judges who was called to save Israel from the Midianites. His small unarmed band of men defeated the powerful Midianite army.

Hannah
God answered her faithful prayers for a son and she gave her child to the high priest to be trained for God's service. He became the prophet Samuel.

Isaac
Son of Abraham and Sarah who was used to test his father's faith. He married Rebekah and was father of twin sons, Jacob and Esau.

Isaiah
A prophet who called on the people to repent and trust in God and who spoke about the coming Messiah. He prophesied in Judah for about fifty years from c740BC.

Jacob
The ancestor of the twelve tribes of Israel. He tricked his elder brother Esau out of his inheritance. His name was changed to Israel after wrestling with the angel of the Lord.

James, brother of Jesus
He was one of Jesus' disciples and a leader in the church at Jerusalem. He is known for his letter that gives practical advice on being a Christian.

James, son of Zebedee
Apostle and brother of John who was one of Jesus' closest disciples. He was the first apostle to die for his faith.

Jeremiah
A prophet who warned of the Babylonian exile and challenged the false prophets but also spoke of the promise of restoration.

Jesus
Born to the Virgin Mary and called the Son of God, or Christ ("Messiah") in the New Testament. He was famous for his teaching and healing, was crucified by the authorities, but rose from the dead. He promised new life to all those who follow him.

Job
A man of wealth who, despite great suffering and misfortune, is remembered for his patience and faith in God.

John, the apostle
Son of Zebedee and brother of James, he was, with Peter and James, one of Jesus' closest disciples. He wrote the Gospel that bears his name, letters and the book of Revelation.

John the Baptist
Son of Zechariah and Elizabeth and a relative of Jesus, who prepared the way for Jesus. He received his prophetic call whilst in the wilderness. He then preached a message of repentance and baptized many people (including Jesus) in the river Jordan. He was executed by Herod Antipas.

Joseph, husband of Mary
A descendant of David, the husband of Jesus' mother, Mary. Joseph was a carpenter who lived in Nazareth.

Joseph, son of Jacob
Jacob's favourite son who was sold into slavery by his jealous brothers. He used his God-given ability to interpret dreams and became a wise ruler in Egypt.

Joshua
Moses' assistant and military commander, he was one of the spies sent to explore Canaan. As Moses' successor, he later led the people of Israel into the Promised Land.

Judas Iscariot
A Jewish zealot and the treasurer for the disciples. He betrayed Jesus for thirty silver pieces, but later, filled with remorse, committed suicide.

Luke
Doctor and close companion of Paul who travelled with him on his journeys. He wrote Luke's Gospel and the Acts of the Apostles.

Mark
He accompanied Paul and Barnabas on their first missionary journey and wrote Mark's Gospel.

Mary the virgin, mother of Jesus
Wife of Joseph, who became the earthly mother of Jesus.

Matthew
Originally a tax-collector employed by the Roman government and one of the twelve apostles, also called Levi. He possibly wrote Matthew's Gospel.

Moses
Born of Hebrew parents in Egypt, he was put in a basket into the river Nile and found and brought up by the king of Egypt's daughter. God later called him at the burning bush to lead the people of Israel out of Egypt. He received the Ten Commandments from God on Mount Sinai but died before entering the Promised Land.

Nehemiah
Cupbearer to the Persian king Artaxerxes, he returned to Jerusalem to rebuild the city walls.

Noah
A good man who obeyed God's command to build an ark to preserve the world's creatures. After the flood, God blessed Noah and his family and commanded them to people the earth.

Paul
Born in Tarsus, Paul was a Jewish Pharisee and a Roman citizen. By occupation, he was a tentmaker. He persecuted the church but was dramatically converted on the road to Damascus. Later on, he went on three missionary journeys through Asia Minor and Greece. He was arrested and taken to Rome. He wrote many letters to encourage and teach the churches which he established.

Peter
Originally called Simon, he was a fisherman who became one of Jesus' closest disciples. Jesus renamed him Peter which means "rock". He denied Jesus three times, but became a leader in the church in Jerusalem and was the first to take the gospel to Gentiles. He wrote two letters that bear his name.

Pontius Pilate
Roman governor in Judea AD26-37. Jesus was brought to him to be tried. Pilate believed Jesus was innocent, but he gave in to pressure from the crowd and allowed him to be crucified.

Ruth
A young Moabite woman, known for her loyalty, who married Boaz the Israelite. Their son, Obed, became the grandfather of David.

Samson
One of the judges who led Israel, known for his outstanding God-given physical strength, which was associated with his uncut hair. He was betrayed by Delilah and died while bringing down the temple.

Samuel
A prophet and last of the judges over Israel. He was born to Hannah, who dedicated him to God. When the people asked for a king, he anointed Saul and, later, David as kings.

Sarah
The beautiful wife of Abraham, originally called Sarai. She longed for a son, and finally, at the age of ninety, God granted her wish and she gave birth to Isaac.

Saul
The first king of Israel, famous for his victories, courage and generosity. But when he grew proud and disobeyed God, David was chosen to be king in his place. In his later years he suffered from fits of insanity, and he finally died in battle against the Philistines.

Solomon
Third king of Israel and son of David and Bathsheba, he was the wealthiest and wisest of all of Israel's kings. He expanded trade and built the temple in Jerusalem. For political reasons he married many foreign princesses who caused him to turn away from worshipping God. When he died, the kingdom was divided into two.

Thomas
A disciple of Jesus, whose name means 'twin'. Best known for his doubts and disbelief, he refused to believe that Jesus had risen from the dead unless he could see and touch the scars for himself.

Timothy
A young Christian from Lystra who was one of Paul's companions on his second missionary journey. He became leader of the church at Ephesus. Paul's two letters to him are full of advice on church leadership.

Zacchaeus
A tax-collector who lived in Jericho. He climbed into a tree so as to be able to see Jesus above the crowds. As a result of his encounter with Jesus, Zacchaeus was a changed man.

TEST YOUR KNOWLEDGE

OLD TESTAMENT

1.   What were the names of the first human beings that God made?
(*page 16*)

2.   Who was Isaac's father?
(*page 28*)

3.   Who got transformed into a pillar of salt as she looked back?
(*page 27*)

4.   Who was thrown into prison, had dreams, but eventually became prime minister of Egypt?
(*page 38*)

5.   Who led the Israelites through the Red Sea?
(*page 46*)

6.   Which woman protected the spies at the city of Jericho?
(*page 56*)

7.   What was the name of Ruth's mother-in-law?
(*page 66*)

8.   What was the name of the priest that Samuel served under?
(*page 68*)

9.   What was the name of David's closest friend?
(*page 76*)

10.   Who is particularly famous for his wisdom?
(*page 85*)

11.   Who was the prophet who followed Elijah?
(*page 93*)

12.   What was the name of the seven-year-old boy who was crowned King of Israel?
(*page 100*)

13.   Who is particularly famous for his suffering and patience?
(*page 106*)

14.   Who was thrown into the lions' den?
(*page 130*)

NEW TESTAMENT

1.   What was the name of John the Baptist's father?
(*page 144*)

2.   What were the three gifts the Magi (wise men) brought to Jesus?
(*page 149*)

3.   In which town did Mary and Joseph live?
(*page 145*)

4.   Where was the wedding at which Jesus changed water into wine?
(*page 158*)

5.   For how much did Judas betray Jesus?
(*page 197*)

6.   What was the occupation of Simon Peter?
(*page 57*)

7.   In which city was Straight Street?
(*page 216*)

8.   What kind of tree did Zacchaeus climb to see Jesus?
(*page 188*)

9.   What does the name "Peter" mean?
(*page 214*)

10.   What was the name of the wife of Herod Antipas?
(*page 174*)

11.   What was the name of the man to whom Jesus said, "You must be born again"?
(*page 170*)

12.   What was written over Jesus' cross at the crucifixion?
(*page 206*)

13. Where was Philip going when he met the Ethiopian official?
(page 215)

14. How old was Jesus when Mary and Joseph found him teaching in the temple?
(page 151)

15. What is the name of the festival at which Christians remember the coming of the Holy Spirit?
(page 209)

16. On which island in the Mediterranean Sea did Paul safely land after being shipwrecked?
(page 223)

GENERAL

1. By what other name is Mount Sinai known?
(page 51)

2. Where did Elijah's contest with the priests of Baal take place?
(page 91)

3. What musical instruments did the people play as they went round the city of Jericho?
(page 58)

4. What was poured over Saul's head when he was made King?
(page 72)

5. What was the name of the town near Jerusalem where Jesus was born?
(page 147)

6. On the road to which city was Paul going when he was blinded by the light of Jesus?
(page 216)

7. In which city was the famous temple of Artemis ?
(page 225)

8. Who was swallowed up by a great fish?
(page 134)

9. What does "gospel" mean?
(page 142)

10. How many books does the Bible contain?
(page 9)

11. Which Roman emperor is famous for his persecution of the Christians?
(page 211)

THE NATURAL WORLD

1. Which bird, representing the Holy Spirit, came upon Jesus at his baptism?
(page 153)

2. What kind of animal, belonging to Balaam, spoke God's words?
(page 54)

3. When Moses threw his staff on the ground, which creature did it turn into?
(page 42)

4. Jesus said that Peter would disown him three times before he heard the sound of which bird?
(page 201)

5. The valuable crop of which tree is used for making oil?
(page 240)

6. What birds did Joseph and Mary bring as a sacrifice when they presented Jesus in the temple?
(page 149)

7. Which birds fed Elijah?
(page 90)

8. On which mountain range did Noah's boat come to rest after the flood?
(page 18)

9. Beside which lake were Simon and Andrew catching fish when Jesus invited them to catch people?
(page 157)

10. In which river did John the Baptist baptize Jesus?
(page 152)

11. Which creature does the prophet Joel use as a warning of God's judgement?
(page 132)

INDEX

ACKNOWLEDGEMENTS

The publishers wish to thank the following artists who have contributed to this book:
Main artists
Mike White (Temple Rogers)
with Richard Hook (Linden Artists); Stewart Lees (S.G.A.); and David Ashby (Illustration).
All other illustrations David Ashby (Illustration); Andy Becket; Jo Brewer; Vanessa Card; Andrew Farmer;
Wayne Ford; Richard Hook (Linden Artists); Stuart Lafford (Linden Artists); Stewart Lees (S.G.A.);
Alan Male (Linden Artists); Gillian Platt (Illustration); Terry Riley; Martin Sanders; Peter Sarson;
Martin Salisbury; Guy Smith; Roger Smith; Sue Stitt.
Maps Mel Pickering (Contour Publishing).

The publishers wish to thank the following for supplying photographs for this book:
Page 8 (T/R) Rosalind Desmond; 14 (T/L) Mary Evans Picture Library; 15 (B/R) York Minster Archives;
17 (T/R) York Minster Archives; 33 (T/R) Dover Publications; 41 (T/R) Jean-Leo Dugast/Panos Pictures;
45 (T/L) Dover Publications; 48 (T/L) Dover Publications; 49 (B/R) Dom Augustine Calmet, Dictionary
of the Holy Bible (1732) Mary Evans Picture Library; 52 (T/L) Dover Publications; 55 (B/R) Rosalind
Desmond; 62 (B/L) Dover Publications; 66 (T/L) Dover Publications; 68 (B/L) The Stock Market; 70 (T)
Dover Publications; 75 (T/R) Dover Publications; 76 (B/L) Rosalind Desmond; 77 (C/R) Rosalind
Desmond; 79 (B/R) Rosalind Desmond; 83 (B/R) Dover Publications; 90 (B/L) Rosalind Desmond; 91
(B/R) Rosalind Desmond; 92 (C/L) Dover Publications, (B/L) York Minster Archives; 93 (T/R) Warren
Faidley/Oxford Scientific Films; 94 (C/L) The Stock Market; (B/L) Rosalind Desmond; 97 (B/R) British
Museum/E.T.Archive; 98 (T/L) Biblioteca Estense Modena/E.T.Archive; 99 (T/R) Professor
D.J.Wiseman; 102 (T/L) The Stock Market; 103 (C/R) Dover Publications; 104 (B/L) The Stock Market;
106 (C/L) E.T.Archive; 107 (B/R) York Minster Archives; 109 (T/R) The Stock Market; 110 (T/L) Ariel
Skelley/The Stock Market; 111 (T/R) Pat Spillane, 111 (C/R) Dover Publications; 114 (C/L) Dover
Publications; 117 (C/R) Dover Publications; 121 (T/R) Professor D.J.Wiseman, (B/R) Dover Publications;
122 (C) British Museum/E.T.Archive; 123 (T) Dover Publications, (T/R) Rosalind Desmond; 124 (C/L)
Dover Publications, (B/L) Rosalind Desmond; 128 (T/L) Professor D.J.Wiseman; 129 (T/R) Dover
Publications; 130 (C/L) Dover Publications, (B/L) Mary Evans Picture Library; 131 (T/R) Professor
D.J.Wiseman; 134 (B/L) Professor D.J.Wiseman; 133 (B/R) Dover Publications; 136 (T/L) Rosalind
Desmond; 137 (C/R) Dover Publications; 139 (T/R) Voronet Monaster, Rumania/E.T.Archive; 145 (T/R)
Rosalind Desmond; 147 (B/R) Rosalind Desmond; 149 (C/R) Dover Publications; 151 (C/R) Rosalind
Desmond; 152 (T/L) Dover Publications; 153 (B/R) Mary Evans Picture Library; 156 (B/L) Dover
Publications; 159 (C/R) Jim Holmes/Panos Pictures, (B/R) Dover Publications; 161 (T/R) York Minster
Archives, (B/R) Rosalind Desmond; 162 (T/L) Dover Publications, (C/L) Rosalind Desmond; 164 (C/L)
Rosalind Desmond; 166 (C/L) Rosalind Desmond; 167 (C/R) Rosalind Desmond, (B/R) Dover
Publications; 170 (T/L) Rosalind Desmond, (C/L) Gamma/Michael Schwarz/Liaison/Frank Spooner
Pictures, (B/L) Dover Publications; 173 (T/R) Mary Evans Picture Library; 174 (B/L) Dover Publications;
175 (B/R) Rosalind Desmond; 176 (C/L) The Stock Market, (B/L) Dover Publications; 177 (T/R) The
Stock Market; 179 (C/R) Rosalind Desmond; 180 (T/L) Rosalind Desmond, (B/L) Rosalind Desmond;
181 (T/R) Dover Publications; 182 (B/L) Dover Publications; 184 (C/L) Basilica Aquiela,
Italy/E.T.Archive; 186 (B/L) Rosalind Desmond; 188 (B/L) Rosalind Desmond; 189 (B/R) The Stock
Market; 191 (B/R) Dover Publications; 192 (B/L) Dover Publications; 193 (B/R) The Stock Market; 195
(C/R) Rosalind Desmond; 196 (T/L) Dover Publications, (B/L) Castello Della Mante
Piemonte/E.T.Archive; 197 (C/R) Mary Evans Picture Library; 198 (B/L) Rosalind Desmond; 199 (T/R)
Dover Publications, (C/R) Rosalind Desmond; 200 (T/L) Rosalind Desmond, (B/L) Rosalind Desmond;
201 (T/R) York Minster Archives, (C/R) Dover Publications; 202 (B/L) York Minster Archives; 204 (B/L)
Rosalind Desmond; 205 (T/R) York Minster Archives, (B/R) Mary Evans Picture Library; 206 (T/L) York
Minster Archives; 208 (T/L) York Minster Archives; 212 (T/L) Abbey of Monteoliveto Maggiore
Siena/E.T.Archive; 213 (T/R) Rosalind Desmond; 214 (C/L) York Minster Archives, 214 (B/L) Dover
Publications; 215 (T/R) Jim Holmes/Panos Pictures; 216 (T/L) Professor D.J.Wiseman; 217 (T/R) York
Minster Archives; 222 (C/R) Rosalind Desmond; 223 (C/R) Liz Dalby; 224 (T/L) Dover Publications,
(C/L) Liz Dalby; 230 (B/L) York Minster Archives; 231 (T/R) Bib Capitolaire Vercelli/E.T.Archive, (C/R)
Panos Pictures; 232 (C/L) Rosalind Desmond; 238 (C) Rosalind Desmond.

All photographs from the York Minster Archives are reproduced
by kind permission of the Dean and Chapter of York.

All other photographs from Miles Kelly Archives.